T0301744

MACROECONOMIC ANALYSIS AND POLICY

A Systematic Approach

MACROECONOMIC ANALYSIS AND POLICY

A Systematic Approach

Joshua E Greene

Singapore Management University, Singapore

W JERSEY · LONDON · SINGAPORE · BEIJING · SHANGHAI · HONG KONG · TAIPEI · CHENNAI · TOKYO

Published by

World Scientific Publishing Co. Pte. Ltd.

5 Toh Tuck Link, Singapore 596224

USA office: 27 Warren Street, Suite 401-402, Hackensack, NJ 07601

UK office: 57 Shelton Street, Covent Garden, London WC2H 9HE

British Library Cataloguing-in-Publication Data
A catalogue record for this book is available from the British Library.

MACROECONOMIC ANALYSIS AND POLICY
A Systematic Approach

ISBN 978-981-3223-82-0

For any available supplementary material, please visit
http://www.worldscientific.com/worldscibooks/10.1142/10542#t=suppl

Desk Editor: Sandhya Venkatesh

Printed in Singapore

PREFACE

This book is the outcome of many years of conducting training programs and courses in macroeconomic analysis for a variety of institutions and several universities. An idea that government officials would find interesting training on macroeconomic accounts and analysis separate from the forecasting done in financial programming courses led to a series of 5 day training programs for government officials, economists at the Asian Development Bank, and a successful half-semester course for master's level students at Singapore Management University. Lectures and exercises used in these programs and courses provided the basis for the contents of this book. Certain chapters were initially intended as part of a volume on financial programming with inflation targeting. When that project was suspended, the organizer graciously agreed that these materials could be used in this book.

I want to thank Bank Negara Malaysia, the Asian Development Bank, Singapore Management University, and the Lee Kuan Yew School of Public Policy at the National University of Singapore for providing the opportunity to conduct training programs or courses on macroeconomic accounts and analysis, and Delano (Dan) Villanueva for initially suggesting that I prepare background materials on the topic. I gratefully acknowledge the willingness of the International Monetary Fund (IMF) to allow the reproduction of tables from selected IMF reports and papers to illustrate concepts presented in various chapters of the book. I also wish to thank World Scientific, the publisher of my book on public finance, for agreeing to publish this book. Finally, I want to thank my wife, Dara, and children, Ashira and Alexander, for their continuing support and encouragement during this project.

Joshua Greene
April 2017

INTRODUCTION
AND OVERVIEW

Understanding a nation's economy requires an appreciation of its macroeconomic accounts — the key data that describe developments in the country's income, inflation, balance of payments, government sector, and monetary activities — along with the main policies that affect macroeconomic activity. Macroeconomic textbooks typically provide an introduction to policies and some discussion of the accounts related to national income, including gross domestic product (GDP) and gross national income or gross national product (GNP). Often, however, little is said about the accounts of other macroeconomic sectors. This book attempts to address this issue, providing an extensive discussion of the accounts of all the major macroeconomic sectors and their linkages, as well as an introduction to the main macroeconomic policies. Understanding these accounts and reviewing the data they contain can provide a basis for identifying macroeconomic problems and suggesting policies to address them, particularly if the economy is not expected to change substantially over the coming period.

Part I of the book describes the data, accounts, and analysis of the four main macroeconomic sectors — real, external, fiscal, and monetary. It also discusses the accounting and economic relations among the sectors, using a flow of funds approach.

Chapter one introduces the macroeconomic accounts and their use in macroeconomic analysis. It identifies key objectives for macroeconomic policy making, in particular attaining macroeconomic stability and economic growth, while reviewing the risks from high inflation and external sector crises. This chapter also provides a brief introduction to the main macroeconomic policies — fiscal, monetary, and exchange rate policy — along with major structural reforms that have proved important in many economies.

Chapter two presents the accounts and key indicators of the economy's real sector. This chapter discusses the various macroeconomic aggregates related to national income and production, including GDP, GNI, gross national disposable income (GNDI), gross national saving (GNS), gross national investment, and the relationship between an economy's savings minus investment (S–I) balance and the current account balance in the balance of payments. This chapter also presents several major indices of inflation, including the consumer price index (CPI) and the GDP deflator.

Chapter three discusses the accounts and key indicators of the external sector, including the balance of payments, the current account balance, the balance in the capital and financial account, the overall balance, and various measures of the exchange rate and external competitiveness. This chapter also introduces indicators of external debt and debt service, along with measures of the adequacy of official reserves and the burden of external indebtedness.

Chapter four introduces the accounts and key indicators of the public (fiscal) sector. Following a description of what the public sector contains, the chapter discusses the elements of government accounts, reviewing the concepts of revenue, expenditure, the fiscal balance, and government financing. The chapter presents several measures of the fiscal balance, noting the purposes of each, and describes the different types of budget finance and their consequences. This chapter also discusses measures of government and public debt and debt service, introducing the notion of fiscal sustainability and its relationship to the ratio of government debt to GDP.

Chapter five discusses the accounts and analysis of the monetary sector, focusing on developments in the banking system. This chapter presents the accounts of the monetary authorities, the consolidated accounts of the commercial banks, and the monetary survey, a consolidation of the previous two accounts that summarizes developments in the banking system. The chapter also introduces such indicators as money velocity, the money multiplier, and the growth in broad money and reserve money or the monetary base.

Chapter six discusses the accounting and behavioral relationships linking the accounts of the four macroeconomic sectors. This chapter shows the various connections across the sectors and introduces the concept of the *flow of funds* — a matrix showing the flows of income, expenditure, and financing among the government, non-government, monetary, and external sectors of an economy. The flow of funds indicates sectoral surpluses and deficits, and how surpluses are used to finance deficits. It can also be used to identify inconsistencies in data across sectors, providing a basis for reviewing macroeconomic statistics.

Part II of the book provides discusses the main macroeconomic policies and how they can be used to address problems identified in the macroeconomic accounts. Separate chapters cover fiscal, monetary, and exchange rate policy and the use of policy combinations to address a variety of macroeconomic difficulties.

Chapter seven provides a concise introduction to fiscal policy. Following a discussion of the various elements of fiscal policy and data on government revenue and expenditure in different economies, this chapter discusses the impact of fiscal policy on a nation's economy, the differences between pro- and counter-cyclical fiscal policy, the implications of fiscal policy for the monetary sector and the balance of payments, how fiscal policy can be used to promote growth and reduce poverty, and special fiscal issues, including a further discussion of fiscal sustainability.

Chapter eight offers an introduction to monetary policy. This chapter presents a basic framework for monetary policy making, involving instruments, operating and intermediate targets, and the choice of policy objective. It also discusses inflation targeting and other monetary policy frameworks, along with the main elements for the transmission of monetary policy. A concluding section of this chapter reviews recent developments in monetary policy, including quantitative easing and a discussion of how several Asian countries have adjusted monetary policy in response to changing macroeconomic circumstances.

Chapter nine provides an overview of exchange rate policy. Following an extensive discussion of different exchange rate regimes, the chapter discusses the relationship between the choice of regime and the type of monetary framework, noting the difficulty of maintaining a fixed rate regime in economies opting for an independent monetary policy and limited restrictions on external capital flows. The chapter also discusses possible objectives for exchange rate policy, assessing the appropriateness of the exchange rate, and using exchange rate policy for various macroeconomic objectives.

Chapter ten, the concluding chapter, discusses how fiscal, monetary, exchange rate, and structural policies can be used jointly to attain macroeconomic objectives. The first part of the chapter introduces the notion of the Swan Diagram to determine the kinds of macroeconomic imbalances in an economy and uses the resulting macroeconomic assessment to suggest combinations of policies to attain both internal balance (low inflation and operating near potential output) and external balance (a sustainable balance of payments). The chapter describes the modalities of the different types of policies, noting their relative advantages and limitations, emphasizing the need for policy coordination. The chapter concludes with several examples of how countries have used combinations of policies to address different types of macroeconomic problems.

CONTENTS

To Dara

Chapter 1

INTRODUCTION TO MACROECONOMIC ACCOUNTS, ANALYSIS, AND RELATED POLICY ISSUES

Macroeconomics is the study of an entire economy. Macroeconomics assumes the existence of many individual economic sectors and the markets governing them. Thus, the focus is on the behavior of the economy as a whole — the aggregate of all the markets for goods and services, as well as the impact of the public sector (government and government-owned entities, called public or state-owned enterprises) and the rest of the world on the economy. Studying an entire economy requires conceiving of **aggregate demand** — the total demand for goods and services in the economy — and **aggregate supply** — the total amount of goods and services made available for sale in the economy. In equilibrium, aggregate demand and aggregate supply should be equal. In practice, aggregate demand and supply can differ, generating a variety of macroeconomic conditions, including short- to medium-term fluctuations in an economy, called business cycles.

Macroeconomic analysis involves studying an economy's main components. These include

- The main sectors of the economy and relevant information about them, recorded in various sectoral accounts;

- Important indicators of macroeconomic performance, representing key variables drawn from the various sectoral accounts; and
- The principal policies used to achieve broad objectives for the economy, typically high rates of economic growth, macroeconomic stability (meaning low inflation), a sustainable external position, and various other objectives, such as low poverty rates, an acceptable distribution of income and wealth, and a safe and sustainable physical environment.

Although each economy has particular sectors of special importance — the petroleum sector, for example, in Saudi Arabia, or the tourist sector in Maldives or Barbados — for purposes of analysis, it is useful to view every economy as having four broad economic sectors, each with its own set of economic accounts. These sectors and their principal accounts are as follows:

1. **The real sector**, often called the national accounts. The real sector comprises production and expenditure in the economy. Its accounts measure the total activity in the economy, described either from the standpoint of production, expenditure, or income. The real sector also records data on inflation in the economy, using such measures as a consumer price index, other price indices, and a price index for overall output or expenditure called the gross domestic product (GDP) deflator. Chapter 2 provides an extensive discussion of the accounts and performance indicators in the real sector.

2. **The external sector**. The external sector covers the relations between the economy and the rest of the world. The economic aspects of these relations are recorded in a set of accounts called the balance of payments. The balance of payments records in detail the amount of trade in goods and services between the economy and other economies. It also shows income, capital, and financial interactions between the economy and the rest of the world, as well as changes in the amount of an economy's official reserves (the stock of gold, foreign exchange, and similar assets held by the country's monetary authority or central bank). The accounts of the external sector also record a country's stock of foreign debt and debt service, including payments of both interest and principal (amortization).

Besides the balance of payments and debt, data for the external sector will typically include indicators of the economy's competitiveness, including data on the country's exchange rate.

3. **The fiscal sector.** The fiscal sector involves the activities of government and government-owned non-financial entities called public or state-owned enterprises. (Publicly owned financial entities are covered in the monetary sector, described below.) The government sector's financial activities are usually recorded in the fiscal accounts of the government sector, typically in a comprehensive budget for the entire sector or for different levels of government (where there are separate budgets for the central and sub-national units of government). There may also be data on the consolidated public enterprise sector — total income, expenses, profits or losses, and any financing needed to cover losses. As with the external sector, fiscal data also include information on government and state-enterprise debt and debt service.

4. **The monetary sector.** The monetary sector comprises the activities of the economy's financial institutions, including its central bank or monetary authority, the commercial (deposit money) banks, and other financial institutions, such as investment banks, finance companies, credit unions, and any microfinance entities. The activities of the main part of the financial sector, the banking system, which comprises the monetary authority and the commercial banks, are recorded in a set of monetary accounts. The accounts record the assets and liabilities of the various institutions covered.

I. AN OVERVIEW OF THE ACCOUNTS AND KEY PERFORMANCE INDICATORS FOR EACH SECTOR

1. **The real sector.** The accounts of the real sector record developments in an economy's income and prices. The accounts for income (which may also record total value added or total expenditure in the economy) represent flows, meaning activities that occur *during a period of time*, such as a year, as opposed to quantities of goods or services at a single point in time. The income (or production or expenditure) accounts of the real sector are measured both in nominal terms (meaning at current prices) and

in real terms (meaning at a constant set of prices). If measured in real terms, these accounts allow comparison of the true volumes or amounts of goods and services produced, or expenditure made, or income earned, from one period to another. Key indicators of real sector performance include the growth (percent change) in real GDP; the output gap or unemployment rate; the ratios of gross investment and gross saving to GDP; and the rates of change in the consumer price index and other price indices.

2. **The external sector**. The accounts of the external sector focus on developments in the balance of payments, external debt, and external debt service, along with the composition and direction of trade (both exports and imports, particularly of goods). Except for the stock of external debt, the accounts record flows, since trade, financial flows, and debt service involve funds received or paid out during a period of time. The accounts of the external sector are typically recorded in nominal terms (at current prices) and are often presented both in domestic currency and in a commonly used foreign currency, such as euros or U.S. dollars. Key indicators of external sector performance include the current account balance in the balance of payments as a percent of GDP; the overall balance in the balance of payments and the level of gross official reserves; the ratios of gross reserves to imports (measured in months of imports) and to short-term debt (debt service due during the coming 12 months); the stock of external debt as a percent of GDP and the amount of debt service as a percent of export earnings (usually of goods and services); and competitiveness measures such as the change in the real exchange rate.

3. **The fiscal sector**. The accounts of the fiscal sector record developments in the government's financial interactions with the rest of the economy and the rest of the world. They may also include developments in the consolidated set of public enterprises. Except for stocks of government and public sector debt, the accounts record flows, since items such as revenues, expenditures, and budget financing entail funds received or paid over a period of time. The fiscal accounts are measured in nominal terms (current prices), although fiscal data are often also reported in percentages of GDP, to allow comparison across years (and with other economies' data). A comprehensive view of the fiscal sector includes not only the accounts of the central

(national) government, but also the consolidated accounts of any state or provincial governments and, if available, of local governments. Including the consolidated accounts of the public (state-owned) enterprises shows the position of the overall public sector. Key indicators of fiscal sector performance include the overall balance of the central and general (consolidated) government budget as a percent of GDP; total revenues and expenditures as percentages of GDP, ideally with breakdowns of revenue into tax and non-tax receipts and expenditure into current and capital expenditure or expense and net acquisition of non-financial assets (again as percentages of GDP); the buoyancy (elasticity) of total revenue and tax revenue to GDP, which shows whether these items keep pace with the growth of nominal GDP; and the ratios of government and public sector debt to GDP.

4. **The monetary sector**. The accounts of the monetary sector show developments in the main financial institutions of an economy, typically focusing on the banking system, which usually represents the bulk of the financial system. Because the accounts record assets and liabilities of different institutions or groups of institutions at a point in time, they record stocks, rather than flows. However, flows in the monetary sector can be constructed by calculating changes in these stocks during a time period. Monetary accounts are recorded in domestic currency, in nominal terms (current prices). As a result, the domestic currency value of foreign currency items, such as international reserves and foreign exchange deposits, can change as the exchange rate fluctuates. Important measures of monetary sector performance include the growth rate of broad money and its main components (e.g., broad money in domestic currency); nominal and real interest rates on loans and deposits; the percentage of loans considered non-performing (i.e., seriously delinquent); the growth in real credit to the private sector (after adjusting for changes in the price level over time); measures of household and corporate debt; and indices of equity (stock) and house prices, which may be useful for identifying asset "bubbles" (price increases to unsustainable levels, far beyond what fundamentals would justify).

II. LINKAGES AMONG SECTORS

The four main economic sectors are related in a variety of ways. Developments in one sector affect other sectors, and policies aimed at one sector (for example, changes in fiscal policy) inevitably affect most sectors. For example, a rise in the population's desire to consume, which increases aggregate demand and total private expenditure (real sector variables), typically raises government revenues, through higher sales or value-added tax collections, thus affecting the fiscal sector. Higher consumption may also boost imports, affecting the external sector (balance of payments). Higher consumption could mean an initial decline in household deposits and/or a rise in consumer loans, affecting the monetary accounts. Thus, a change originating in the real sector spreads to other sectors.

Changes originating in other sectors also affect other sectors. A rise in government pension payments will boost income, and most likely consumer expenditure, thus affecting the real sector. Higher pensions would probably raise imports, affecting the balance of payments. In addition, a rise in government pensions should mean at least an initial rise in household deposits, probably followed by increases in business deposits, thereby affecting the monetary accounts. Depreciation of the exchange rate typically reduces imports, at least over time, and may also boost exports, as competitiveness increases, thereby affecting the trade balance and current account of the balance of payments (external sector). Lower imports would reduce customs (import) duties, thereby affecting the government budget (fiscal accounts), while a stronger current account balance would likely raise international reserves, thereby affecting the monetary sector. Finally, relaxing monetary policy, by cutting the central bank's policy interest rate, will likely expand lending, thereby affecting the monetary sector. Higher lending, whether for consumption or investment, should add to economic growth and income, thereby affecting the real sector. Moreover, higher investment may lead to more imports of investment (capital) goods, thereby affecting the balance of payments.

III. MACROECONOMIC OBJECTIVES AND POLICIES TO ATTAIN THEM

As mentioned earlier, economies typically aim at achieving certain broad macroeconomic objectives designed to deliver a high or improved standard living for citizens or residents. Attaining a high standard of living typically requires an acceptable rate of real economic growth, sufficient to raise per capita income and to provide enough jobs to keep the unemployment rate low.[1] A well-performing economy also attains relative price stability (low inflation)[2] and a "sustainable" external position, meaning a balance of payments that can be maintained without need for a major change in exchange rate or trade policy and that does not lead to high ratios of external debt to GDP. Finally, most economies are concerned not only about the average level of income per capita but also about in its distribution. Thus, economies typically aim at reducing the percentage of people in poverty, and many also try to reduce income inequality by providing benefits targeted at low- to middle-income households and, in some cases, imposing higher taxes on upper-income households and the wealthy. As noted earlier, many countries also enact policies aimed at achieving other broad economic objectives, such as reducing pollution or improving the physical environment.

Considerable history suggests that achieving price stability and a sustainable external position are important for being able to sustain growth. Countries like Turkey, which for many years before 2000 experienced high inflation, had trouble keeping growth rates high so long as prices were elevated. In the case of Turkey, a few years of moderate (3–5 percent) real growth was frequently followed by an economic collapse, as the failure of the exchange rate to offset inflation led to a loss of competitiveness and an inability to finance imports and external debt. Similarly Romania, where inflation exceeded 300 percent early in the 1990s, experienced poor growth until inflation fell to more reasonable levels. More generally, many researchers have found that, above a minimum level (perhaps 1–3 percent for advanced economies and somewhat higher rates for developing and emerging market countries), higher inflation corresponds with lower growth rates.[3] One reason may be that higher inflation discourages private investment, encourages

---

[1] An economy's unemployment rate measures the ratio of those looking but unable to find work to those in the labor force. The unemployment rate can fluctuate not only with changes in the level of employment but also with changes in the number of those seeking work, as people enter or leave the labor force.

[2] Most economies aim at a low, rather than zero, rate of inflation, to allow increases in wages and prices to help attract resources to expanding sectors. These increases, averaged across the economy, result in small amounts of inflation.

[3] See, for example, Khan, M., and A. Senhadji (2001), "Threshold Effects in the Relationship Between Inflation and Growth," *IMF Staff Papers*, Vol. 48, No. 1, pp. 1–21 (December).

inefficient activities aimed at preserving the value of financial assets, and promotes capital flight to other economies with less inflation or a shift in assets to more stable currencies. As for external stability, balance of payments crises have imposed huge economic losses on many countries at all levels of economic development. In Asia, Indonesia, Malaysia, Thailand, and the Republic of Korea all suffered major declines in real GDP during 1998 because of large capital outflows (although Korea's situation stabilized within a year after short-term loans were renewed). Real GDP fell nearly 11 percent in Argentina during 2002 after continuing fiscal imbalances and an end to International Monetary Fund (IMF) support forced the country to abandon pegging its exchange rate to the U.S. dollar. In 2009 Iceland's real GDP fell nearly 7 percent, as huge losses in the banking sector triggered a collapse in the krona and a sharp decline in real imports and consumption.

Attaining attractive growth rates, low inflation, and a sustainable balance of payments requires a skilled mix of well-coordinated macroeconomic policies. These include

- Monetary policy (the choice and level of the monetary policy instrument, typically an overnight interest rate, along with the type of monetary framework and level of reserve requirements);
- Fiscal policy (the level and composition of revenues and expenditures, the level of budget balance or deficit, and the composition of budget financing);
- Exchange rate policy (the choice of exchange rate regime and policies affecting the level of the real exchange rate); and
- Structural policies (a wide array of specific measures involving trade, labor, competition, financial sector regulation, pricing, state enterprises, and governance, many of which affect the economy's investment climate). In recent years, financial sector regulation has become especially important, as banking crises have led to severe recessions in many economies, including Iceland, Ireland, Mexico, Spain, the United Kingdom, and the United States, with regional and even global spillovers, particularly after the U.S. financial crisis starting in late 2007.

Experience has shown that certain policies are critical for attaining and preserving macroeconomic stability (low inflation and a sustainable balance of payments). These include

- Monetary policy focused on attaining low inflation;
- Fiscal policy (in particular a level of the government budget deficit) that limits the demand for government financing and maintains a low to moderate ratio of public debt to GDP;
- An exchange rate regime appropriate for the economy (this will depend on the economy's circumstances, including the composition of its trade) that attains and maintains a competitive real exchange rate; and
- Supporting structural policies that provide an attractive investment climate; assist monetary, fiscal, and exchange rate policy; and foster public support for macroeconomic stability.

Experience has also shown that certain policies are essential for promoting economic growth.[4] These include attaining and maintaining macroeconomic stability, along with implementing various growth-promoting policies. Countries with sustained high growth rates have typically achieved low inflation and a strong balance of payments; attained high rates of investment and national savings, including reasonable rates of public investment; used markets and market prices to allocate most economic resources; achieved close integration with the world economy through liberal trade policies; established strong governance; and focused policies on promoting growth. Following from the above list, countries with high growth rates have typically developed and maintained good physical infrastructure, including reliable transport systems and sources of electricity. They have also developed strong and effective institutions, including the rule of law and respect for private property; an effective and impartial judicial system; an effective and stable financial system; an education system that produces graduates well prepared to fill job openings in the economy; political stability and good governance (effective and honest political administration); and a fiscal environment able to respond to new challenges. Together, these and related features, such as the ability to resolve insolvency effectively, relative simplicity in paying taxes, and

---

[4] For a comprehensive analysis of high-growth economies and the policies they have implemented, see Commission on Growth and Development (2008), *The Growth Report: Strategies for Sustained Growth and Inclusive Development* (Washington: World Bank).

the ease of obtaining construction permits, credit, electricity, and trading across borders, have a strong bearing on an economy's investment climate,[5] which in turn affects the level of investment. Indeed, structural reform is often the key to raising growth rates.

A. Monetary Policy

Monetary policy has the benefit of being quick and easy to set, although it may operate with a long lag. Monetary policy can be particularly effective at slowing inflation, particularly where inflation is believed to be closely related to the rate of monetary growth. By using its policy instrument to raise interest rates, the monetary authorities can reduce inflation by curbing aggregate demand, either through reducing the volume of loans (which decreases production, sales, employment, and income), reducing asset prices (which cuts spending, since people feel poorer when their net worth declines), or appreciating the exchange rate (which reduces exports). Appreciating the exchange rate also reduces inflation by cutting the price of imports in domestic currency. Although in the long run expanding the money supply can be expected only to raise prices, in the short run, where the authorities have credibility and the economy is operating below potential output, using the policy instrument to relax monetary conditions can boost economic activity by reducing interest rates, raising asset prices, and depreciating the exchange rate.

Where monetary policy has scope to operate — in economies where most transactions take place in domestic currency and the monetary authority is not a currency board or part of a broader currency union — the process of monetary policy depends on the following issues:

1. **Toward which objective is policy focused?** Monetary policy can focus on achieving price stability, achieving a targeted exchange rate, or attaining a growth objective, such as a particular rate of economic growth or a certain level of employment or unemployment rate. Pursuing more than one objective at once is very difficult, since separate policy instruments are needed to attain each objective and one policy instrument — usually open

---

[5] For details, see the World Bank's "Doing Business" website, www.doingbusiness.org.

market operations (buying and selling government securities or central bank bills, including "repurchase" and "reverse repurchase" operations) — generally dominates monetary policy. The laws governing the monetary authorities differ across countries, so different countries pursue different objectives. Some target the exchange rate, while others focus mainly on attaining price stability. A few countries, such as the United States, pre-scribe multiple objectives for their monetary authority, allowing the authority to shift between focusing on price stability and focusing on attaining high employment or a high growth rate, depending on conditions in the economy.

2. **Which monetary framework is used?** Countries can choose among several frameworks in conducting monetary policy. Some target the growth rate of a monetary aggregate, such as broad money (*M*2 or *M*3). A few, such as the United States during the decade or so after World War II, target a certain level of market interest rates. More than 30 countries have adopted a framework called inflation targeting, in which monetary policy instruments are used to attain a forecast rate of inflation at some point in the future.[6] Implementing inflation targeting requires countries to have a reasonable model linking changes in their policy instrument to forecast rates of inflation. They must also announce their inflation targets, publish the proceedings of monetary policy deliberations, and be capable of com-mitting to their targets by avoiding "fiscal dominance" (having large fiscal deficits that dictate the stance of monetary policy).

3. **Which instrument is used to conduct monetary policy?** Most coun-tries today use indirect instruments, in particular open market operations, to conduct monetary policy. Indirect instruments have the advantage of providing a market solution to expanding or contracting the monetary base, because the desired change in the policy rate can be achieved by interacting with only those banks that wish to buy securities from the monetary authority (thereby reducing reserves and raising interest rates) or sell securities to the monetary authority (thereby adding reserves and

---

[6] See Jawan, S. (2012), "Inflation Targeting: Holding the Line," *Finance and Development.* Available at: http://www.imf.org/external/pubs/ft/fandd/basics/target.htm. Accessed July 16, 2017.

lowering interest rates). In the past, more countries used direct instruments, such as establishing interest rate ceilings or ceilings on credit for each bank. Direct instruments typically proved less efficient than indirect instruments, because they constrained all banks, regardless of their lending position or extent of excess reserves.

Effective monetary policy ordinarily requires that the monetary authority be perceived as being independent, i.e., capable of pursuing its policy objective without requiring government approval. Under inflation targeting, some countries require the monetary authority and government jointly to agree on a targeted rate of inflation. Once the objective is set, however, the monetary authority should be free to use its policy instruments to achieve the objective without government interference.

B. Fiscal Policy

Fiscal policy, which usually takes longer to establish than monetary policy, should be well coordinated with monetary policy and aim at attaining potential output, meaning maximum employment consistent with relative price stability. Fiscal policy should also aim at attaining public debt sustainability: keeping the ratio of public debt to GDP at a low to moderate level, generally not exceeding 40–50 percent of GDP (the level at which many developing and emerging market economies have begun to experience defaults). Countries in the Euro zone have adopted 60 percent of GDP as the ceiling for public debt under the Maastricht Treaty, although countries have been allowed to exceed the limit under extenuating circumstances, such as those arising from the Financial Crisis of 2007–2009. In several advanced economies, public debt has exceeded 100 percent of GDP (e.g., the United States, Japan), and governments are struggling with how to reduce the debt ratio to a more sustainable level.

Most economies aiming to curb inflation or reduce the deficit in the current account of the balance of payments make tightening fiscal policy — reducing the government's budget deficit — part of the policy response. In many economies cutting expenditure is a key part of tightening fiscal policy. Economists usually advocate cutting so-called "unproductive" expenditure — outlays whose benefits are small relative to their costs. However, political concerns often lead economies to sacrifice valuable spending, such as outlays for operations and maintenance, rather than reducing public employment, cutting subsidies, or scaling back inefficient but politically useful capital projects. In some economies, fiscal consolidation also includes measures to raise revenues. Such measures are particularly valuable in countries where the ratio of revenues to GDP is very low — under 15 percent — and the government has difficulty finding enough revenue to fund basic services, such as public education and the provision of infrastructure. Although revenue raising measures usually involve increasing taxes, in some economies efforts to raise non-tax revenues, for example, by making state enterprises more efficient and profitable, can be useful. Measures to improve tax administration and increase compliance with the law can also help, although it is often difficult estimating how much revenue such measures can generate.

C. Exchange Rate Policy

Exchange rate policy should be used to promote competitiveness and a sustainable external current account balance, one in which any deficit is easily financed by assured capital inflows that keep the ratio of external debt to GDP modest (preferably below 40 percent), with a low ratio of debt service (principal and interest) to exports of goods and services (ideally less than 10–12 percent). If the authorities choose to fix the exchange rate, the rate should be market clearing, avoiding any incentives to create a parallel market that can distort activity and encourage corruption. To judge competitiveness, the authorities should assess the real effective exchange rate against a broad set of the economy's trading partners. Signs that a currency may be over-valued or under-valued include (1) a large and noticeable parallel market in foreign exchange; (2) a large and persistent current account deficit or surplus; and (3) a large and continuing real appreciation or depreciation in the exchange rate. The IMF now uses a method called "External Balance Assessment" (EBA), which relies on regression-based analyses to determine whether an exchange rate is over- or under-valued, to assess the appropriateness of the exchange rate.[7]

---

[7] For details, see Phillips, S., and others (2013), "External Balance Assessment (EBA) Methodology," IMF Working Paper 13/272 (Washington: December). Available at: http://www.imf.org/external/pubs/ft/wp/2013/wp13272.pdf. Accessed July 16, 2017. Previously the IMF used a different approach, the so-called (Consultative Group on Exchange Rate Issues) "CGER" methodology, which employed three different methods — the

The choice of exchange rate regime is a key issue for exchange rate policy. Regimes vary along a spectrum from so-called "hard fixed" regimes, involving membership in a currency union (such as the Euro zone) or creation of a currency board (where currency creation is linked to the level of foreign reserves) to floating exchange rate regimes, whether managed or freely floating. In the middle are so-called intermediate regimes, such as a managed crawl (where the exchange rate appreciates or depreciates at a set pace against a reference currency or set of currencies), floating within bands (where the exchange rate can move inside certain limits), or an adjustable peg (where the currency is fixed against a reference currency but can adjust if the authorities choose or conditions warrant — the system in effect for most advanced economies between 1945 and 1973). Small economies with a single, dominant trading partner (such as Bhutan, Nepal, or some of the Pacific Islands) may find it useful to peg their currencies to that of the trading partner. However, they need to monitor their currencies, to avoid a steady real appreciation (or depreciation) that could make the existing peg unsustainable. Economies with a history of high inflation sometimes find it useful to peg to the currency of a major trading partner with low inflation, such as the Euro zone. Again, such a peg works only if the economy keeps domestic inflation in check, to prevent the currency from becoming seriously over-valued. Economies adopting an inflation targeting regime typically adopt a floating exchange rate, to allow an independent monetary policy and open capital account (few restrictions on capital movements).

D. Price Adjustment Issues

Many economies fix the prices of critical goods and services, such as petroleum, electricity, or certain food items, to curb the power of monopolies or try to preserve the purchasing power of consumers. While price

---

macroeconomic balance, equilibrium real exchange rate, and external sustainability approaches — to assess the appropriateness of the real exchange rate. Under the CGER methodology, a currency would typically be labeled over- or under-valued if all three methods pointed in the same direction. For more information, see Lee, Jaewoo, and others (2008), *Exchange Rate Assessments: CGER Methodologies*, Occasional Paper 261 (Washington, DC: International Monetary Fund, April).

ceilings are a well-established part of regulating monopolies, efforts to limit prices of other goods can create difficulties when the prices differ substantially from those that would prevail in free markets. Keeping prices below market-clearing levels can lead to shortages, as firms reduce production while consumers seek higher purchases. In some cases, price ceilings lead to high imports. In others, setting low prices for crops may cause farmers to avoid selling to state marketing boards and even smuggle goods outside the country, as in Ghana during the early 1980s. Pricing the output of state enterprises below cost-recovery levels can create losses, requiring the government budget to provide transfers and leading firms to borrow heavily from the banking system. Alternatively, firms may raise prices for other goods, establishing a complex pattern of cross-subsidization that leads to an inefficient allocation of resources. For all these reasons, governments should think carefully about setting prices below costs.

Interest rates also raise important pricing issues, since the rate of interest represents the price of borrowing or the reward for depositing money. Setting interest rates below the perceived rate of inflation, which creates negative real rates, discourages saving while encouraging borrowing, exacerbating the imbalance between the demand and supply of funds for lending. Thus, economies should avoid allowing interest rates to become negative in real terms, particularly for deposits.

Finally, the real exchange rate itself represents an important price in the economy. An overvalued exchange rate discourages exports while encouraging imports. Thus, it helps weaken the current account balance. However, an undervalued exchange rate raises the price of imports in domestic currency, thereby adding to inflation. Thus, economies do better when the real exchange rate is at an appropriate level — neither overvalued nor under-valued.

E. Structural Policies

Structural policies play an important role in supporting monetary, fiscal, and exchange rate policies and contribute importantly to an economy's investment climate. At any one time, certain structural issues are particularly important in an economy. For example, during the 1990s, in many eastern European countries, privatization, state enterprise reform, price liberalization, and rationalizing subsidies were critical steps in the transition from central planning to a market economy. In other countries, such as Indonesia, eliminating monopolies and strengthening competition among market participants were important. Many economies at all income levels have grappled with financial sector reform. Others have implemented reforms in tax administration, budgeting, and public expenditure management. External sector reforms, including trade liberalization and, *where appropriate* (usually only after strengthening the financial sector, with adequate regulation and supervision), capital account liberalization, can also be valuable. Better corporate and public sector governance, including a more efficient judicial and legal system and more transparent and effective delivery of government services, can play a critical role in improving the investment climate. Combatting money-laundering and terrorist financing is important for strengthening the rule of law. Finally, research shows that reducing corruption can boost investment and raise a country's growth rate.[8] Addressing whichever of these issues is problematic can be important for economic adjustment and promoting growth.

IV. SUMMARY AND CONCLUSIONS

Macroeconomic analysis is the study of an economy's main components: the accounts used to measure performance, key performance indicators, and the main policies driving the economy. For the purposes of analysis, the economy can be subdivided into four main sectors: the real sector, whose performance is measured by the national accounts; the external sector, where performance is measured by the balance of payments and data on external debt; the fiscal sector, whose outcome is measured by budget and debt data on all levels of government, possibly augmented by the consolidated accounts of the pubic (state-owned) enterprises; and the monetary sector, whose activities are usually summarized in the monetary survey, which combines the accounts of the

---

[8] Mauro has estimated that a one standard deviation reduction in corruption, based on the "Business International" index (subsequently acquired by the Economist Intelligence Unit), is associated with increases of 0.5 percent in a country's real growth rate and 5 percentage points in its ratio of investment to GDP. See Mauro, P. (1995), "Corruption and Growth," *Quarterly Journal of Economics*, Vol. 110, No. 3, pp. 681–712 (August).

monetary authority and the consolidated deposit money (commercial) banks. The four sectors are related in many ways, and activities originating in one sector generally affect all other sectors.

An economy's performance can be assessed by analyzing developments in key indicators drawn from the accounts of the real, external, fiscal, and monetary sectors. Key indicators from the real sector include the growth rate of real GDP, the ratios of national savings and total investment to GDP, and the percentage changes in the consumer price index, the GDP deflator, and possibly other price indices. Important indicators from the external sector include the ratio of the current account balance to GDP, the size of the overall balance in the balance of payments, trends in the real effective exchange rate, and the ratios of external debt to GDP, debt service (principal plus interest) to exports of goods and services, and gross reserves to short-term debt service. Useful indicators from the fiscal sector include the ratios of revenue, expenditure, the overall fiscal balance, and total government debt (foreign plus domestic) to GDP. Important monetary and financial indicators include the growth rate of broad money, nominal and real interest rates on loans and deposits, the percentage of nonperforming loans, indices of housing and asset prices (to test for asset price "bubbles"), and measures of corporate and household indebtedness.

Most economies strive for high growth, low inflation, and a sustainable balance of payments, often accompanied by efforts to reduce poverty, preserve the environment, and limit income inequality. Governments try to attain these objectives using monetary, fiscal, and exchange rate policy, along with structural policies in such areas as financial sector regulation, trade and competition policy, and measures to strengthen company and public sector governance. The careful use of structural policies can promote stabilization and improve the investment climate, thereby supporting economic growth.

Chapter 2

REAL SECTOR ACCOUNTS AND ANALYSIS

As mentioned in Chapter 1, an economy's output, growth, and inflation are measured in the real sector of the economy. This chapter discusses the main elements of the real sector, including measures of actual and potential output and other macroeconomic aggregates; economic growth; and prices.

I. ECONOMIC OUTPUT, GROWTH, AND EMPLOYMENT

A. Macroeconomic Aggregates: Gross Domestic Product

Gross domestic product (GDP) is the most fundamental of the macroeconomic aggregates that describe an economy's output, income, and total expenditure. GDP represents the total market value of final goods and services an economy produces. GDP is also the total value added by an economy: the value of all goods and services produced, less the value of all inputs used in producing these items.

GDP can be measured in three ways. One is from the supply side ("GDP by sector of origin"), by aggregating value added in the various production sectors of the economy (agriculture; industry, including manufacturing, mining, construction, and utilities; and services, including trade, hotels, restaurants, finance, housing, the non-profit sector, and government). Another is from the demand side ("GDP by category of expenditure"), aggregating consumption and investment in the private and public sectors, along with net exports (exports of goods and services, minus imports of goods and services). The third is the income approach: aggregating all factor incomes: wages, interest, rent and profit, consumption of fixed capital (depreciation), and net indirect taxes (indirect taxes such as value added taxes (VATs) and excise taxes, less subsidies). Virtually all countries publish data on GDP by sector of origin, in both real and nominal terms, and most publish data on GDP by expenditure, at least in nominal terms. Typically, only advanced economies publish data on GDP by source of income. Tables 2.1–2.3 provide illustrative data on GDP by expenditure, sector of origin, and income, respectively.

All three approaches to GDP should, in principle, yield the same result, although in many countries the data reveal small discrepancies between different approaches (e.g., GDP by sector of production and GDP by category of expenditure). The reason is that, in principle, income should equal expenditure in every economy, because every transaction has a buyer and a seller, and every unit of spending by some buyer is a unit of income for some seller. The equality of income and expenditure can be illustrated with a simple "circular-flow" diagram for a closed economy, with no government, no external trade, and no capital inflows or outflows (Figure 2.1). Within this diagram, every expenditure by one party is a source of income for another, and vice versa. Adding government to the diagram would insert some outflows (e.g., tax payments) and inflows (e.g., transfer payments to individuals) but leave the basic structure unchanged if government is introduced as another party in the economy. Introducing foreign trade and payments would introduce additional outflows (e.g., exports of goods, payments for imports) and inflows (e.g., receipts for exports, imports of goods). However, enlarging the diagram to include the "rest of the world" would again lead to a circular flow — this time, for the global economy.

When considering GDP by category of expenditure, the following information is noteworthy.

1. **Consumption** involves purchases of goods and services by firms, households, and government (including state enterprises) for items that could, in principle, be consumed in a year, plus consumer durables such

TABLE 2.1   INDONESIA: GDP BY EXPENDITURE, 1998–2002 (IN BILLIONS OF RUPIAH; AT CURRENT PRICES)

	1997	1998	1999	2000	2001	2002
Domestic demand	629,423.9	818,090.6	970,754.3	1,100,017.5	1,307,362.6	1,445,971.4
Consumption	451,737.8	575,047.2	749,282.0	824,136.2	993,296.8	1,119,806.2
Private	408,785.8	539,053.6	704,110.9	768,996.2	993,948.8	1,055,458.4
Public (central govt)	42,952.0	35,993.5	45,171.1	55,140.0	59,348.0	64,347.8
Investment	177,686.1	243,043.4	221,472.3	275,881.3	314,065.8	326,165.2
Fixed captial	177,686.1	243,043.4	221,472.3	275,881.3	314,065.8	326,165.2
Private sector	—	193,920.4	171,242.1	227,193.2	272,480.8	290,542.1
government (central govt)	—	49,123.0	50,230.2	48,688.1	41,585.0	35,623.1
Net exports of goods + services	−1,728.5	137,658.8	128,977.7	164,901.4	160,292.5	164,593.7
Exports of goods and services	174,871.3	539,398.9	434,129.1	600,669.5	632,742.4	597,478.8
Imports of goods and services	176,599.8	401,740.1	305,151.4	435,768.1	472,450.0	432,885.1

Source: Data provided by the Indonesian authorities.

TABLE 2.2 SINGAPORE: GDP BY SECTOR OF ORIGIN, 2011–2016 (IN MILLIONS OF SINGAPORE DOLLARS AT CURRENT MARKET PRICES)

	2011	2012	2013	2014	2015	2016
GDP	346,649	361,365.9	378,531.6	390,447.7	408,096.6	410,271.9
Goods Producing Industries	85,981	89,813.7	88,420.9	94,560.3	100,516	100,491.7
Manufacturing	65,901.1	67,869.5	65,837	69,573.6	74,790	75,295.7
Construction	14,811.6	16,450.5	17,201	19,341.1	19,897.2	19,346.2
Utilities	5,148.4	5,373.2	5,253.5	5,499	5,686.6	5,709.2
Other Goods Industries	119.9	120.5	129.4	146.6	142.2	140.6
Service Producing Industries	226,980	235,504.7	251,757.3	257,418.8	266,346.1	266,525
Wholesale and Retail Trade	66,597.8	64,807	66,070.1	59,985.8	56,975.8	54,618.7
Transportation and Storage	22,222.7	23,660.9	24,666.9	27,075.3	29,690	29,198
Accommodation and Food Services	6,986	7,504.3	7,818.6	8,249.2	8,392.9	8,602.8
Information and Communications	12,356.9	13,429.9	14,543.4	15,538.2	15,610.6	16,265.2
Finance and Insurance	35,295.4	37,289.7	42,292.2	45,773.9	49,902.6	50,242.4
Business Services	47,661.1	51,309.6	56,139.2	58,199.8	61,082	60,584.1
Other Services Industries	35,860.1	37,503.3	40,226.9	42,596.6	44,692.2	47,013.8
Ownership of Dwellings	13,797.2	14,992	16,308.8	16,861.9	17,177.2	16,819.9
Gross Value Added At Basic Prices	326,758.2	340,310.4	356,487	368,841	384,039.3	383,836.6
Add: Taxes on Products	19,890.8	21,055.5	22,044.6	21,606.7	24,057.3	26,435.3

Source: Singapore Department of Statistics (SINGSTAT).

TABLE 2.3 KOREA: GDP BY INCOME, 2007–2012 (IN BILLIONS OF KOREAN WON AT CURRENT PRICES)

	2007	2008	2009	2010	2011	2012
Compensation of Employees	448,994	474,954	493,686	526,279	560,153	680,757
Operating Surplus	284,556	295,368	310,604	363,901	375,979	201,476
Consumption of Fixed Capital	128,904	135,876	142,094	150,911	163,653	339,895
Taxes on Production and Imports	117,375	125,296	122,907	136,918	140,532	10,722
(less) Subsidies	4,816	5,042	4,254	4,734	5,157	718,967
Gross Domestic Product	975,013	1,026,452	1,065,037	1,173,275	1,235,161	679,786

Source: Korean Statistical Information Service (Kosis), Table 10.2.1, from data provided by the Bank of Korea.

The circular flow diagram – for a simple closed economy

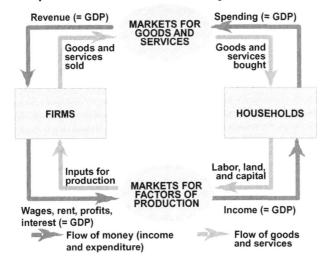

FIGURE 2.1. THE CIRCULAR FLOW OF INCOME AND EXPENDITURE IN A SIMPLE ECONOMY

Source: Derived from yyp.earecom.press, circular-flow diagram.

as automobiles and appliances. Government consumption includes government payments for wages, salaries, and purchases of other goods and services — typically, most expenditure for the operation and maintenance of government activities and programs. By convention, government consumption includes outlays for armaments and most other military spending, except for constructing military installations. Government consumption *excludes* transfer payments, subsidies, and interest payments because they are not made in exchange for currently produced goods or services.

2. **Investment** involves purchases of goods and services by firms, households, and government (including state enterprises) for long-lived assets. Private investment comprises spending by the private sector on capital equipment, inventories, and structures, including new housing. Government investment involves government expenditure on capital (long-lived) projects, including government facilities and public infrastructure (highways, water projects, public utilities, schools, public hospitals, military installations, etc.). Purchases of land are not counted, however, since these are considered changing the form of asset holding. The IMF's 2001 *Government Finance Statistics Manual*, with its net worth approach to government accounts, makes this clear. As noted earlier, purchases of military equipment are part of government consumption.

3. **Net exports** comprise exports of goods and non-factor services, minus imports of goods and non-factor services. Non-factor services comprise items such as freight and insurance on imports, transportation, receipts and payments for travel, and government payments for embassies and other foreign services. Net exports *exclude* repatriated wages and profits. They also *exclude* external interest payments and interest receipts. Repatriated wages and profits, and external interest receipts and payments, are part of net factor service income and included in a different macroeconomic aggregate — Gross National Income (GNI).

B. Other Macroeconomic Aggregates

Gross National Income (GNI) — formerly called Gross National Product (GNP) — is GDP plus net factor income from abroad. Net factor income from abroad (NFY) includes net earnings (or payments) from wages, interest, and profits earned or remitted overseas. NFY includes compensation of non-residents working outside their home countries. Thus, the foreign earnings of a citizen or permanent resident of a country who works in another country for a few months but then returns home are part of NFY. Remittances by those residing for more than a year in another country are classified as current transfers.

Gross National Disposable Income (GNDI) equals GNI plus net foreign transfers to the economy. Net foreign transfers include both official transfers (e.g., grants from foreign donors) and private transfers (gifts to or from persons living abroad). As noted above, net foreign transfers include remittances by citizens and residents living abroad for more than a year at a time. In a number of countries (including Jordan, Lesotho, Philippines, Vietnam, and some Pacific Island countries), remittances comprise an important source of income for the economy, sometimes exceeding 10 percent of GDP.

Gross National Savings (GNS) represents the difference between GNDI and consumption. GNS is the money left over from GNDI after total spending on consumption. Gross domestic savings (GDS) is the difference between GDP and consumption, while government savings represent the difference between government revenue (in particular, government disposable income, meaning revenue apart from sales of land and similar assets, less payments for interest, subsidies, and transfers, and any net lending under government programs) and government consumption. All three savings measures are useful for identifying domestic sources of financing for investment. Too little national savings can constrain investment or force the economy to rely on foreign savings for investment. A shortfall of government savings from investment means that government must run a deficit, borrowing either domestically or abroad, to finance its activities.

The **Output Gap** measures the difference between real GDP and the economy's potential output — the level at which the economy can operate at relative price stability (i.e., low inflation). The output gap is calculated as actual GDP minus potential GDP. A positive output gap means a country is operating above potential, while GDP is below potential if the output gap is negative, as shown in Figure 2.2.

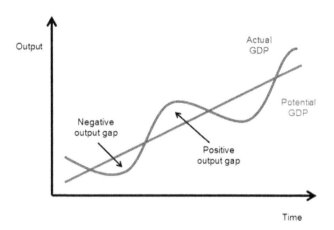

FIGURE 2.2. THE OUTPUT GAP

Source: moneymorning.com.au/20090629/output-gap-indicates-there-wont-be-any-inflation.html

Estimating the output gap requires an estimate of potential output. Potential output can be estimated in one of two ways: econometrically, by applying a filter to past data on real GDP, or by estimating a production function for the economy using estimates of total capital, total labor, and total factor productivity using a Cobb–Douglas or other production function. The data filtering approach, applying the Hodrick–Prescott or other filters (e.g., Baxter–King, Christiano–Fitzgerald symmetric or asymmetric) to past data, is the most common method. EViews and other econometric software packages provide ways of using these filters to estimate potential output and, thus, the output gap, for an economy.

C. Linkages between Income and Absorption, or Savings and Investment, and the Current Account

It is useful to know that the difference between GNDI and absorption (total consumption plus total investment), and the difference between GNS and investment, has a direct relationship with the current account balance in the balance of payments. These relationships can be seen with the help of a few equations.

Begin with the definition of GDP by expenditure:

$$GDP = C + I + X - M$$

Add net factor service income (NFY) to both sides of the equation, creating GNI:

$$\text{GNI} = C + I + X - M + \text{NFY}$$

Then add net foreign transfers (TRF) to both sides, creating GNDI:

$$\text{GNDI} = C + I + X - M + \text{NFY} + \text{TRF}$$

Now subtract absorption (A), comprising consumption and investment, from both sides of the equation:

$$\text{GNDI} - A = X - M + \text{NFY} + \text{TRF} = \text{CAB}$$

It turns out that GNDI minus A equals $X - M + \text{NFY} + \text{TRF}$, which in turn comprise the elements of the current account balance in the balance of payments. Thus, GNDI minus A equals the current account balance. This has the following implications:

1. If GNDI $- A$ is positive, meaning that GNDI exceeds consumption plus investment, the current account is in surplus.
2. If GNDI $- A$ is negative, so that GNDI is less than consumption plus investment, the current account is in deficit.
3. If GNDI $- A$ is zero, meaning that GNDI equals the sum of consumption and investment, the current account balance is exactly zero.

An even more useful set of relationships involves the savings minus investment balance and the current account balance. Begin with the definition of GNDI and subtract consumption from both sides of the equation, obtaining an expression for GNS, or simply S:

$$\text{GNDI} - C = \text{GNS} = S = I + X - M + \text{NFY} + \text{TRF}$$

Now, subtract investment from both sides of the equation:

$$S - I = X - M + \text{NFY} + \text{TRF} = \text{CAB}$$

Notice that $S - I$ also equals the current account balance of the balance of payments. This implies that

4. If $S - I$ is positive, meaning that GNS exceeds total investment, the current account is in surplus.
5. If $S - I$ is negative, so that GNS is less than total investment, the current account is in deficit.
6. If $S - I$ is zero, meaning that GNS equals total investment, the current account balance is exactly zero.

The $S - I$ balance can be disaggregated into separate $S - I$ balances for the public and private, or government and non-government, sectors, to determine how each sector contributes to the economy's $S - I$ balance, and thus the current account balance in the balance of payments:

$$S - I = (S - I)_g + (S - I)_{ng}.$$

Since government savings equals government revenue, less payments for subsidies, transfers, interest, net lending, and consumption, the government's $S - I$ balance equals

$$S_g - I_g = \text{Rev} - C_g - \text{Transfers} - \text{Interest} - \text{Subsidies}$$
$$- \text{Net Lending} - \text{Investment} = \text{Budget Balance}$$

Government consumption, plus transfers, plus interest, plus subsidies, plus net lending, plus government investment, comprise all the elements of government expenditure. Thus, the government's $S - I$ balance equals the budget balance (or the budget balance excluding net lending, if net lending is not included in government expenditure, as in the 2001 *Government Finance Statistics Manual*). This has an interesting implication: a government budget deficit generally contributes to a deficit in the current account of the balance of payments. Unless reducing the deficit reduces non-government savings by the same amount, a government can reduce the economy's current account deficit by reducing its own budget deficit. More generally, a country's authorities can reduce an excessive deficit in the current account by bringing national savings and investment into better balance. In the short run, this will likely require measures to reduce consumption (thereby raising savings) and investment. Over time, however, savings can rise as economic growth raises income (GNDI, and particularly GDP within GNDI).

D. Economic Growth and Employment

Economic growth is an enormous subject. For purposes of national income accounting, it is worth noting a few factors that research has shown can accelerate growth and, thus, boost income.

1. **Promoting investment**. Most studies show a strong correlation between growth and investment. Other things being equal, countries with higher rates of investment — both public and private — tend to grow faster. The Spence Commission on Growth has noted that investment averaged at least 25 percent of GDP, with public outlays on infrastructure and education typically about 1/3 of total investment, in the 13 countries with the highest sustained growth rates from World War II through 2005.[1]

2. **Strengthening the investment climate**. While countries have many ways to promote investment, legal and regulatory changes that make it easier for private sector firms to do business can be a powerful way to strengthen the investment climate. Each year, the World Bank assesses more than 180 economies on the ease of doing business, using such criteria as the time needed to open a business, the cost and time required to pay taxes, the ease of obtaining credit, electricity, and construction permits, and the time and cost needed to resolve business disputes (i.e., have a case heard in court). The data appear in the World Bank's Doing Business website, www.doingbusiness.org, which allows countries to compare themselves against others in their region and competitors elsewhere.

3. **Boosting competitiveness**. Countries can also accelerate growth by taking steps to boost their competitiveness, thereby encouraging exports and attracting more investment. The World Economic Forum (WEF) publishes an annual report ranking more than 135 economies along 12 dimensions of competitiveness, including the quality of institutions, infrastructure, macroeconomic stability, and financial market development. Annual reports can be found at the WEF's website, www.weforum.org.

---

[1]Commission on Growth and Development (2008), *The Growth Report: Strategies for Sustained Growth and Inclusive Development* (Washington: World Bank).

Employment, like growth, is a vast subject with an extensive literature of its own. For purposes of macroeconomic analysis, an economy's level of employment depends on many factors, including the size and composition of the labor force, how close the economy is to potential output, the structure of economic activity, and how well the labor force matches the needs of employers. In many developing and some emerging market economies, a poor investment climate has made it hard for employers to create enough jobs to meet the demand, including jobs for university graduates. In some countries, a poor match of training with job openings contributes to high unemployment: not enough graduates in science and other technical fields, for example. In still other countries, economic expansion in urban areas has encouraged mass migration from rural areas, creating an excess supply of marginally skilled workers for the limited number of jobs available in urban manufacturing.

Traditionally, economies have boosted high-wage employment by promoting investment, providing a stable and competitive macroeconomic environment, and supporting productive education and training, so that employers can find enough workers with the relevant skills to meet production goals. While government programs can promote job matching, addressing large-scale unemployment typically requires a long-term and multi-pronged program aimed at strengthening education, improving on-the-job training, and facilitating job matching, often by promoting internship programs that ease the transition of young adults from school to the workforce. Successful programs also require being able to operate the economy near potential output, so that the demand for labor is high. In some advanced economies, an aging population may complicate the ability of firms to meet their demand for appropriately skilled workers. In these countries, measures to promote immigration or the use of skilled foreign labor may be important for sustaining production and growth.

II. INFLATION AND PRICES

Inflation is a sustained increase in the overall price level. The sustained nature of the increase distinguishes inflation from a one-time shock to the price level that could come, for example, from a sudden jump in food or fuel prices that is later reversed. In practice, one-time price shocks can generate inflation if the jump in prices is passed through to other prices in the economy, creating a noticeable rise in consumer and other prices and causing firms, workers, and households to revise their expectations about the future rate of inflation. This change in expectations can cause the overall rate of inflation to accelerate and remain elevated over time. Thus, ensuring that one-time price shocks do not change expectations and lead to a more general rise in prices is an important concern for the economy's policy makers, in particular the monetary authority (central bank).

Economists often distinguish between headline inflation, the rate of increase of the general price level, and core or underlying inflation, which measures inflation after volatile elements such as prices for food and fuel are removed from the main price index. In some countries, they may also include the price of housing. Occasionally core inflation will be defined as the inflation rate after removing the impact of one-time events, such as one-time changes in a value added or sales tax, a reduction in fuel subsidies, or the exchange rate. Removing volatile elements can have a large effect on the rate of inflation over time. In Thailand, for example, the 25 percent or so of the consumer price index (CPI) removed in calculating core inflation has accounted for the preponderance of variation in the overall rate of consumer price inflation in many years.

Most economies have several indices for measuring inflation. The most common is the consumer price index (CPI), a weighted average of prices for items purchased by a representative consumer or household. The CPI is generally calculated as an average for the entire economy, although in some small island economies there may only be a CPI for the capital city. In some larger economies, separate CPIs are calculated for different geographic areas or for specific demographic groups, such as the elderly, whose market baskets may differ from the average for the entire population. Besides the CPI, most economies have either a wholesale price index (WPI), which records changes in the prices of goods at the wholesale (pre-retail) level; a producer price index (PPI), which measures changes in a sample of goods at the production (e.g., factory) stage; or both. In addition, all economies have a GDP deflator, which measures the inflationary component of changes in nominal GDP and allows calculation of the real (volume) change in GDP (the real rate of economic growth). The GDP deflator is normally compiled as a weighted average either of deflators for each of the main production sectors (agriculture, industry, and services) or the deflators for the components of GDP by expenditure (private and public consumption, private and public investment, exports of goods and services, and imports of goods and services). In each index, the weights used to calculate the overall price change are the weights of each component (e.g., food, fuel, clothing, housing, services, and other items, for the CPI) in the overall index. Because each price index has different components, the rate of change in each index may differ, although the differences are often small, particularly if the overall rate of inflation is low (e.g., less than 2 or 3 percent).

The CPI records changes in a market basket of consumer goods. Thus, it reflects changes in the price of domestically produced goods and imports that are part of household consumption, but not the price of exports. The basket is usually fixed for a period of time and updated every few years to reflect changes in consumer spending. The WPI and PPI, which reflect prices at the wholesale or producer level, respectively, may be a useful guide to production costs. In addition, changes in the PPI or WPI changes may signal changes in the CPI in the coming months, as retailers adjust their own prices in response to higher prices at the production or wholesale level.

The GDP deflator differs from the CPI because it includes prices of exports and investment. In addition, it includes the average price of all imports, not just those that households consume, as well as the prices of goods produced in the economy that are not part of household consumption. Because of different coverage and different weights of those items that appear in both the GDP deflator and the CPI, the two indices will move at different rates. When export and import prices rise more than the prices of domestically consumed goods, and exports and imports are both large in relation to GDP, the GDP deflator may rise more than the CPI. By comparison, the GDP deflator may rise less than the CPI if the exchange rate appreciates (which reduces the domestic price of both exports and imports) and trade is large in comparison to GDP while imports are only a small part of household consumption.

Although the GDP deflator can be measured from both the production (supply) and expenditure (demand) side, forecasting the deflator is often easier from the expenditure side, because it may be easier to forecast deflators for consumption, exports, imports, and investment than to forecast the deflators for the various production sectors (agriculture, industry, and services). Consumption deflators, particularly the deflator for private consumption, may mirror changes in the CPI. Data on prices of key exports and imports may be known, so that a weighted average of all export and all import prices in foreign currency can be compiled. In addition, it may be possible to make a plausible forecast of the exchange rate. The investment deflator should be a weighted average of imported and domestic prices, with weights reflecting the share of imported and domestic components of investment goods. In countries like China that produce many of the goods needed for investment, the weight of import prices in the investment deflator will be small. In Pacific Island countries that import most goods, import prices will have a weight of close to 100 percent in the investment deflator. Recent data may offer guidance on what weights to use for the shares of domestic and import prices in the deflator.

It is worth remembering the difference between nominal and real GDP. Nominal GDP measures the economy's value added at current prices, while real GDP measures value added using constant prices. Changes in nominal GDP reflect changes in both prices and physical output, while changes in real GDP record changes only in the economy's physical output.

The same difference applies to other real and nominal variables (e.g., consumption, investment). Nominal consumption reflects changes in both real consumption amounts and in the consumption deflator, while real consumption measures changes in the volume of consumption, meaning consumption at constant prices. The same is true for nominal and real investment. Moreover, the deflators for private and public consumption, and private and public investment, may differ, because each involves different items. The private consumption deflator reflects the set of goods and services purchased by households and private firms, while the government consumption deflator reflects the prices of government wages and salaries, along with the costs for operations and maintenance in government programs and installations. The private investment deflator reflects the cost of inputs for private investment, while the deflator for public investment reflects the costs associated with government investment projects, such as those for infrastructure.

III. MISCELLANEOUS ISSUES

A. Rebasing National Accounts Data

Data for GDP at constant prices can vary, depending on the year chosen for basing the series. In general, the longer the time since the last rebasing of data, the greater the risk that the data may no longer provide an accurate view of trends in real GDP. An economy's structure changes over time, and the share of GDP attributable to goods and services whose prices have risen more rapidly often represents a smaller proportion of GDP as time passes. To avoid biasing estimates, data for GDP should be "rebased" periodically, so that increases in the GDP deflator take into account the current structure of production. Some advanced economies, such as the United States, have addressed the issue by creating a "chain weighted" data series for GDP, which allows the composition of GDP to change every year.

B. Relating Changes in the Nominal Value of a Variable to Changes in Price and Quantity

Often, analysts need to project the nominal value of GDP, consumption, or another macroeconomic aggregate by using projections for real growth and the appropriate price deflator. Alternatively, the real growth in a variable needs to be calculated from data on the changes in the nominal value and the change in the deflator, or the change in the deflator from the growth in the nominal and real quantities. For all these operations, the following formula should be used:

$$(1 + \Delta\%V/100) = (1 + \Delta\%P/100) * (1 + \Delta\%Q/100) \qquad (2.1)$$

where $\Delta\%V$ represents the percent change in the nominal value in whole numbers (e.g., 9 percent), $\Delta\%P$ represents the percent change in the relevant deflator or price index, and $\Delta\%Q$ represents the percent change in the volume or "real" quantity of the variable.

This formula provides a more accurate answer than simply adding the percentage changes in P and Q, since it takes account of the small cross product term $\Delta\%P \times \Delta\%Q$ omitted from the simple addition of percentage changes in *P* and *Q*. From the above formula the variables of interest are solved as follows:

$$\Delta\%V = [(1 + \Delta\%P/100) \times (1 + \Delta\%Q/100) - 1] \times 100$$
$$\Delta\%Q = [(1 + \Delta\%V/100)/(1 + \Delta\%P/100) - 1] \times 100$$
$$\Delta\%P = [(1 + \Delta\%V/100)/(1 + \Delta\%Q/100) - 1] \times 100$$

Equation (2.1) shows, for example, that the percent change in nominal GDP resulting from real growth of 5 percent and a rise in the GDP deflator of 3 percent is not 8 percent, but a slightly higher value, 8.15 percent: $(1.05 \times 1.03 - 1) \times 100 = (1.0815 - 1) \times 100 = 0.0815 \times 100 = 8.15$ percent. Similarly, the real growth in GDP associated with a nominal rise of 10 percent and a rise in the GDP deflator of 5 percent is slightly less than 5 percent: $(1.1/1.05 - 1) \times 100 = (1.0476 - 1) \times 100 = 0.0476 \times 100 = 4.76$ percent.

IV. SUMMARY

The real sector of the economy involves output (production), employment, and inflation. Developments in the real sector are recorded in the national accounts, with data on output, expenditure, and income presented both in real terms (at constant prices) and nominal terms. Real sector data represent flows.

Gross domestic product (GDP) is the best known and arguably most important of the aggregates recorded in the real sector. GDP can be measured in three ways: as output (value added) by sector of production; as expenditure (subdivided into consumption, investment, and exports less imports of goods and services); and as income (wages, profits, interest, and returns to property ownership). In principle all three approaches should yield the same result, although differences in how items are measured can lead to statistical discrepancies. Gross national income (GNI) adds net factor income from abroad (income of short-term consultants, profit remittances, and net interest payments) to GDP. Including net foreign transfers (grants to governments plus net worker remittances) leads to an even broader income measure, gross national disposable income (GNDI). Subtracting total consumption (C) from gross national disposable income yields gross national savings (S). S − I (total investment) and GNDI − (C + I) each equal the current account balance in the balance of payments. Thus, a current account deficit implies that GNDI is less than the sum of C plus I, or that S is less than I, while a current account surplus implies that GNDI exceeds C plus I and S is greater than I.

Inflation represents a sustained increase in prices, as opposed to a one-time jump in prices that is later reversed. Inflation can be measured using various price indices, of which the consumer price index (CPI) is the best known and most widely used for monitoring price developments. Other useful price indices include the wholesale price index (WPI) and the producer price index (PPI), each of which reflect price changes at the pre-retail stage and may provide indications of future changes in the CPI. The GDP deflator is the index used to convert GDP from current prices to constant prices. Because the GDP deflator reflects changes in the prices of exports and investment goods as well as consumption, inflation as measured by the percent change in the GDP deflator can differ from inflation as measured by the percent change in the CPI. CPI inflation is typically measured as the percent change either in the annual average value of the CPI (annual inflation) or as the percent change in the CPI in one month from the value twelve months earlier (the 12 month inflation rate). The rise in the GDP deflator typically reflects the percent change in the deflator from one quarter to another, or the percent change in the average annual value of the deflator from one year to the next.

Because GDP at current prices equals the product of GDP at constant prices multiplied by the GDP deflator, one can easily calculate the value of any one of these items given values for the other two. Calculating the percent change in nominal GDP is best calculated using the formula (1 + percent change in nominal GDP) = (1 + percent change in real GDP) times (1 + percent change in the GDP deflator), with all percent changes in decimal form (e.g., 5 percent = 0.05), to capture the interaction between the two percent changes. Simply adding the percent changes in real GDP and the GDP deflator excludes the value of this interaction term and thus understates the true change in nominal GDP.

Chapter 3
EXTERNAL SECTOR ACCOUNTS AND ANALYSIS

The external sector of an economy comprises its economic relations with the rest of the world. The economy's balance of payments (BOP) summarizes these interactions. Other important information can be found in tables detailing the economy's external debt service payments and stock of external debt; the composition and direction of its external trade; and various measures of external competitiveness, including its nominal and real effective exchange rates (REER) opposite its trading partners.

I. BALANCE OF PAYMENTS

The BOP is an accounting statement that summarizes, for a specific time period, the economic transactions (flows) of an economy with the rest of the world. The accounts are prepared based on residency, which depends on whether an individual or household resides in an economy for at least a year at a time. The transactions included refer to a certain period of time, typically either a quarter or a full calendar or fiscal year. Transactions are valued using market prices. In developing and emerging market countries the BOP is often presented in two currencies: in the national currency and in a widely used foreign currency such as the Euro or U.S. dollar, to provide a reference when the national currency can fluctuate noticeably against leading currencies.

A. Accounting Principles

The BOP reflects certain accounting principles.

1. Every external economic transaction results in two entries of equal size in the BOP: one on the credit side, recorded as a positive entry, and one as a debit, shown with a negative sign. By convention, the approach followed by the Fifth BOP Manual records reductions in assets or increases in liabilities as credits, while increases in assets or reductions as liabilities are shown as debits.[1] An intuitive explanation is that many financial flows involving a rise in liabilities, such as inward foreign direct investment (FDI) or the receipt of loan proceeds, reflect financial flows into the economy. Similarly, flows reflecting a decrease in liabilities or a rise in assets (claims on other economies) involve outward financial flows, such as outward foreign investment or a repayment of external loans.

2. Another BOP convention is that payments associated with trade in goods (exports and imports) are divided into pure payments for the goods themselves, i.e., exports or imports f.o.b. ("free on board"), and payments for insurance and freight associated with the goods. Payments for exports and imports f.o.b. are recorded in the trade account of the BOP, while payments for insurance and freight (part of "non-factor" services) are recorded in the services account.

3. The BOP has still more useful conventions. Exports of goods and services are recorded as credits, while imports of goods and services are shown as debits. Income and transfers received are reported as credits, while income remitted and transfers paid out represent debits. In addition, because an increase in foreign assets is shown as a debit, an increase in foreign reserves is recorded as a debit (−), while a decrease is shown as a credit (+). By this convention, a rise in reserves is analogous to an import, in that we "purchase" higher reserves using the proceeds from exports of goods, services, income, and financial flows to increase reserves rather than, say, purchasing imports. Likewise, a decrease in reserves generates recorded "receipts."

---

[1] International Monetary Fund (1993), *Balance of Payments Manual, Fifth Edition* (Washington), https://www.imf.org/external/pubs/ft/bopman/bopman.pdf. Accessed July 17, 2017.

4. The BOP classifies transactions into two categories: "real" and "financial." Real transactions comprise transactions in goods, services, income, and current transfers, according to the Fifth BOP Manual. They are shown in the top portion of the BOP, called the current account. Financial transactions, which reflect changes in the economy's foreign assets and liabilities, appear in the capital and financial account. Since foreign assets and liabilities are stocks (amounts at a specific point in time), the capital and financial account records *changes* in these stocks during the time period that the table covers. The main elements in the financial account, using the classifications in the Fifth BOP Manual, are foreign direct investment (FDI), portfolio flows, medium and long-term capital (loans), and other capital flows (mainly short-term loans, such as trade credit, and flows by banks between their correspondent accounts abroad and their home offices).

5. The more recent Sixth BOP Manual[2] has changed some of the above accounting conventions. In the current account, the four subcategories are now called goods, services, primary income, and secondary income, with primary income replacing the earlier income subaccount and secondary income replacing current transfers. For each subaccount, the new approach sums credits and debits to provide net balances for goods, services, primary income, and secondary income. In the capital and financial account, the Sixth Manual categories financial account transactions under one of four headings: direct investment, portfolio investment, financial derivatives, and other investment (which typically includes government borrowing). Countries record transactions for the financial account on a *net* basis, reported separately for assets and liabilities (e.g., net transactions in financial assets show the acquisition of financial assets less reductions in assets) for each of the main types of financial flows. The balance for each type of flow is reported as the *net acquisition of assets less net incurrence of liabilities*. The sum of these balances is the financial account balance ("net lending (+) / net borrowing (−)") and is *subtracted* when calculating the overall BOP balance, because a net inflow (implying net borrowing) appears with a negative sign, while a net outflow (indicating net lending) appears with a positive sign.

---

[2] International Monetary Fund (2007), *Balance of Payments and International Investment Position Manual, Sixth Edition* (BPM6), https://www.imf.org/external/pubs/ft/bop/2007/pdf/bpm6.pdf. Accessed July 17, 2017.

B. Schematic Presentations of the Balance of Payments

Figure 3.1 below provides a schematic summary of the BOP, showing the trade balance, current account balance, elements of the capital and financial account, the overall balance, and changes in net international reserves (NIR), with specific items categorized either as credits or debits. Besides FDI and various types of loans, the capital and financial account also includes changes in portfolio assets and liabilities, primarily holdings of corporate equity (shares of stock) and debt (corporate bonds and commercial paper).

Figure 3.2 provides a more detailed list of the common elements of the BOP, including Errors and Omissions (the difference between the overall balance and transactions identified in either the current account or the capital and financial account) and Exceptional Financing, which typically involves debt relief or arrears on external payments. Errors and omissions result from the diversity of data sources; missing data, for example, financial transactions outside the banking system (in the informal sector); or

Balance of Payments: Components

Credit (+)	Debit (–)
Exports of goods	Imports of goods
Trade Balance	
Exports of Non-Factor Services	Imports of Non-Factor Services
Income received from abroad (interest, profits)	Income paid abroad (interest, dividends)
Transfers received from abroad	Transfers sent abroad
Current Account Balance	
Increase in foreign liabilities:	Increase in foreign assets:
a. FDI from abroad	a. FDI invested abroad
b. Portfolio equity liabilities	b. Portfolio equity assets
c. Other financial liabilities	c. Other investment assets
(loans, trade credit, bank borrowing, etc.)	(or repayment of previous debts)

Overall Balance

Decreases in reserves	Increases in reserves
Net Changes in International Reserves	

FIGURE 3.1. PRINCIPAL ELEMENTS OF THE BOP

Overview of the Balance of Payments

ITEM	CREDIT	DEBIT
I. Current Account		
A. Goods	Exported	Imported
B. Services		
Transportation	Exported	Imported
Travel	Exported	Imported
Other	Exported	Imported
Government, not included elsewhere	Exported	Imported
C. Income (Factor services)		
Compensation of employees	Received	Paid
Investment income, incl. profits	Received	Paid
Of which: interest on external debt	Received	Paid
D. Current Transfers	Received	Paid
II. Capital and Financial Account		
A. Capital Account		
Capital transfers	Received	Paid
Acquisition/disposal of non-produced, non-financial assets	Disposed of	Acquired
B. Financial Account		
Foreign direct investment	Received from abroad	Sent abroad
Government and publ. enterprise loans	Borrowed from abroad	Repaid or lent abroad
Portfolio flows (equity and non-equity)	Received from abroad	Sent abroad
Other (can split between banks and others)		
Medium- and long-term	Borrowed from abroad	Repaid or lent abroad
Trade credit, other short-term loans	Borrowed from abroad	Repaid or lent abroad
III. Errors and Omissions	Net (equal to IV less sum of I and II)	
OVERALL BALANCE (= I. + II. + III. = -IV.)		
IV. CHANGE IN NET INTERNATIONAL RESERVES		
Change in reserve assets (Increase = -)	Decrease	Increase
Exceptional financing (debt relief)	Received	Repaid

FIGURE 3.2.   DETAILED PRESENTATION OF THE BOP (FIFTH BOP MANUAL APPROACH)

the under- or overvaluation of transactions, including smuggling. Exceptional financing includes the rescheduling of external debt obligations (scheduled payments postponed in agreement with creditors); debt forgiveness (voluntary cancellation by creditors); and arrears on debt service (scheduled payments unilaterally postponed, without creditor agreement). Net credit from the International Monetary Fund (IMF) also appears in this part of the BOP, which is typically called "below the line."

Finally, Figure 3.3 provides a more analytical presentation of the BOP, distinguishing "autonomous" transactions (driven by market forces) from transactions that finance these autonomous transactions (changes in reserves and exceptional financing). Figure 3.3 also groups elements of the current account into net exports of goods and (non-factor) services (X–M), which are included in GDP; net factor income (Y_f), which is part

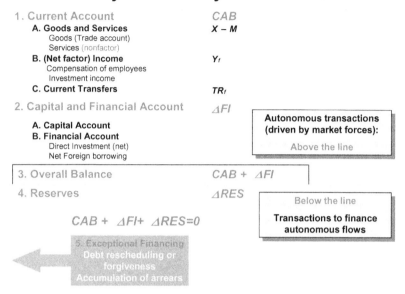

FIGURE 3.3. ANALYTICAL PRESENTATION OF THE BALANCE OF PAYMENTS

of Gross National Income (GNI); and net transfers (TR_f), which are part of Gross National Disposable Income (GNDI). Table 3.1, taken from the Staff Report for the IMF's 2015 Article IV Consultation with the Republic of Korea, provides an example of a BOP table compiled according to the Fifth BOP Manual. Table 3.2, taken from the Staff Report for the IMF's 2016 Article IV Consultation with the Philippines, provides an example of a BOP table compiled according to the Sixth BOP Manual.

C. Issues Concerning Specific Balances in the Balance of Payments

1. Current Account

The current account balance is always matched by net claims on the rest of the world (the change in the capital and financial account, ΔFI, and the change in NIR, ΔRES):

$$CAB + \Delta FI + \Delta RES = 0$$

TABLE 3.1   SAMPLE BOP TABLE, FIFTH BOP MANUAL FORMAT: REPUBLIC OF KOREA

	2012	2013	2014	2015	2016
				Projections	
Current account balance	50.8	81.1	89.2	104.8	88.6
Trade balance	49.4	82.8	92.7	119.0	113.5
Exports	603.5	618.2	621.3	593.5	617.3
(growth rate, in percent)	2.8	2.4	0.5	−4.5	4.0
Imports	554.1	535.4	528.6	474.5	503.8
(growth rate, in percent)	−0.7	−3.4	−1.3	−10.2	6.2
Services	−5.2	−6.5	−8.2	−13.7	−22.6
Income	12.1	9.1	10.2	5.8	4.9
Current transfers	−5.5	−4.2	−5.5	−6.3	−7.1
Financial and capital account balance	−41.1	−68.2	−76.2	−101.3	−95.6
Financial account	−41.0	−68.2	−76.2	−101.3	−95.6
Portfolio investment, net 1/	6.7	−9.3	−33.6	−36.5	−33.5
Direct investment, net	−21.1	−15.6	−20.7	−22.5	−24.4
Inflows	9.5	12.8	9.9	9.9	9.9
Outflows	−30.6	−28.4	−30.6	−32.4	−34.3
Other investment, assets	−8.6	−37.1	−32.2	−40.9	−37.3
Other investment, liabilities	−18.0	−6.2	10.3	−1.4	−0.3
Capital account	0.0	0.0	0.0	0.0	0.0

(*Continued*)

TABLE 3.1 *(Continued)*

	2012	2013	2014	Projections 2015	Projections 2016
Net errors and omissions	0.8	−1.0	1.2	0.0	0.0
Overall balance	10.6	11.9	14.2	3.5	−6.9
Financing	−13.2	−16.3	−17.9	−5.6	4.6
Change in reserves (increase -)	−13.2	−16.3	−17.9	−5.6	4.6
Memorandum items:					
Current account balance (in percent of GDP)	4.2	6.2	6.3	7.3	5.9
Trade balance (in percent of GDP)	4.0	6.3	6.6	8.3	7.6
Gross reserves minus gold	323.2	341.7	358.8	364.4	359.8
(in months of imports of goods and services)	5.9	6.4	6.7	7.4	6.8
External debt	408.9	423.5	425.4	426.6	428.8
(in percent of GDP)	33.4	32.4	30.2	29.9	28.6
Short-term external debt (inc. trade credits)	128.0	111.8	115.3	110.0	105.8
Nominal GDP (U.S. dollars)	1222.8	1305.5	1410.8	—	—

Source: IMF (2015), *Republic of Korea: 2015 Article IV Consultation — Staff Report*, p. 32.
1/ Includes financial derivatives net.

TABLE 3.2 SAMPLE BOP TABLE, SIXTH BOP MANUAL FORMAT: PHILIPPINES

	2011	2012	2013	2014	2015	Proj. 2016	Proj. 2017
Current account balance	5.6	6.9	11.4	10.8	8.4	5.5	4.9
Trade balance of good and services	−13.9	−12.7	−10.6	−12.8	−17.5	−20.7	−22.2
Goods	−20.4	−18.9	−17.7	−17.3	−21.7	−25.8	−28.1
Exports, f.o.b.	38.3	46.4	44.5	49.8	43.3	41.8	43.5
Imports, f.o.b.	58.7	65.3	62.2	67.2	65.0	67.6	71.6
Services	6.6	6.2	7.0	4.6	4.2	5.0	5.9
Receipts	18.9	20.4	23.3	25.5	28.2	30.8	33.8
Payments	12.3	14.3	16.3	20.9	23.9	25.8	27.9
Primary income, net	0.9	0.2	1.0	0.7	2.3	2.1	2.0
Receipts, *of which:*	7.6	8.3	8.4	8.8	9.5	9.8	10.2
Resident workers abroad	5.9	6.5	7.0	7.4	7.8	8.5	9.3
Payments	6.7	8.1	7.4	8.1	7.2	7.7	8.2
Interest payments	2.8	3.0	2.9	2.8	2.5	2.6	2.5
Secondary income, net	18.6	19.5	21.1	22.8	23.5	24.2	25.1
Receipts, *of which:*	19.0	20.1	21.7	23.4	24.3	25.1	26.1

(Continued)

TABLE 3.2 *(Continued)*

	2011	2012	2013	2014	2015	Proj. 2016	2017
Nonresident workers remittances	17.1	18.0	19.3	20.8	21.7	22.3	23.2
Payments	0.5	0.6	0.6	0.7	0.8	0.9	1.0
Capital account	0.2	0.1	0.1	0.1	0.1	0.1	0.1
Financial account 2/	–5.3	–6.8	2.2	9.6	2.5	0.4	0.5
Direct investment	0.3	1.0	–0.1	1.0	–0.1	–1.0	–1.1
Portfolio investment	–3.7	–3.2	–1.0	2.7	4.8	2.7	2.3
Equity	–1.0	–1.7	0.1	–1.0	1.0	0.5	0.3
Debt	–2.6	–1.5	–1.1	3.7	3.7	2.3	2.0
Financial derivatives	–1.0	0.0	–0.1	0.0	0.0	0.0	0.0
Other investment, *of which*:	–1.0	–4.5	3.4	5.9	–2.1	–1.3	–0.6
Currency and deposits	2.3	–1.5	1.4	3.5	0.5	0.8	1.0
Loans	–3.6	–2.3	1.4	2.0	–2.5	–1.6	–0.7
Errors and omissions	0.3	–4.6	–4.2	–4.1	–3.3	–2.5	–2.3
Overall balance	11.4	9.2	5.1	–2.9	2.6	2.7	2.1
Memorandum items;							
Current account/GDP	2.5	2.8	4.2	3.8	2.9	1.8	1.4
Short-term debt (original maturity)	12.1	16.5	16.9	16.2	15.1	15.4	15.8

Short-term debt (residual maturity)	15.6	21.1	20.5	19.0	20.7	21.1	21.5
Gross reserves	75.3	83.8	83.2	79.5	80.7	84.0	86.5
(in percent of short-term debt by remaining maturity) 3/	482.5	397.9	406.2	418.9	396.9	397.5	401.7
External debt (in billions)	75.6	79.9	78.5	77.7	77.5	78.1	79.1
(in percent of GDP)	33.7	32.0	28.9	27.3	26.5	25.1	22.7
Debt service ratio 4/	13.6	9.9	11.1	8.4	7.4	11.2	10.7
Export value (percent change) 1/	4.1	21.2	-4.0	11.9	-13.1	-3.4	4.1
Import value (percent change) 1/	9.5	11.3	-4.8	8.0	-3.2	4.0	6.0
Gross external financing needs 5/	9.8	8.7	9.7	9.7	10.6	15.1	16.3
Remittances value (percent change)	7.2	6.3	7.4	7.2	4.6	4.6	5.4

Source: IMF (2016), *Philippines: 2016 Article IV Consultation — Staff Report*, p. 43.

1/ In BPM6.

2/ An increase in either assets or liabilities is always positive and a decrease is always negative. Net investment is assets minus liabilities. A negative financial account balance means that the change in liabilities is greater than the change in assets while a positive financial account balance means that the change is assets in greater than the change in liabilities.

3/ As a percent of short term debt.

4/ In percent of goods and nonfactor services exports.

5/ Current account deficit, plus amortization on medium- and long-term debt, plus short-term debt at the end of the previous period.

Moreover, a current account surplus is reflected either in an increase in claims on non-residents or in the acquisition of reserve assets by the monetary authority (central bank). Similarly, a current account deficit is reflected either in increases in country's liabilities to non-residents or in decreases in the monetary authority's reserves (reserve assets).

2. Capital and Financial Account

The capital and financial account balance indicates the size of the autonomous (market driven) sources of funds from abroad. This is to be distinguished from the overall balance, which indicates whether NIR have risen (in the case of a surplus) or declined (if there is a deficit). A surplus in the BOP also indicates that autonomous (market driven) sources of funds from abroad were sufficient to cover any deficit in the current account balance, or that a current account surplus was sufficient to cover any deficit in the capital and financial account, after incorporating unexplained flows (errors and omissions).

II. USEFUL INDICATORS FOR ASSESSING THE EXTERNAL SECTOR

Several variables are quite useful for assessing developments in the external sector. These include the terms of trade, the current account balance as a percent of GDP, the overall balance of the BOP, and measures of competitiveness such as the real exchange rate (RER).

A. Terms of Trade

The terms of trade is the ratio of export prices to import prices: P_X/P_M, where P_X is an index of export prices, P_M is an index of import prices, and both indices are expressed in the same currency (e.g., Euros, U.S. dollars). The terms of trade is typically expressed as an index relative to its value in a base year, so that it shows the net change (positive or negative) over time. A rise in the terms of trade indicates a rise in the purchasing power of an economy's exports, while a decline signals the opposite.

For example, when oil prices rise relative to the prices of other commodities and of manufacturers, the terms of trade improve for oil exporters and worsen for other economies.

The terms of trade were especially relevant during the period of widespread colonialism, when developing economy colonies typically exported primary products to the home country, which in turn exported manufactures and other finished goods to its colonies. Colonial residents often complained that the home country used restrictive trade practices to keep the price of finished products high and the price of primary commodities low. Price increases for finished products and fixed prices for primary commodities meant that the terms of trade for colonies deteriorated, while the terms of trade for the home country improved. In recent years, the terms of trade has proved useful in explaining the economic rise of oil exporters and the changing fortunes of other commodity exporters, such as Australia, which has benefitted from rising exports of raw materials to China.

B. The Current Account Balance

The current account balance of the BOP indicates an economy's ability to finance imports and payments of services, income (e.g., interest payments), and transfers through receipts from exports of goods, services, income (e.g., profit remittances), and transfers (e.g., worker remittances). A current account surplus means that the economy has funds available from its "real" transactions for use in lending, outward foreign investment, repaying outstanding external debt, or accumulating NIR. A current account deficit means that the economy needs to finance its transactions in goods, services, income, and transfers through some combination of FDI, portfolio (equity and debt) flows, external borrowing, or drawing down reserves. To facilitate comparison across time, the current account balance is typically reported as a percent of GDP.

A deteriorating current account balance, in particular a rising current account deficit, can signal that the economy's external position is unsustainable. An unsustainable external position arises when continued current account deficits, reflecting the behavior of the government and the private sector, would require a drastic adjustment of economic policies to avoid a crisis possibly involving a collapse of the exchange rate or default on external debt obligations. The current account balance can become a source of concern when two conditions hold:

(1) when the deficit appears to be structural, rather than temporary, for example, when export earnings appear unable to cover imports and debt service obligations over the foreseeable future; and

(2) when the deficit can only be financed through short-term external borrowing or a protracted reduction in official reserves or other net foreign assets.

Thus, a continuing, large current account deficit (e.g., 8 percent or more of GDP) could be a source of concern in an economy with limited reserves and little FDI. By comparison, a deficit resulting from a temporary decline in the price of a key export, in an economy with reserves equivalent to a year or more of imports, or a temporary deficit linked to construction projects financed by FDI, would ordinarily not create problems.

External sustainability (ES) also depends on such factors as the economy's capacity to meet its external financial obligations and the availability of external financing. Private external financing may only be available when the economic looks strong, however. This is one reason why many emerging market economies have accumulated substantial external reserves, to avoid having to rely on foreign credit lines that can easily be cut during an economic downturn or crisis.

If the current account position appears unsustainable, then adjustment is needed, hopefully without sudden disruption, i.e., a crisis. Otherwise, financial markets will most likely force a correction sooner rather than later, with high costs for the economy (e.g., a plunge in the exchange rate, shortages, and possible recession). Various measures can be used to address an unsustainable current account. The authorities can impose tariffs or quantitative controls on imports, although this would likely violate covenants with the World Trade Organization. Another option is to impose controls on external payments, which would create problems *vis-à-vis* the IMF. Alternatively, the authorities can depreciate the currency (to promote exports) or tighten monetary and fiscal policy, to reduce demand and thereby decrease imports. These measures are more likely to receive international support, although they are generally unpopular and may create political risks for the authorities.

C. The Overall Balance and External Sustainability

Still another useful indicator is the overall balance of the BOP. As noted earlier, the overall balance ordinarily indicates the change in NIR of the economy's monetary authority. A deficit indicates a decline in NIR, unless exceptional financing, such as IMF credit or debt relief, is available. Unless the current reserve level is considered very strong — well above short-term debt liabilities and equivalent to many months of imports, c.i.f. — deficits can be worrisome. Thus, countries typically monitor the overall balance of the BOP.

From the standpoint of the overall balance, ES depends on whether reserves and autonomous capital inflows are sufficient to cover any current account deficit or capital outflows. For countries with a fixed exchange rate regime, a key question is whether reserves are sufficient to defend the peg. The answer depends on a variety of issues, including the outlook for the current account balance and the more general question of the economy's competitiveness.

D. Indicators of External Competitiveness: The Real Exchange Rate

Various indicators can help assess a country's external competitiveness. These include the ability to earn current account surpluses, or keep deficits small and financed in ways that do not create an excessive accumulation of external debt; developments in the real exchange rate (RER); and trends in the unit labor cost of key exports. The third indicator, trends in the unit labor cost of key exports, is more commonly available in advanced economies and can be combined with trends in productivity to assess competitiveness. In developing and emerging market countries, unit labor cost data are often not available. In these economies it is useful to measure trends in the RER.

The RER measures the "real" purchasing power of one economy's currency relative to one or more foreign currencies. A bilateral RER indicates the "real" purchasing power of the economy's currency relative to a single foreign currency. A real effective exchange rate (REER) measures the purchasing power of the economy's currency *vis-à-vis* a set of foreign currencies, typically a weighted average of those for the economy's main trading partners, with the weights comprising each partner's share in the economy's total exports (export-weighted REER), total imports (import-weighted REER), or total trade (trade-weighted REER). The basic formula for a simple bilateral RER is as follows:

$RER^{h/f} = ER^{f/h} * (P^h/P^f)$, where

h represents the home economy;

f represents the foreign economy;

$ER^{f/h}$ is the (nominal) bilateral exchange rate, expressed in units of foreign currency per unit of home currency;

P^h is the value of a domestic price index, such as the domestic consumer price index (CPI) or GDP deflator; and

P^f is the value of a comparable foreign price index, e.g., the foreign CPI if the domestic CPI is used.

The RER is typically normalized so that its value for a base period (e.g., 2016) is set at 100. A rise in the RER indicates a real appreciation, while a decrease signals a real depreciation.

Because the RER depends both on the nominal rate and the relative price indices in the home and foreign economies, the RER can change if either the nominal exchange rate or the relative values of the home and foreign price indices change. For example, the RER can appreciate if the nominal rate appreciates, if inflation is higher in the home economy than abroad, or if the difference between home and foreign inflation rates exceeds the nominal depreciation in the exchange rate. When assessing the RER, the nominal rate used must reflect the market exchange rate. Thus, the presence of a parallel foreign exchange market with significantly different rates from the official rate would suggest that the official rate is not representative.

Unless domestic productivity is rising rapidly, an appreciation in the RER normally signals a decline in competitiveness. Continuing real appreciation can raise questions about the sustainability of the economy's external position, while steady real depreciation may signal efforts by the authorities to make the economy's exports "super-competitive." As mentioned in Chapter 1, the IMF now uses a method called "External Balance Assessment" (EBA), which relies on regression-based analyses, to assess the appropriateness of the exchange rate.[3] Until a few years ago the IMF used a slightly different approach called the "Consultative Group on Exchange Rates" "(CGER)" methodology. This methodology uses three different approaches to assess the exchange rate:

- the *macroeconomic balance* (MB) approach, which assesses the exchange rate change eliminating differences between currently projected medium-term current account balance and an "equilibrium" balance;
- the *equilibrium real exchange rate* (ERER) approach, which involves calculating the difference between the current RER and the RER estimated as a function of "fundamental" variables at their medium-term equilibrium values; and
- the ES approach, which estimates the change in RER that would move the current account balance to a level stabilizing net foreign assets at a benchmark value.

The IMF's Occasional Paper No. 261 has more detailed information on the three approaches.[4]

E. Capital Flows

The volume and nature of capital flows for an economy can also be a valuable indicator of ES. Relatively large capital flows (e.g., equivalent to 10 percent or more of GDP) may signal the economy's dependence on foreign capital to finance investment, for example, and thus indicate a source of vulnerability. The type of capital flows also matters. FDI, for

---

[3] For details, see Phillips, S., and others (2013), "External Balance Assessment (EBA) Methodology," IMF Working Paper 13/272 (Washington: December). Available at: http://www.imf.org/external/pubs/ft/wp/2013/wp13272.pdf. Accessed July 17, 2017.

[4] See Lee, Jaewoo, and others (2008), *Exchange Rate Assessments: CGER Methodologies* (Washington, DC: International Monetary Fund, April).

example, is typically for the long-term and involves risk sharing with the investor, since the investor receives funds only if the project is profitable. Medium- to long-term debt (debt maturing in more than 1 year) cannot typically be withdrawn on short notice. However, debt service is due regardless of the economy's export earnings or internal strength. Portfolio capital flows, such as purchases of shares (equity) on a domestic stock market, also involve risk-sharing with the investor, although this type of investment can usually be liquidated quickly. Short-term borrowing or short-term deposits pose the greatest risk, because debt service is always due, funds can be quickly withdrawn, and short-term loans need not be renewed ("rolled over"), leaving the economy at risk of (possibly large) capital outflows.

F. External Debt Indicators

The size of an economy's external debt stock and its debt service ratio indicate the burden of its external borrowing. The gross external debt represents the economy's outstanding contractual liabilities to non-residents, while its debt service comprises payments for principal and interest on all external debt. If short-term debt is rolled over, meaning that debt coming due during a year is replaced by new debt, the debt service comprises all interest payments and principal on medium and long-term debt. Debt-creating flows in the capital and financial account of the BOP should be viewed in the context of a country's gross external debt. The following equation defines the relationship among the debt stock at the end of a period, the previous period's debt stock, amortization, principal payments, and new borrowing:

$D_t = (1 + R_{t-1}) * D_{t-1} + B_t - A_t$, where

D = stock of debt

R = interest rate on debt

B = new loans

A = amortization of debt (principal payments)

External debt sustainability depends, in principle, on whether future debt service obligations can be met without rescheduling debt or seeking debt relief. But sustainability is doubtful if the debt/GDP ratio tends to rise without limit. External debt also becomes worrisome if the ratio of external debt to GDP or debt service to exports of goods and services becomes too high. The following table identifies some "rules of thumb" that have been developed to assess the severity of external debt for emerging market countries:[5]

Severity of External Debt: Rules of Thumb for Emerging Market Countries

Ratio (in percent)	Less indebted	Moderately indebted	Heavily indebted
NPV of debt service/GNI	Below 40	40–80	Above 80
NPV of debt service/Exports (G&S)	Below 120	120–200	Above 200–250
Debt service/Exports (G&S)	Below 12	12–20	Above 20–25

In the above table NPV represents the net present value, GNI is gross national income, and Exports (G&S) represents exports of goods and (non-factor) services. The key ratios are NPV of debt service to GNI, NPV of debt service to Exports of goods and services, and Debt service (principal plus interest payments) to Exports of goods and services. The level of external debt, as a percent of GDP, also matters. In practice, many emerging market economies worry if their ratio of external debt to GNI or GDP exceeds 50 percent. For countries that have defaulted on external debt, a debt-to-GNI ratio exceeding 35 percent, or in some cases even less, has proved problematic.[6]

G. External Reserve Levels

Levels of gross or net international reserves also help indicate the strength of an economy's external position. The reason is that reserve assets provide

---

[5] Somewhat different standards have been established for low-income countries. See International Monetary Fund (2013), "Staff Guidance Note on the Application of the Joint Bank-Fund Debt Sustainability Framework for Low-Income Countries," www.imf.org/external/np/pp/eng/2013/110513.pdf. Accessed July 17, 2017.

[6] See Reinhart, Carmen, and others (2003), "Debt Intolerance," NBER Working Paper 9908 (Cambridge, MA: National Bureau of Economic Research, August).

a kind of "insurance" against various contingencies. Reserve assets, for example, can help finance a BOP deficit, at least for a temporary period. Reserves also support an exchange rate peg. In addition, reserves provide confidence in the domestic currency and economy generally.

The level of required reserves depends in part on the nature of the exchange regime. Countries with fixed exchange rate regimes presumably need more reserves, because reserves are reduced during a BOP deficit. With a floating rate regime, the exchange rate can depreciate if the BOP is in deficit. In practice, however, the stability of the exchange rate and how much it adjusts can reflect the size of reserves. Countries with very low reserve levels may experience sharper exchange rate adjustments during a BOP deficit than those with larger reserves, because of greater concerns about ES when reserves are low.

A traditional measure of reserve adequacy is the ratio of gross reserves to imports, c.i.f., measured in months of imports. When capital account restrictions were more prevalent, before the 1990s, the minimum "safe" level of reserves was 3 months of imports, c.i.f. Even today, countries where reserves are below this level are considered quite vulnerable to external shocks.

Today, with most countries experiencing larger and more volatile capital flows, broader measures of financial vulnerability have become more common. Factors affecting vulnerability include the following:

- the exchange rate regime and the credibility of the authorities' policies;
- the openness of the economy (in trade and capital flows);
- the variability and volume of foreign exchange transactions;
- the economy's access to short-term borrowing facilities; and
- the maturity structure of external liabilities.

One indicator that many analysts examine is the ratio of reserves to short term debt, meaning the ratio of readily accessible external reserves to principal and interest payments due during the coming 12 months (including any short-term debt falling due). Research has suggested that countries in which gross reserves fell below short-term debt on average experienced greater difficulties than those where reserves exceeded short-term debt.[7]

---

[7] See Calafell, Javier, and Rodolfo Padilla del Bosque (2002). "The Ratio of International Reserves to Short-Term External Debt as Indicator of External Vulnerability: Some Lessons

III. SUMMARY

An economy's external sector involves the economy's relations with the rest of the world. The balance of payments records most of the developments in the external sector. Transactions in goods (exports and imports), services (service credits and debits), income (profit remittances, overseas earnings by residents, and net interest payments), and current transfers (official transfers and remittances by citizens residing abroad for more than year) appear in the current account of the balance of payments, while transactions involving capital flows appear in the capital and financial account, mainly the latter. Stocks of external debt are recorded separately, as are drawings and repayments of principal (amortization) of external debt, although net foreign borrowing is reported in the financial account of the balance of payments, while net interest payments appear in the current account (in net income).

Various conventions apply to recording entries in the balance of payments. In the most commonly used approach, based on the Fifth BOP Manual, earnings from exports of goods and services, along with inflows of income and transfers, appear as credits. Payments for imports of goods and services, along with outflows of income and transfers, are shown as debits. Capital flows that increase foreign liabilities or reduce foreign assets, such as inflows of FDI, portfolio capital (equity and debt), and foreign borrowing, are shown as credits. Flows that reduce foreign liabilities or increase foreign assets, such as outward foreign direct investment, portfolio investment in other economies, and the repayment of external loans, appear as debits. In the absence of exceptional financing (debt relief plus net drawings from the IMF), the change in net international reserves equals the overall balance in the balance of payments, with surpluses recorded as debits (because the economy has increased its claims on the rest of the world) and deficits recorded as credits. The overall balance equals the sum of the current account balance, the capital and financial account balances, and errors and omissions (movements in the overall balance not explained by the sum of the current, capital, and financial

---

from the Experience of Mexico and Other Emerging Economies." Available at: https://www.g24.org/wp-content/uploads/2016/01/THE-RATIO-OF-INTERNATIONAL-RESERVES-TO-SHORT-TERM.pdf. Accessed July 16, 2017.

account balances). In the newer Sixth BOP Manual, entries in the various financial account components are shown as changes in net assets and net liabilities. In addition, the income account is called "primary income", while current transfers are called "secondary income".

The current account balance has traditionally been viewed as recording developments in real transactions, with the capital and financial account showing financing for the current account, although in a world of widespread capital flows developments in the capital and financial account can have as much or more bearing on the overall balance as developments in the current account. Developing and emerging market economies often have current account deficits, reflecting the need for external resources to supplement domestic savings in financing investment. Deficits equivalent to just a few percentage points of GDP are typically not problematic, if financed by foreign direct investment or concessional borrowing. The same applies to deficits resulting from a one-time drop in export prices that is quickly reversed. However, protracted deficits financed by short-term borrowing on commercial terms may signal an unsustainable position that requires adjustment. The problem may arise from excessive domestic spending, which can be addressed by tightening fiscal and monetary policy. It could also reflect a more fundamental lack of competitiveness, possibly signaled by a steady appreciation in the real exchange rate (which takes into account changes in both the nominal exchange rate and relative inflation rates between an economy and its trading partners) or the maintenance of an overvalued official exchange rate, accompanied by a parallel (black) market in foreign currency. A deficit in the overall balance indicates a loss in net international reserves, which can weaken confidence in the currency and reduce the ability to maintain current consumption when the current account weakens.

Traditionally, countries have aimed at maintaining international reserves equivalent to at least three months of imports, c.i.f. However, with greater capital flows, larger reserves may be needed, particularly to support a fixed exchange rate. In addition, experience during the Asian Crisis of 1997–98 has led many economies to maintain reserves at least equal to the value of debt service plus any short-term debt maturing within a year.

Economies are also advised to limit the accumulation of external debt. Various measures have been developed to indicate relative debt burdens and levels of debt distress in emerging market and low-income countries, with figures of 25 percent or more for the ratio of debt service to exports of goods and services signaling severe indebtedness in emerging market countries.

Chapter 4

FISCAL ACCOUNTS AND ANALYSIS

The fiscal sector of the economy comprises the economic activities of government- and state-owned enterprises (Figure 4.1). These activities are recorded in the budgets of the central, provincial or state, and local governments, as well as the budgets of non-financial public enterprises. Financial public enterprises, such as state-owned banks and the central bank or monetary authority, are usually treated in the monetary sector of the economy. However, the IMF's most recent (2014) Government Financial Statistics (GFS) manual includes them in the public sector.[1] In many economies, the activities of the central government comprise not only the budget of the central administration, but also a separate social insurance or social security system, plus trust funds or separate budgets for some decentralized agencies. In some of these economies, the budgets for the central administration, social insurance or social security fund, and decentralized agencies are combined into a unified budget, to show the full extent of central government activities.

Besides regular fiscal activities, a number of economies conduct quasi-fiscal operations. These are activities that look like regular budgetary programs but take place outside the regular budget. Quasi-fiscal operations are less transparent than regular budgetary activities and are not subject to the normal rules and procedures governing programs in the budget. Thus,

---

[1] International Monetary Fund (2014), *Government Finance Statistics Manual* (Washington).

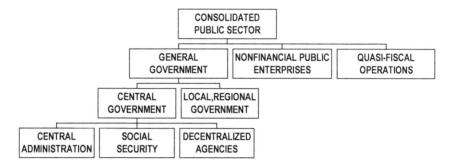

FIGURE 4.1. SCHEMATIC VIEW OF THE PUBLIC SECTOR, EXCLUDING FINANCIAL PUBLIC ENTERPRISES

they are often hard to control. Exchange rate guarantees provided to importers by a central bank, which ensure the availability of foreign exchange at a fixed rate even if the market rate is less favorable, are a typical quasi-fiscal operation. The guarantees offer the equivalent of a subsidy to importers, which would normally be a budgeted activity. Because the central bank provides the subsidy, the activity takes place off-budget, and the amount of the subsidy is typically not limited. Accordingly, this activity is considered a quasi-fiscal operation. It affects the regular budget insofar as it reduces central bank profits and thus the amount the central bank remits to the budget (as part of non-tax revenue).

I. BUDGET ACCOUNTS: TRADITIONAL AND MORE MODERN FORMATS

Figure 4.2 describes the standard format of elements in most countries' government budgets, based on the IMF's 1986 GFS Manual[2] and using an economic classification of government expenditure. Table 4.1 provides an example. The top of the table comprises government revenue and grants, subdivided into tax and non-tax revenue, along with grants (transfers from other governments or international organizations); expenditures and net lending, distinguishing between current and capital outlays as well as net

---

[2] International Monetary Fund (1986), *Manual on Government Finance Statistics* (Washington).

Standard Budget Format (1986 GFS)

- Revenue and grants
  - Tax revenue
  - Non-tax revenue
  - Grants
- Expenditure and net lending
  - Current outlays
  - Capital outlays
  - Net lending (2001 GFS puts in financing)
- Financing
  - Foreign (net)
  - Domestic
    - Bank (net), Non-bank (net)

NB: Accounts are on a cash basis – so arrears (unpaid obligations) and contingent liabilities are omitted!

FIGURE 4.2. TRADITIONAL PRESENTATION OF GOVERNMENT BUDGET ACCOUNTS

TABLE 4.1. ILLUSTRATES THE TRADITIONAL PRESENTATION USING DATA FROM INDONESIA

	1998	1999	2000	2001	2002
		(In billions of rupiah)			
Total revenue and grants	140,917.0	179,387.3	244,552.6	301,078.9	300,072.9
Tax revenue	93,023.0	109,787.6	143,890.6	185,543.1	210,177.9
Nontax revenue 2/	47,894.0	69,599.7	100,662.0	115,057.6	89,593.0
Grants	0.0	0.0	0.0	478.2	302.0
Current expenditure	99,155.0	131,821.8	201,841.9	232,380.8	189,346.1
of which					
Personnel (central govt.)	21,717.0	29,814.0	37,376.8	38,713.1	39,784.7
Subsidies	36,774.3	45,788.0	74,514.3	77,442.9	40,006.3
Interest on external debt	22,446.2	22,004.7	35,399.7	35,201.0	21,902.7
Interest on domestic debt	4,500.0	18,150.0	36,787.9	66,000.0	64,481.3
Development and net lending 3/	61,580.5	65,796.8	68,996.1	128,250.4	135,543.0
Total including development and net lending	160,735.5	197,618.5	270,838.1	360,631.2	324,889.1
Overall balance	-19,818.5	-18,231.2	-26,285.4	-59,552.3	-24,816.2
Financing (net)	19,818.5	18,231.2	26,285.4	59,552.3	24,816.2
Domestic 4/	-78,640.9	-23,562.1	-1,169.8	48,968.4	13,925.0
Bank	-25,733.9	2,091.4	119,489.3	13,092.3	-21,935.1
BI			-19,446.7	30,743.3	5,181.9
Commercial banks			138,936.0	-17,651.0	-27,117.0
Nonbank	-52,907.0	-25,653.5	-120,659.1	35,876.2	35,860.1
Financial asset sales	0.0	12,900.0	20,714.1	.....	.....
Nonfinancial asset sales	1,633.0	3,727.2	.....	.....	.....
Bonds	0.0	0.0	.....	.....	.....
Other	-54,540.0	-42,280.7	.....	.....	.....
Foreign (net)	98,459.4	41,793.3	27,455.2	10,583.9	10,891.1
Primary balance	7,127.7	21,923.5	45,902.2	41,648.6	61,567.8

Source: Data provided by the Indonesian authorities.

Government Operations: 2001 GFS

I. Transactions affecting net worth
  1. Revenue (increase net worth)
  2. Expense (reduce net worth)

  3. Gross Operating Balance = 1 − 2
    2.8 Consumption of fixed capital (depreciation)

  4. Net Operating Balance ➡ Change in net worth = 3 − 2.8
II. Transactions in nonfinancial assets
    5.1 Net acquisition of nonfinancial assets
      5.1.1 Fixed assets
      5.1.2 Change in inventories
      5.1.3 Other

  6. Net lending/Borrowing = 4 − 5.1

III. Transactions in financial assets and liabilities = 5.2 − 5.3 = 6
    5.2 Net acquisition of financial assets (or 5.3 − 5.2 = − 6)
    5.3 Net incurrence of liabilities
      5.3.1 Foreign
      5.3.2 Domestic

FIGURE 4.3. FISCAL ACCOUNTS UNDER THE 2001 GFS MANUAL

lending (loans by government for policy purposes, less repayments of loan principal); and financing (total revenue and grants less total expenditure and net lending), comprising foreign financing, domestic financing from the banking system, and domestic financing from other sources, all on a net basis (loan proceeds received less amortization payments). Note that loan repayments are treated as part of financing, rather than expenditure. All transactions are reported on a cash basis, meaning that arrears — government purchases not paid during the fiscal year — are not counted as expenditures.

Figure 4.3 shows a somewhat different presentation of budget data based on the IMF's more recent 2001 GFS Manual.[3] In this format, designed for consistency with the UN's System of National Accounts (SNA), entries are on an accrual basis and follow a format more analogous to that of private firms. The top part of the table comprises revenue (items that tend to increase government's net worth), expense (items that reduce

---

[3]International Monetary Fund (2001), *Government Finance Statistics Manual 2001* (Washington).

net worth), and the gross operating balance or revenue less expense. Deducting depreciation on government assets (ignored in the 1986 presentation) yields the government's net operating balance or change in net worth. The second section of the table comprises transactions in non-financial assets, comprising the net acquisition of fixed assets (similar to capital expenditure under the 1986 classification), changes in inventories (also ignored in the 1986 classification), and other items. Combining the net operating balance with the net acquisition of fixed assets yields what the 2001 Manual calls "Net lending or borrowing," roughly analogous to an accrual version of the overall fiscal balance under the 1986 GFS. The final section of the table comprises transactions in financial assets and liabilities, including the net acquisition of financial assets and the net acquisition of financial liabilities (both foreign and domestic). Table 4.2 provides an example of a fiscal table that reflects the 2001 GFS approach.

In both budget formats, revenues comprise all non-repayable receipts (i.e., receipts that do not create an obligation of repayment), except grants. The main elements of revenue are tax revenues, representing compulsory and unrequited receipts collected by the government for public purposes, and non-tax revenues, which include the operating surpluses of public enterprises, profits of the monetary authority, property income, administrative fees, charges, and fines. Property income includes fees and royalties for leasing government-owned land, which in many oil-producing countries represents the main source of revenue. Receipts from privatization (the sale of government assets) are typically excluded from revenue and shown elsewhere — for example, as part of non-bank budget financing in the 1986 GFS format — because the assets can only be sold once. In the 2001 GFS format, privatization proceeds would have no direct impact, because they involve replacing one type of asset (government shares in an enterprise) with another (cash).

Expenditures can be classified either on an economic or a functional basis. Using the economic classification and the 1986 GFS format, expenditures can be categorized as either current, capital, or net lending. Current expenditure includes payments for wages and salaries, purchases of other goods and services (typically spending for operations and maintenance under government programs), subsidies (payments to reduce the market price of goods and services), transfers (payments to individuals, firms, or institutions), and interest payments. Capital expenditure comprises the acquisition of fixed assets

TABLE 4.2   INDONESIA: SUMMARY OF GENERAL GOVERNMENT OPERATIONS, 2011–2016

	2011	2012	2013	2014	2015 Prel. Est.	2016 Proj.
	(In trillions of rupiah)					
Total revenue and grants	1,332	1,486	1,610	1,740	1,698	1,758
Taxes	953	1,075	1,192	1,274	1,374	1,449
Taxes on income, profit, and capital gains	431	465	506	546	597	633
Taxes on goods and services	355	433	493	527	568	588
VAT and luxury taxes	278	338	385	409	424	462
Excise	77	95	108	118	145	126
Taxes on international trade and transactions	54	50	47	44	36	39
Taxes not elsewhere classified	113	127	145	156	173	190
Grants	5	6	7	5	3	2
Other revenue	374	406	411	461	321	307
Total expenditure	1,387	1,623	1,822	1,967	2,017	2,116
Expense	1,161	1,343	1,481	1,642	1,610	1,714
Of which:						
Compensation of employees	406	465	511	564	631	708
Purchases/use of goods and services	125	141	170	177	237	216
Interest	93	101	113	133	156	196
Fuel subsidies	256	306	310	342	119	79
Social benefit	84	88	103	110	110	115

Net acquisition of nonfinancial assets	226	280	341	324	406	402
Net lending/borrowing	−55	−137	−212	−227	−319	−358
Net acquisition of financial assets	47	−1	7	35	115	12
Of which: policy lending	4	4	4	3	0	0
Net incurrence of liabilities	102	136	219	262	434	370
			(in percent of GDP)			
Total revenue and grants	17.0	17.2	16.9	16.5	14.7	13.9
Taxes	12.2	12.5	12.5	12.1	11.9	11.5
Taxes on income, profit, and capital gains	5.5	5.4	5.3	5.2	5.2	5.0
Taxes on goods and services	4.5	5.0	5.2	5.0	4.9	4.7
VAT and luxury taxes	3.5	3.9	4.0	3.9	3.7	3.7
Excise	1.0	1.1	1.1	1.1	1.3	1.0
Taxes on international trade and transactions	0.7	0.6	0.5	0.4	0.3	0.3
Taxes not elsewhere classified	1.4	1.5	1.5	1.5	1.5	1.5
Grants	0.1	0.1	0.1	0.0	0.0	0.0
Other revenue	4.8	4.7	4.3	4.4	2.8	2.4
Total expenditure	17.7	18.8	19.1	18.7	17.5	16.8
Expense	14.8	15.6	15.5	15.6	14.0	13.6

(Continued)

TABLE 4.2   *(Continued)*

	2011	2012	2013	2014	2015 Prel. Est.	2016 Proj.
Of which:						
Compensation of employees	5.2	5.4	5.4	5.3	5.5	5.6
Purchases/use of goods services	1.6	1.6	1.8	1.7	2.1	1.7
Interest	1.2	1.2	1.2	1.3	1.4	1.6
Fuel subsidies	3.3	3.6	3.3	3.2	1.0	0.6
Social benefit	1.1	1.0	1.1	1.0	1.0	0.9
Net acquisition of nonfinancial assets	2.9	3.2	3.6	3.1	3.5	3.2
Net lending/borrowing	−0.7	−1.6	−2.2	−2.2	−2.8	−2.8
Net acquisition of financial assets	0.6	0.0	0.1	0.3	1.0	0.1
Of which: policy lending	0.1	0.0	0.0	0.0	0.0	0.0
Net incurrence of liabilities	1.3	1.6	2.3	2.5	3.8	2.9
Memorandum items:						
General government debt (In percent of GDP)	23.1	23.0	24.9	24.7	27.5	28.4
Nominal GDP (In trillions of rupiah)	7,832	8,616	9,525	10,543	11,516	12,629

Source: International Monetary Fund (2016), *Indonesia: 2015 Article IV Consultation*, Table 6, p. 39.

(government development programs) and capital transfers (transfers to other units of government for development programs and the acquisition of assets). Net lending, as noted earlier, comprises government loans for policy purposes, less repayments of principal. Under the 2001 GFS approach, the acquisition of fixed assets belongs to a separate category of government financial transactions, while net lending appears "below the line," as part of net transactions in financial assets, rather than in Expense or the acquisition of non-financial or financial assets. The functional classification of expenditure, by contrast, combines all types of expenditures related to a single functional area, such as health or education. Typical functional categories of expenditure include outlays for defense, public order, foreign affairs, general administration, courts and justice, health, education, and income support, among others.

II. KEY CONCEPTS OF FISCAL ANALYSIS

A variety of indicators can help in analyzing and assessing fiscal performance. This section discusses several of these, including different measures of the fiscal balance, the implications of alternative forms of budget finance, the concept of fiscal space, and the analysis of revenues and expenditures. This section also provides a brief discussion of fiscal sustainability.

A. Alternative Measures of the Fiscal Balance

Journalists and the public are most familiar with what has been called the "conventional fiscal balance": revenues less expenditures. In fact, economists have developed many different fiscal balances, each designed to address a different purpose.[4] This section highlights some of the most useful.

1. *Conventional Fiscal Balance:* the conventional fiscal balance or overall fiscal balance, as noted above, is defined as the difference between total government revenues and grants and total expenditures, including net lending, all measured on a cash basis. The great advantage of the conventional fiscal balance is that it indicates the government's financing requirement: how much is needed to cover the shortfall of revenues from

---

[4]Blejer, M. I., and A. Cheasty (1991), *How to Measure the Fiscal Deficit* (Washington: IMF).

expenditures. In the case of a surplus, the conventional balance indicates how much the stock of existing government debt is reduced or, if the government has no debt, the amount by which the government's financial balances rise, during the indicated period. Since it is determined on a cash basis, the conventional balance ignores the impact of arrears. Thus, it can understate the true fiscal imbalance when the government has substantial arrears, as occurred in many countries of the Commonwealth of Independent States during the early 1990s.[5] Being a measure of cash transactions, this fiscal balance reflects the 1986 approach to GFS.

2. *Primary balance*: the primary balance (PB) or primary fiscal balance is the difference between total revenues and grants and total non-interest expenditures (total expenditures less interest payments). The PB has two main purposes. First, by excluding interest payments, it identifies the fiscal impact of "new" government activities: those activities undertaken in the current period, without reference to the interest cost from past deficits. Second, the PB turns out to be the main variable for determining fiscal sustainability, i.e., whether the ratio of government debt to GDP is stable or tends to rise without limit. This second point is demonstrated later in this chapter. Because the PB excludes interest payments, it can record a surplus even if the conventional fiscal balance shows a deficit. A primary surplus can occur, for example, if the government has a high debt burden and, thus, large interest payments, as was common in Indonesia during the early 2000s.

3. *Public sector borrowing requirement*: the public sector borrowing requirement combines the conventional fiscal balance with the overall balance of the state enterprise sector: the combined surplus or deficit of state-owned non-financial enterprises. Thus, it measures the overall financing burden that the public sector imposes on the economy's financial system. The public sector borrowing requirement can be especially useful in an economy with a large state enterprise sector, particularly if many of these entities incur losses. In Romania during the early 1990s, for example, the combined losses of the state enterprise sector far exceeded

---

[5]Cheasty, A., and J. M. Davis (1996), "Fiscal Transition in Countries of the Former Soviet Union: An Interim Assessment," *MOCT-MOST: Economic Policy in Transitional Economies*, 6(3), pp. 7–34.

the government's budget deficit. Thus, the public sector borrowing requirement was a more informative measure of the public sector's burden on the banking system.

4. *Cyclically adjusted budget balance*: the cyclically adjusted budget balance is an attempt to correct for the impact of the business cycle in assessing the stance of fiscal policy. The cyclically adjusted balance is calculated by estimating budget revenues and expenditures at potential output (or full employment), rather than at the current level of GDP. For an economy in recession, estimating revenues and expenditures at potential output could well lead to a smaller fiscal deficit, since revenues would likely be higher and any recession-linked expenditures (such as unemployment benefits) would be smaller. By comparison, the cyclically adjusted balance could show a smaller surplus or larger deficit for an economy with a positive output gap, since revenues would be above those at potential output while cyclically sensitive expenditures might be lower. Determining the cyclically adjusted balance requires an estimate of the economy's output gap — the difference between actual GDP and potential GDP. This in turn requires having an estimate of potential output (see Chapter 2 on real sector analysis). The cyclically adjusted budget balance also requires knowing the elasticity of revenues and expenditures to changes in the output gap: the percentage by which revenues and expenditures change for each 1 percent rise or fall in the output gap.

The following example shows how the cyclically adjusted budget deficit can be calculated. Assume that revenues are 200 billion units of national currency and expenditures are 220 billion units of currency, with GDP at 1,000 billion units of currency, which implies a deficit of 2 percent of GDP. Suppose that potential GDP has been estimated at 1,100 billion currency units, implying that the economy is about 9.1 percent short of potential. Suppose also that the elasticity of revenue to GDP at constant prices is 1, but that the expenditure elasticity is zero, as might be true in many developing and emerging market countries that lack unemployment insurance. If the economy were at potential GDP, GDP would be 10 percent higher (1,100, rather than 1,000). With a revenue elasticity of 1, revenues would also be 10 percent higher at potential output, i.e., 220 billion currency units rather than 200 billion. In this case, at potential output the budget would be in balance:

revenues and expenditures would both be 220 billion currency units. Thus, the cyclically adjusted budget balance would be zero.

The cyclically adjusted budget balance can be useful for judging the budget's fiscal stance, i.e., whether the budget is tending to expand or contract the economy when assessed at potential output. As suggested earlier, a small budget deficit in an economy with a negative output gap could be considered contractionary at potential output. Similarly, a budget with a small surplus when the economy is overheating, i.e., has a positive output gap, could be considered expansionary at potential output. The cyclically adjusted budget balance also provides a way to assess long-term trends in fiscal policy, by smoothing out the effects of business cycles on projected levels of the budget balance. For this reason, many fiscal reports, including recent issues of the IMF's *Fiscal Monitor*, often report projections of the cyclically adjusted fiscal or primary balance.[6]

5. *Fiscal balances in the 2001 approach to GFS.* The 2001 approach to GFS, which involves accrual accounting and measuring the effect of fiscal operations on the government's net worth, has its own set of budget balances. These include

a. *Net operating balance*: the net operating balance is the difference between government revenue and budget expense, as defined in the 2001 GFS Manual (2001 GFS). This balance is somewhat analogous to a firm's operating balance and takes into account the effects of depreciation, but not capital expenses.

b. *Net primary operating balance*: the net primary operating balance is the net operating balance after removing net interest payments (interest payments less interest receipts).

c. *Net lending or borrowing*: in the 2001 GFS, net lending or net borrowing is the sum of the net operating balance plus any change in non-financial government assets. This can be considered the accrual version of the conventional fiscal balance, although net lending in the 1986 GFS is eliminated from expenditure and any privatization proceeds are excluded.

---

[6] See, for example, IMF (2016), *Fiscal Monitor, October 2016*, Tables A3, A4, A11, and A12 (Washington).

d. *Net PB*: the net PB in the 2001 GFS is the above-mentioned net lending or borrowing, excluding net interest flows (both revenues and expenditures). This is the accrual equivalent of the primary fiscal balance mentioned earlier (which is consistent with the 1986 GFS), although net lending by government and privatization proceeds are removed.

e. *Cash surplus or deficit*: the cash surplus or deficit is the same as the conventional fiscal balance in the 1986 GFS.

B. Effects of Alternative Types of Budget Financing

How the government budget deficit is financed matters. Different types of financing have different risks and implications.

1. Foreign financing of the budget — net borrowing from abroad — increases external debt. In addition, because foreign lenders have usually been reluctant to buy the debt of developing and emerging market economies when issued in local currency, foreign financing generally exposes the budget to currency risk: the possibility that the local currency value of debt will escalate as the domestic currency depreciates. For this reason, economists urge developing and emerging market economies to avoid foreign financing where possible, even though foreign loans often have lower interest rates (because lenders face less currency risk).

2. Domestic budget financing comprises three main types: financing provided by the monetary authority or central bank; financing from commercial banks; and financing from non-bank sources. All increase the stock of domestic government debt, but each has different consequences.

a. **Central bank financing**, where the monetary authority buys government securities or offers "ways and means" financing (e.g., overdraft lending) to the government, involves the creation of high powered money, since the monetary authority has to create (i.e., print) money to purchase the securities. Thus, this type of financing can be inflationary if the economy is operating at or above potential output. For this reason, advanced economies generally avoid central bank financing, and some countries even prohibit such financing in their constitutions. Since 2009, however, a number of leading economies, including the United States, have used central bank financing as part of their tool kit to revive the national economy, with little impact on the inflation rate through early 2017.

b. **Commercial bank financing** occurs when commercial banks buy government securities or extend ways and means (overdraft) financing to government. The macroeconomic consequences of commercial bank financing depend on what commercial banks do with these securities. If the banks buy and hold these securities as assets, their purchases reduce the available financing for non-government, and particularly private sector, borrowers. As such, they crowd out non-government borrowing and raise the interest rates such borrowers face. However, commercial banks can also use these securities as collateral for loans from the monetary authority, drawing on the authority's discounting (or rediscounting) facility. To the extent such refinancing occurs, commercial bank financing has the same effect as central bank financing.

c. **Non-bank financing** occurs when firms, individuals, and financial institutions other than commercial banks purchase government securities. Under normal circumstances, these parties cannot access the central bank's discounting facility. Thus, their purchases act as pure crowding out, eliminating financial resources that might otherwise be used to support private sector borrowing. In the United States, for example, some insurance companies help finance apartment construction, so their purchases of government securities would reduce the availability of such financing. Since 2009, investment banks in a few advanced economies have had access to the central bank's rediscount facility, but this is an unusual exception to the norm.

3. **Drawing on foreign reserves**: in some situations, a country can use foreign reserves to provide budget financing. During 2003, for example, the People's Republic of China (PRC) drew the equivalent of US$45 billion in foreign exchange reserves to provide financing to recapitalize two state-owned policy banks.[7] This option is available only to countries with

---

[7] See Knowledge @ Wharton (2005), "Reform of China's Banks, Burdened by Bad Loans, Is Priority for Government," (June 1)." Available at: http://knowledge.wharton.upenn.edu/article.cfm?articleid=1202. Accessed July 16, 2017.

massive foreign exchange reserves. Most economies would find it difficult using reserves for this purpose. Indeed, doing so could undermine confidence in the national currency and threaten a currency crisis, much as a sharp decline in a commercial bank's capital could put downward pressure on the price of its stock (equity).

4. Incurring arrears: a government can also finance its accrual deficit by running arrears, that is, failing to pay contractual obligations. However, doing so undermines confidence in the government, reduces the number of those willing to be contractors, and can raise the prices government pays for goods and services from those that will deal with it. Arrears on debt service can disrupt government financing and make it hard for a government in deficit to continue operating. Thus, arrears should normally be avoided, except possibly as a temporary measure before reaching agreement with creditors on debt restructuring or forgiveness.

C. Fiscal Space

Fiscal space has been defined as "room in a government's budget that allows it to provide resources for a desired purpose without jeopardizing the sustainability of its financial position or the stability of the economy."[8] Governments with fiscal space typically have budget surpluses or deficits small enough to allow a small deterioration in the fiscal balance without undermining fiscal sustainability or macroeconomic stability.

A government can create fiscal space by raising taxes, securing outside grants, cutting lower priority expenditure, or borrowing, provided the borrowing does not raise debt to an unacceptable level or threaten a steady rise in the government's debt-to-GDP ratio. In creating fiscal space, the government must ensure it has the capacity in both the short term and the longer term to finance its expenditure programs while also servicing its debt. Following are several examples of how governments can create fiscal space for desired programs.

---

[8]Heller, P. (2005), "Understanding Fiscal Space," IMF Policy Discussion Paper 05/4 (Washington: International Monetary Fund, March)." Available at: http://www.imf.org/external/pubs/ft/pdp/2005/pdp04.pdf. Accessed July 16, 2017.

1. *Expenditure substitution*: a government could reduce spending for a lower-priority program to make available funds for a new and higher-priority project. Indonesia, for example, cut petroleum subsidies in 2005 and used some of the proceeds to provide a cash transfer program to low-income families.

2. *Revenue increases*: a government can raise revenue to finance a new program or increase spending for an existing one. In 2006, for example, the Philippines raised the rate of its value-added tax (VAT) by 2 percentage points and used the resulting revenue to boost education expenditure.

3. *Expanding borrowing in a low-debt environment*: where the government's debt-to-GDP ratio is sufficiently small, a modest increase in the deficit could be used to provide fiscal space for a desired program. In 2009, for example, the People's Republic of China (PRC) raised its budget deficit by about 2 percentage points of GDP to finance fiscal stimulus, to limit the adverse effects of the global financial crisis on the economy. Because the central government's debt-to-GDP ratio was less than 30 percent of GDP, this increase in the deficit did not threaten the sustainability of the government's fiscal position.

D. Revenue Analysis

Fiscal revenues can be analyzed in different ways. For example, one can examine the structure of revenues: what percentage of revenue comes from different types of taxes and how much comes from non-tax sources. The U.S., the U.K., and Australia, for example, rely heavily on taxation from income and profits. Many countries also have payroll taxes, meaning taxes levied on wages on salaries, to fund government-sponsored social insurance schemes. Most countries also obtain a sizable share of revenues from taxes on goods and services. The most important of these are value added taxes (VATs) or sales taxes, and excise taxes levied on specific products, typically alcoholic beverages, tobacco, and petroleum products. Lower-income countries often receive a large share of revenues from taxes on international trade, especially import duties, while property taxes are important for funding local government in many countries. Finally, most economies also obtain at least some revenue from non-tax sources, such as profits from state-owned enterprises (including the monetary authority), leases from government-owned property, vehicle permits and road use fees, and earnings from a state lottery. In many oil-producing countries, royalties from profit-sharing arrangements and land rental fees comprise a majority of all government revenues.

One can also examine the ratios of total revenues and tax revenues to GDP and compare these ratios to those in other, similar economies. Many middle-income countries, for example, obtain revenues in the range of 20–25 percent of GDP, while advanced economies tend to have revenues of at least 30 percent of GDP, with higher ratios in Europe. Revenue-to-GDP ratios below 15 percent may signal insufficient revenue to support basic public sector activities, such as quality universal primary and secondary education, reasonable health care facilities for the poor, and an efficient and effective legal system. Low tax-to-GDP ratios may signal basic problems with tax administration, enforcement, and compliance or, in the case of oil-producing countries, heavy reliance on revenues from exhaustible natural resources.

Examining how well revenues keep pace with economic activity can also be informative, since governments are often keen to increase spending as the economy expands. The **buoyancy** of total revenue or tax revenue to GDP, defined as the ratio of the percentage change in total or tax revenue to the percentage change in nominal GDP, is one such measure. A buoyancy of one or more indicates that revenues are rising at least as fast as economic activity. Even more useful is the **elasticity** of total revenue or tax revenue to GDP, the ratio of the percentage change in revenue to the percentage change in GDP after eliminating any changes in tax law, tax administration, or compliance with the tax code. The elasticity measures the "built-in" response of revenues to changes in economic activity, indicating by how much revenues "automatically" rise, without intervention by government through tax increases or compliance-boosting activities, when the economy expands. An economy whose revenue system has an elasticity of at least one is better able to withstand spending pressures and maintain a sustainable fiscal position than one in which the elasticity is noticeably less than one. Such revenue systems typically rely mainly on broadly based sources, such as income, profits, and value added taxes with few exemptions and exclusions.

Closely related to the elasticity of revenue systems is the quality of tax administration. High-quality administration depends not only on strong enforcement, but also on the ease of complying with the law and on ensuring that taxpayers make regular "advance" or estimated payments toward their full year tax liability throughout the fiscal year (which reduces the erosion in revenues from inflation). Having broad-based taxes, with few exemptions or exclusions, a limited number of tax rates, and objective measures of assessment (to avoid possibilities for special treatment) and avoiding nuisance taxes (taxes that yield little revenue but have heavy enforcement and compliance costs) also helps.[9]

E. Expenditure Analysis

Expenditures, like revenues, can also be analyzed. For example, one can look at the structure and composition of expenditures. Besides examining the shares of expenditure devoted to various functions such as health, housing, defense, and education, the allocation of spending across various economic categories can also be assessed: what percentage of outlays goes for wages and salaries, purchases of other goods and services, subsidies, transfers, interest payments, and capital expenditure, to use 1986 GFS expenditure categories. Countries that devote large shares of expenditure to interest payments, such as India and Pakistan, for example, often have little money left to spend for infrastructure, while other countries with lower debt service burdens, such as Malaysia and Thailand, have sometimes allocated 25 percent or more of total outlays to capital expenditure. In many advanced economies such as the United States, Spain, and Italy, heavy expenditures for mandatory benefit programs, such as public pensions and health care schemes, limit funding available for other activities. In a few economies, civil war and strategic threats require high military expenditures, meaning less money for civilian programs.

---

[9] For more discussion of administrative issues, including the so-called "Tanzi diagnostic test" of tax administration, see Ouanes, A., and S. Thakur (1997), *Macroeconomic Analysis and Accounting in Transition Economies* (Washington: International Monetary Fund), Box 3.5, p. 70.

Ratios of total expenditure and various categories of expenditure to GDP can also be informative, indicating the extent of economic activity taking place in the public sector. The rage of spending various tremendously across countries, with expenditures ranging from more than 50 percent of GDP in some European nations to less than 20 percent in some low-income countries in South Asia. Ratios of specific types of spending to GDP can also signal the adequacy of government efforts to fund certain activities. Many countries strive, for example, to devote at least 4 percent of GDP to education and 2 percent to health care (through subsidies, insurance programs, and public health facilities).

One can also examine the effect of exchange and interest rate changes on expenditure. A large devaluation, for example, will likely raise interest costs on external debt and the cost of capital projects that involve imported equipment and foreign technical experts. It will also raise amortization costs on external debt, possibly reducing net foreign financing of the budget. Monetary tightening or a rise in world interest rates can raise interest costs on domestic as well as foreign debt. Estimating these effects can be important in projecting future government budgets.

Assessing the productivity of government expenditure can also be useful, particularly for governments undergoing adjustment or seeking fiscal space to finance new activities. Productivity is typically assessed by comparing the discounted value of benefits to the discounted sum of costs for a program, with high ratios signifying high-productivity activities and low ratios — in particular, ratios less than one — signaling (economically) unproductive expenditure.

Economists have done extensive work helping governments identify unproductive expenditure.[10] While specific programs vary from country to country, typical examples include

- poorly targeted subsidies, which have high costs and deliver only a fraction of their benefits to the intended beneficiaries;
- health or education outlays that reach relatively few people, such as funding expensive hospitals in a capital city rather than rural health

---

[10]See, for example, International Monetary Fund (1995), "Unproductive Public Expenditures: A Pragmatic Approach to Policy Analysis," IMF Pamphlet No. 48. Available at: http://www.imf.org/external/pubs/ft/pam/pam48/pam4801.htm. Accessed July 16, 2017.

centers or creating tuition-free universities (attended mainly by children of the elite) while underfunding primary or secondary education;

- low-yield development projects, such as railways with little traffic, that provide few benefits apart from the political gains for those sponsoring them;
- massive hiring of low-skilled government employees, an expensive way of providing income transfers to the poor; and
- exceptionally high military expenditures in a country facing few military threats.

The above activities can be contrasted with programs more likely to have high productivity: outlays for useful operations and maintenance, such as road maintenance; productive infrastructure, including the construction of roads and railroads to overcome transport bottlenecks; and primary health and education programs, particularly in low-income areas.

F. Fiscal Sustainability[11]

Fiscal sustainability is the ability to maintain current fiscal policy without risk of a crisis or severe disruption. While sustainability can depend on the government's ability to meet upcoming debt service obligations (liquidity) or its fundamental solvency (could debt, in principle, be paid off), in practice sustainability turns on whether the government's debt-to-GDP ratio will stabilize or rise without limit. A fiscal position in which the debt-to-GDP ratio tends to rise without limit is considered unsustainable.

Of the many analytical tools developed to assess fiscal sustainability, arguably the most useful is the change in the government or public debt-to-GDP ratio. This formula is as follows:

$$d_t - d_{t-1} = -pb_t + \frac{r-g}{1+g} d_{t-1}$$

where d is the government or public debt/GDP ratio, pb is the primary balance (PB)/GDP ratio, r is the real interest rate, and g is the real rate of

---

[11] For an extended discussion, see Greene, Joshua (2012), *Public Finance: An International Perspective* (Singapore: World Scientific), Ch. 5.

GDP growth, all measured in decimals (e.g., a debt-to-GDP ratio of 60 percent is 0.60, etc.), t is the current time period, and $t-1$ denotes the previous period. The values of r and g are values during the same period as the PB. The above formula implies that, to stabilize the government's debt-to-GDP ratio, the PB in period t must satisfy the following mathematical condition:

$$pb_t \geq (r_t - g_t)/(1 + g_t) * d_{t-1}.$$

For example, if $r = 0.04$, $g = 0.02$, $d_{t-1} = 0.6$, pb_t must $= 1.18$ to stabilize the debt-to-GDP ratio and be higher to reduce the ratio.

III. CASE STUDY OF FISCAL ANALYSIS: SINGAPORE

Singapore presents an interesting case for fiscal analysis. As Table 4.3 shows, Singapore typically attains a budget surplus. However, the authorities' budget figures, reflecting rules in the Singapore constitution for protecting Past Reserves, exclude from revenue the proceeds from land sales and the part of investment income that accrues to Past Reserves. Thus, the authorities' budget accounts normally report a smaller surplus, or larger deficit, than would arise from using international standards.

Singapore's budget surpluses reflect a longstanding policy of maintaining a limited social safety net, with discretionary policy measures rather than mandatory spending programs ("entitlements") to assist vulnerable groups. Unlike most advanced economies, Singapore has no unemployment insurance. Retirement income is provided through the use of the Central Provident Fund (CPF), a mandatory savings program into which employers and employees each contribute a portion of the employee's wage earnings. A portion of CPF balances is set aside to provide funds for certain medical payments (Medisave) and the cost of basic health insurance ("Medishield"). Part may also be used to pay mortgage bills from the purchase of a state-built housing unit. The remainder is available to fund retirement, and account holders are required to have a minimum sum in order to receive retirement benefits. Singapore uses a variety of methods, including support for polyclinics and government hospitals, providing medical benefits for low-income citizens (Medifund), and organizing health insurance programs (Medishield Life and Eldershield), whose premiums are paid by enrollees, to help citizens and permanent residents

TABLE 4.3   SINGAPORE: SELECTED FISCAL INDICATORS, FISCAL YEARS 2012-13–2017/18

	2012/13	2013/14	2014/15	2015/16	2016/17		2017/18	
					Budget	Prel.	Budget 1/	Proj.
(In billions of Singapore dollars)								
1. Statement of government operations								
Revenue	81.4	82.3	84.9	89.8	90.9	91.4	88.4	88.8
Taxes	50.1	51.1	54.1	55.6	59.2	58.2	59.4	59.6
Other revenue 2/	31.2	31.2	30.8	34.1	31.8	33.2	29.0	29.2
Of which: interest income	1.7	1.9	2.6	3.1	3.9	4.0	4.1	4.1
Expenditure	52.7	57.0	63.3	74.7	80.4	77.8	82.3	82.9
Expense	37.9	42.7	46.5	52.5	57.1	55.5	58.9	59.3
Compensation of employees	6.2	6.8	7.4	8.0	8.7	8.5	8.9	9.0
Use of goods and services	14.6	15.2	16.1	17.5	18.7	18.5	19.3	19.4
Expense not elsewhere classified	17.0	20.7	23.0	26.9	29.7	28.5	30.7	30.9
Grants, subventions & capital injections to organisations	6.7	7.1	7.9	9.4	11.4	10.6	12.5	12.6
Transfers	10.3	13.6	15.1	17.5	18.3	17.9	18.2	18.3
Net acquisition of nonfinancial assets	14.9	14.6	16.8	22.3	23.3	22.2	23.4	23.6
Development expenditure	13.5	13.0	15.3	20.8	20.9	20.2	20.4	20.5

Land-related expenditure	1.3	1.3	1.4	1.4	2.4	2.0	3.1	3.1
Gross operating balance	43.5	39.6	38.4	37.3	33.8	35.8	29.5	29.5
Net lending/borrowing	28.6	25.3	21.6	15.0	10.5	13.6	6.1	5.9
Net acquisition of financial assets	—	—	—	—	—	—	—	—
Net incurrence of liabilities	—	—	—	—	—	—	—	—
(In percent of GDP)								
Revenue	22.3	21.6	21.5	22.0	21.9	22.0	20.8	20.9
Taxes	13.8	13.4	13.7	13.6	14.3	14.0	14.0	14.0
Other revenue 2/	8.2	8.2	7.8	8.4	7.7	8.0	6.8	6.9
Expenditure	13.7	15.0	15.8	18.9	20.8	20.0	19.8	19.9
Expense	10.4	11.2	11.8	12.9	13.8	13.4	13.8	13.9
Net acquisitions of nonfinancial assets	4.1	3.7	4.2	5.5	5.6	5.4	5.5	5.6
Gross operating balance	11.9	10.4	9.7	9.1	8.2	8.6	6.9	6.9
Net lending/borrowing	8.7	6.5	5.7	3.1	1.1	2.0	1.0	1.0
Memorandum Items:								
Primary balance 3/	0.8	0.0	–0.6	–2.4	–2.9	–2.2	–3.0	–3.1
Cyclically adjusted primary balance	0.7	–0.2	–0.7	–2.3	–3.1	–2.4	–2.9	–3.0
Expenditures on social development 4/	6.0	6.4	6.9	7.9	8.7	8.7	—	—

TABLE 4.3 (*CONTINUED*)

	2012/13	2013/14	2014/15	2015/16	2016/17		2017/18	
					Budget	Prel.	Budget 11/	Proj.
Land sales revenue	5.0	4.5	3.8	3.8	2.4	2.8	1.9	2.0
Spending from Endowment and Trust Funds (9)	0.8	1.0	1.0	1.2	1.3	1.3	—	—
Fiscal impulse 5/	-1.5	1.3	-0.1	2.2	1.4	0.8	0.5	—
Authorities' budgetary accounts 6/								
Operating revenue (1)	15.3	14.9	15.4	15.9	16.5	16.5	16.3	—
Total expenditure (2)	13.5	13.5	14.3	16.5	17.7	17.2	17.7	—
Primary fiscal balance (3) = (1) – (2)	1.9	1.4	1.1	-0.6	-1.2	-0.7	-1.3	—
Special transfers (excl. transfer to endowment funds) (4)	0.4	0.8	1.0	1.1	0.6	0.7	0.6	—
Basic balance (5) = (3) – (4)	1.5	0.6	0.1	-1.7	-1.8	-1.3	-1.9	—
Transfer to Endowment and Trust Funds (6)	2.0	1.5	2.2	1.5	0.9	0.9	0.9	—
Net investment returns contributions (7)	2.2	2.2	2.2	2.4	3.5	3.5	3.3	—
Overall balance (8) = (5) – (6) + (7)	1.6	1.3	0.1	-0.8	0.8	1.2	0.4	—
II. Stock positions	2012	2013	2014	2015	2016			
(In billions of Singapore dollars, unless otherwise indicated)								
Gross financial assets 7/	—	817	834	878	841			
Gross debt 8/	385	390	987	421	463			
Gross debt (in percent of GDP) 8/	107	103	99	103	113			

Memorandum items:

Government deposits at the Monetary Authority of Singapore 7/	147	163	114	115	124
Temasek asset holdings 7/ 9/	198	215	223	266	242
GIC asset holding 10/			more than 140		

Notes: Data provided by the Ministry of Finance; and IMF staff estimates and projections.

1/ The fiscal year runs from April 1 through March 31. The presentation of the table is based on GFSM 2001.

2/ Includes revenue from lands sales and investment income.

3/ Overall balance excluding investment income, capital revenue, and interest payments.

4/ Includes development and operating expenditure on educations, health, national development, environment and water resources, culture, community and youth, social and family development, communications and information, and manpower (financial security). Includes spending on social development purposes from endowment and trust funds set up by the government.

5/ The fiscal impulse is the change in the cyclically adjusted operational balance, excluding top ups to endowments and trust funds.

6/ The authorities' budgetary accounts are based on Singapore's Constitutional rules governing the protection of Past Reserves. It includes the net investment returns contribution, which reflects the amount of investment returns that is taken into the Budget. It excludes receipts such as proceeds from land sales and the remaining part of investment income that accrues to Past Reserves and cannot be used to fund government expenditures without the approval of the President. While such receipts are not reflected in the Overall Balance, the information is presented annually to Parliament and included in Budget documents.

7/ Gross asset stock figures are as at the end of March for each year as reported in the "Statement of Assets and Liabilities" in the budget documents.

8/ Gross debt stock figures are as at the end of the calendar year. Government debt is issued to develop domestic capital markets and to provide an investment vehicle for the mandatory savings scheme.

9/ The government of Singapore is the sole equity shareholder of Temasek.

10/ The Government Investment Corporation (GIC) is a private company wholly owned by the government of Singapore.

11/ The IMF Staff projections for GDP are used to calculate the number for the 2016/17 budget in the authorities' budgetary accounts in percent of GDP.

Source: International Monetary Fund (2017), *Singapore: 2017 Article IV Consultation: Press Release; Staff Report (IMF Country Report 17/240)*, Table 6 (July). Data for 2017/18 are IMF Staff estimates.

manage health care expenses. The poor receive help through a variety of discretionary social service programs. In addition, the working poor can participate in the Workfare Income Supplement Scheme (WIS), which provides income supplements and contributions to CPF accounts for workers earning less than a certain monthly income.

The above policy choices enable Singapore to keep budget expenditure low relative to most advanced economies. They also allow a relatively high level of spending for capital projects (4 percent or more of GDP in most years), which supports economic growth. As Table 4.3 indicates, in recent fiscal years expenditure has averaged 20–21 percent of GDP, well below the average for advanced economies (about 40 percent).[12] Accordingly, revenue can be kept low, averaging 21–22 percent of GDP in recent years, while still maintaining a balanced budget. Besides low expenditure levels, Singapore also benefits from a high level of non-tax revenue, largely from investment income and land sales (although the latter is not included in the authorities' budget accounts). These provisions, along with heavy taxes on motor vehicles and alcohol, allow taxes on income and profits to be low by international standards. The corporate income tax rate is 17 percent, while the top marginal rate on personal income is 22 percent. In addition, income from interest, dividends, and capital gains is excluded from tax, making the income tax more like a mildly progressive consumption tax. These tax provisions add to the attractiveness of Singapore's investment climate.

With expenditures kept moderate and revenues geared to cover outlays, Singapore has the fiscal space to address new challenges facing the public sector. Thus, Singapore is typically in a position to provide support to the poor and elderly through one-time benefit payments, including supplementary "top ups" to CPF Medisave accounts. In addition, Singapore will likely find it easier than many other advanced economies to meet the rising medical expenses resulting from an aging population.

IV. SUMMARY

The fiscal sector records the activities of the government and state-owned (public) enterprises, with emphasis on those operating outside the

---

[12]See IMF (2016), *Fiscal Monitor*, October 2016, Statistical Table A6.

financial sector. Government includes the activities of central, provincial or state, and local governments, including any special purpose funds or trust funds with specified activities and their own sources of revenue. The fiscal sector also includes quasi-fiscal operations, activities such as subsidies that would normally appear in a government budget but take place outside government, often by central banks at the request or command of government. Fiscal activities are typically recorded in the budgets of governments or state-owned enterprises, although the government's net worth, including stocks of government and public debt, is typically recorded separately. Occasionally the activities of some government agencies or ministries are only recorded "off budget." In addition, some government units obtain financing from special purpose vehicles (SPVs), which also reduce the transparency of government operations. Monitoring sub-national as well as central government budgets is particularly important in countries such as Argentina, Brazil, China, India, and the United States, where provincial and local government represents a large share of total government activity.

Fiscal accounts are compiled either on a cash basis, using the 1986 GFS manual, or on an accrual basis, in the newer 2001 and 2014 GFS formats. The accounts typically include revenue, expenditure, a fiscal balance, and sources of financing. Revenue comprises taxes, non-tax items such as fees and charges or income from government property (including state-owned enterprises), plus grants. Expenditure, when classified on an economic basis, is typically divided between current and capital outlays. When classified using the 1986 Government Finance Statistics manual, it also includes net lending (government lending to other sectors for policy purposes). Current expenditure comprises payments for wages and salaries, other purchases of goods and services, subsidies, transfers (to persons and institutions), and interest (domestic and external). Capital spending includes payments for capital projects and capital transfers to other levels of government. Financing is presented on a net basis and subdivided into external and domestic, with domestic financing further divided between that from the banking system (the monetary authority and commercial banks) and financing from other domestic sources (non-bank financing). In the format of the 2001 and 2014 GFS manuals,which are designed to show the impact of transactions on the government's net worth, current expenditure is called "expense," while capital outlays are the main element in the "net acquisition of non-financial assets." In addition, financing is part of the "net acquisition of financial assets," along with net lending to persons and institutions under government loan programs.

Fiscal accounts typically show one of several balances. The best known is the overall or conventional balance, equal to total revenue and grants less total expenditure (including net lending) on a cash basis. This balance indicates the government's financing requirement, apart from covering amortization payments. However, it ignores arrears (unpaid obligations). The primary balance, which equals total revenue and grants less non-interest expenditure, records the impact of new fiscal obligations and is useful for assessing fiscal (public debt) sustainability. The current balance, representing total revenue and grants less current expenditure, indicates the government's ability to finance current outlays from revenue. The public sector borrowing requirement adds to the overall balance the financing needs of state-owned enterprises, showing the financial burden of the public sector on the banking system. The cyclically adjusted balance, which adjusts revenue and expenditure for the effects of the business cycle (output gap), can be used to assess the government's fiscal stance. Fiscal accounts prepared in accord with the with the 2001 and 2014 GFS manuals show accrual versions of these balances, with net lending/borrowing being the accrual version of the overall balance and the net primary balance the accrual version of the primary balance.

Among the many useful fiscal concepts are fiscal space and fiscal sustainability. Fiscal space means the government's ability to address new challenges without creating debt problems or undermining macroeconomic stability. The government can create fiscal space by raising more revenue, replacing lower priority with higher priority outlays, or (if the public debt is low — typically less than 30 percent of GDP), borrowing, preferably on concessional terms. Fiscal or public debt sustainability involves the ability to maintain current policy without risk of a crisis. A sustainable fiscal position is one in which the ratio of public (government) debt is not excessive (typically less than 40 to 50 percent of GDP for emerging market countries) and does not tend to rise without limit. Avoiding a rise in the public debt ratio usually involves attaining a primary surplus or keeping any primary deficit small, with the amount depending on the relative size of real GDP growth and the average real interest rate on government debt.

Revenue can be assessed in various ways, including the ratio of total revenue and total taxes to GDP, along with the composition of revenues among major sources. Assessing the buoyancy of revenue, the ratio of the percent change in total revenue to the percent change in nominal GDP, can be particularly useful, because the deficit is likely to rise as a percent of GDP if the buoyancy is less than 1, while spending pressures may keep total outlays constant or rising as a share of GDP. Data on expenditure as a percent of GDP and the allocation of expenditure between current and capital outlays can also prove informative. In addition, it is useful to assess the productivity of expenditure, because governments often find it easier to cut spending for operations, maintenance, and infrastructure rather than containing spending for wages and salaries or poorly targeted subsidy and transfer payments.

Chapter 5

MONETARY SECTOR
ACCOUNTS AND ANALYSIS

The monetary accounts provide information on an economy's financial system. As indicated in Figure 5.1, the financial system comprises the activities of the banking system and of other financial institutions, such as savings banks, finance companies, credit unions, and microfinance agencies. The banking system, in turn, comprises the activities of the monetary authorities and of the commercial (deposit money) banks, the financial entities that normally have access to the rediscounting and lender-of-last-resort facilities of the monetary authorities. The monetary authorities and the consolidated commercial banks each have their own sets of accounts, while the accounts of the entire banking system are recorded in the monetary survey. The financial survey in turn provides a consolidated view of the economy's entire financial system, comprising both the banks and other financial institutions.

I. THE IMPORTANCE OF MONETARY ACCOUNTS

The monetary accounts are important because they provide information on an economy's financial system. The financial system is a critical part of an economy, because it provides intermediation for the resources flowing between different economic sectors. The various monetary accounts help explain these flows, which mirror the flows of real resources among the sectors. Unlike the accounts of the real, external, and fiscal sectors,

The Monetary Accounts

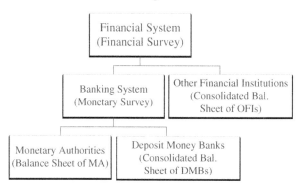

FIGURE 5.1. THE STRUCTURE AND ACCOUNTS OF AN ECONOMY'S FINANCIAL (MONETARY) SECTOR

however, the accounts themselves measure *stocks* — data at a point in time. Identifying flows requires calculating *changes* in these stocks over a period of time — for example, the changes from the end of one calendar quarter to the end of the following quarter. Like the national and external accounts, monetary accounts are measured in local currency. This can create challenges, because certain elements in the accounts — for example, foreign currency deposits — measure the current domestic currency value of items whose real value is determined in a foreign currency.

Monetary accounts are also important in other ways. They focus on variables that are central to macroeconomic analysis (such as money, credit, and foreign assets and liabilities). Monetary accounts are usually available with little delay and are among the most reliable of macroeconomic statistics, since banks must report on them regularly and typically do so, even in low-income economies. In addition, the monetary accounts are a central element of the theoretical foundation for adjustment programs supported by the International Monetary Fund (IMF). Most IMF-supported adjustment programs assume a basic accounting identity: that the sum of all banking system assets, foreign plus domestic (usually expressed as net foreign and net domestic assets), equal the sum of all monetary liabilities (the broad money stock). Moreover, net foreign assets in the banking system comprise the sum of the country's net international reserves and all other net foreign assets, primarily those of the commercial banks. For a given amount of broad money and net foreign assets of the commercial banks, attaining a specific increase in net international reserves requires limiting the growth of net domestic assets. Hence, IMF-supported adjustment programs almost always include agreed limits on the growth in net domestic assets, and sometimes limits on key components of net domestic assets, such the growth in net banking system credit to government.

II. KEY ELEMENTS OF THE BANKING SYSTEM

In most developing and emerging market economies, the banking system accounts for most financial transactions. Thus, it is worthwhile focusing on the banking system and its key elements: the monetary authorities and the commercial (deposit money) banks.

A. The Monetary Authorities

The monetary authorities, comprising either a central bank or a more limited institution such as a currency board (whose currency-issuing powers are limited by law to a certain percentage of its gold and foreign exchange holdings), represent the central monetary institution in most economies. The monetary authorities have the following functions:

1. The monetary authorities issue currency, even if they are not the agency that actually prints notes or mints coins. In fact, the monetary authorities are responsible not only for currency issuance, but also for establishing the minimum level of reserves that commercial banks must hold against various liabilities. The combined liability of the monetary authorities is called either reserve money or the monetary base. The term monetary base (or base money), which includes both banks' reserves and currency in circulation, is used when reserve money is used to describe only the amount of banks' reserves.

2. The monetary authorities hold the country's foreign reserves. In most economies the monetary authorities are charged with the responsibilities for storing and maintaining records on the country's official reserves, even if the reserves are considered property of the government.

3. The monetary authorities act as banker to the government. The monetary authorities are often the agency responsible for receiving the proceeds of foreign loans, even if the government issues securities. In most countries, the monetary authorities are the ones maintaining accounts with the IMF and receiving the proceeds of IMF loans, even if the proceeds are then credited to the accounts of the government.

4. The monetary authorities conduct monetary policy, typically buying and selling government securities or their own instruments to control a critical (usually overnight) interest rate as a way of influencing the rate of inflation, the exchange rate, or, in some cases, the level of economic activity.

5. The monetary authorities oversee the monetary system. At a minimum, the authorities monitor developments in the system, using the information to determine changes in monetary policy. In many economies, the monetary authorities are also responsible for regulating some or all of the banking system, although in others a separate agency is charged with financial regulation.

6. The monetary authorities serve as lender of last resort to the system. They provide resources to banks short of liquidity for meeting reserve requirements and, more importantly, the demands of depositors for liquid funds to prevent a panic. Commercial banks short of liquid funds can approach the monetary authorities for assistance, typically providing collateral in the form of government securities or other approved assets in return for receiving cash or other freely usable funds. As a general rule, monetary authorities follow a practice of lending freely, at a penalty rate of interest, against good collateral, to prevent bank failures. The penalty interest rate, along with disapproval and sometimes other measures (such as assuming managerial authority for a bank), is designed to discourage banks from seeking this assistance except during times of extreme stress.

Figure 5.2 provides an analytical (stylized) balance sheet of the monetary authorities. On the asset side of the balance sheet are net foreign assets and net domestic assets. Net foreign assets comprise net international reserves and some other, less liquid, foreign assets and liabilities. Net domestic assets comprise mainly the domestic credit provided by the monetary authorities. The credit includes the net credit provided to the government, in the form of holdings of government securities and less

Analytical Balance Sheet of the Monetary Authorities

Assets	Liabilities
Net Foreign Assets	**Reserve Money***
Net Domestic Assets - Domestic credit (net) Claims on the government(net) Claims on the DMBs Claims on other domestic economic sectors - Other items (net)	- Currency issued Held in banks Held outside banks - Deposits of deposit money banks

*Sometimes "reserve money" is used to describe only bank reserves, while "base money" or "the monetary base" is used to describe reserves plus currency outside banks.

FIGURE 5.2. ANALYTICAL BALANCE SHEET OF THE MONETARY AUTHORITIES

formal (e.g., overdraft or ways and means) facilities provided to government, minus the government's deposits at the monetary authorities; the claims on deposit money banks from rediscounting or lender-of-last-resort activities; and any claims on other domestic economic sectors, such as state enterprises, although in most economies these other claims are relatively small. Net domestic assets also include other items net, a variety of miscellaneous items including the value (a liability) of the capital and premises of the monetary authorities, including any branches or regional offices, and the revaluation account, which records the impact of exchange rate changes on the domestic currency value of the authorities' net foreign assets. The liability side of the balance sheet comprises reserve or base money: the value of currency in circulation plus the value of banks' reserves, including reserves held in accounts at the monetary authorities and currency at banks' premises (sometimes called "cash in vault"). Since this is a balance sheet, total assets equal total liabilities.

Because assets equal liabilities in the balance sheet, developments in reserve (or base) money can be explained not only by changes in the amount of currency issued or in the deposits of the commercial banks at the monetary authorities, but also by developments in the monetary authorities' assets. Indeed, increases in reserve (base) money are more typically explained by changes in one or more elements on the asset side. An increase in reserve (base) money can reflect net capital inflows that raise the net foreign assets of the monetary authorities. Reserve (base) money can also grow if the monetary authorities increase their net claims on government by purchasing government securities, either directly from government or from commercial banks through open market operations. Reserve (base) money can also rise if the monetary authorities extend credit to deposit money banks through discounting or lender-of-last-resort activities. Finally, reserve (base) money can expand less transparently if other items net increase.

B. Deposit Money (Commercial) Banks

The other element in the banking system is the set of deposit money (commercial) banks, both state and privately owned. Deposit money banks have a number of important functions.

1. They represent an important part of the payments system, enabling buyers and sellers to use accounts to make payments, thereby eliminating the need physically to transfer funds at sellers' offices.

2. They provide financial intermediation for savers and investors, thereby transforming the maturities of financial assets. By assessing the creditworthiness of potential borrowers, deposit money banks enable savers to earn income on their assets without having to find "bankable" investments. The assets into which deposits are placed inevitably have longer maturities than most deposits. This leads to one source of "mismatching" in the banking system, whereby short-maturity deposits (most available immediately on demand) are converted into assets with maturities from 90 days to several years ("maturity mismatch"). Further mismatching can occur if the banks borrow or accept deposits (or other liabilities) in foreign currency and then use these liabilities to lend in domestic currency ("currency mismatch").

3. They are the primary creators of deposit money, by extending credit. When banks accept deposits and then lend them out (after setting aside

required reserves), banks expand broad money, since borrowers either deposit the funds until needed or use them to make payments to suppliers or creditors who, in turn, deposit them, allowing more loans to be made. This process of lending out new deposits allows an initial extension of credit ultimately to make several times that amount of "deposit money." At the limit, if banks choose to maintain only the minimum required reserves, and these reserves represent n percent of deposits (with n less than 100), up to $1/(n/100)$ times the amount of the initial deposit can be created.

4. The actions of deposit money banks — in particular their policies on deposit taking and lending — affect money supply and liquidity. The more willing banks are to accept deposits and make loans, the greater is the amount of broad money that can be created for any initial amount of currency issued or expansion of reserve (base) money. The less willing they are to make loans, the smaller will be the rise in broad money. Similarly, the less willing banks are to receive deposits (or the public is to make them), the smaller will be the rise in broad money.

5. Operating within the constraints set by the monetary authorities, deposit money banks help to transmit monetary policy from the monetary authorities to the public. The amount by which a given increase in reserve (base) money leads to a rise in broad money depends in large part on the willingness of banks to lend.

Figure 5.3 provides an analytical (stylized) balance sheet of the accounts of the consolidated deposit money (commercial) banks. As shown in Figure 5.3, the assets of commercial banks comprise net foreign assets (foreign exchange holdings and holdings in correspondent accounts, less foreign liabilities), domestic credit (net claims on government and claims on the private and state enterprise sectors), and other items net (mainly bank capital, the value of bank premises, and the revaluation account, which records the impact of exchange rate changes on the domestic currency valuation of net foreign assets, foreign exchange deposits, and any loans made in foreign currency). The liabilities of commercial banks comprise deposits, any liabilities to the monetary authorities, and miscellaneous liabilities not included in other items net. In most market

Analytical Balance Sheet of Deposit Money Banks

Assets	Liabilities

Net Foreign Assets
 	
Reserves
  Required reserves
  Excess reserves
	Deposits
	  Demand
	  Time and savings
	  Foreign currency

Domestic credit
  Claims on government (net)
  Claims on other domestic
      sectors
	Liabilities to MA
	
	Other less liquid liabilities

Other items (net)	

FIGURE 5.3. ANALYTICAL (STYLIZED) BALANCE SHEET OF THE DEPOSIT MONEY BANKS

economies, the main elements of commercial bank balance sheets will be credit provided to the private sector (firms and households) and deposits (demand, savings, and foreign currency deposits).

Figure 5.4 presents an analytical (stylized) version of the **monetary survey**. The monetary survey summarizes the position of the entire banking system at a point in time. It consolidates the accounts of the monetary authorities with those of the commercial banks, netting out the claims and obligations that the monetary authorities and the commercial banks have on each other. As a consolidated balance sheet, it provides data on monetary and credit developments for the entire banking system. It thus allows policy makers to monitor monetary sector developments and adjust policy, if necessary.

As shown in Figure 5.4, the banking system's assets comprise net foreign assets (those of the monetary authority and the commercial banks) and net domestic assets (net claims on government, claims on the private sector, and other items net, which include the various items mentioned as other items in the accounts of the monetary authorities and the commercial banks). The liabilities of the banking system comprise broad money: currency in circulation, demand deposits, time and savings

Analytical Balance Sheet of the
Banking System: Monetary Survey

Assets	Liabilities
Net Foreign Assets	**Broad Money (M2)**
Net Domestic Assets	- **Narrow Money (M1)** • Currency in circulation
- **Net Domestic credit**	• Demand Deposits
• Net claims on government • Claims on the Private Sector	- **Quasi-Money (QM)** • Time and savings deposits • Foreign currency deposits
- **Other items (net)**	

FIGURE 5.4. ANALYTICAL (STYLIZED) MONETARY SURVEY

deposits, and foreign currency deposits. The first two of these are sometimes called "narrow money," while the last two have been called "quasi-money," reflecting an earlier era when customers needed to provide notice to have access to time, savings, and foreign currency deposits. Table 5.1 provides an example of the monetary survey and the balance sheet of the central bank, using data for Pakistan.

III. IMPORTANT ANALYTICAL CONCEPTS

Understanding the monetary sector requires appreciating certain useful analytical concepts. This section introduces money demand and supply; the quantity theory of money and money velocity; and the money multiplier. In addition, the valuation adjustment — an important element in addressing the impact of exchange rate changes on the monetary accounts — is discussed.

A. Money Demand and Supply

Households and firms hold money for two main reasons: to finance economic transactions (the transactions motive), thereby eliminating the need for barter; and as one of the assets in their financial portfolios (the portfolio motive).

TABLE 5.1   PAKISTAN: MONETARY SURVEY AND ANALYTICAL BALANCE SHEET OF THE STATE BANK OF PAKISTAN, 2005/2006–2009/2010

	2005/06	2006/07	2007/08	Est. Sep.	Proj. Dec.	Proj. Mar.	Jun.	Proj.
					2008/09	2008/09	2009/10	2009/10
				(In billions of Pakistani rupees)				
Monetary survey								
Net foreign assets (NFA)	710	985	669	486	295	229	438	530
Net domestic assets (NDA)	2,697	3,080	4,021	4,188	4,536	4,638	4,759	5,494
Net claims on government, *of which:*	796	889	1,473	1,522	1,593	1,596	1,535	1,636
Budget support	708	816	1,325	1,430	1,473	1,485	1,417	1,508
Commodity operations	108	99	127	113	100	91	137	147
Credit to nongovernment	2,191	2,576	3,018	3,172	3,410	3,573	3,794	4,528
Private sector	2,130	2,496	2,904	2,995	3,221	3,373	3,636	4,349
Public sector enterprises	61	81	114	177	189	200	159	179
Privatization account	–3	–3	–3	–3	–3	–3	–3	–3
Other items, net	–287	–382	–467	–503	–463	–528	–567	–667
Broad money	3,407	4,065	4,689	4,674	4,831	4,867	5,197	6,024
Currency	740	840	982	1,107	1,168	1,190	1,156	1,301
Rupee deposits	2,471	3,018	3,443	3,282	3,369	3,372	3,737	4,379
Foreign currency deposits	196	207	263	285	295	305	303	343
State Bank of Pakistan (SBP)								
NFA	565	788	481	308	101	57	236	276

NDA	436	422	990	1,250	1,346	1,412	1,314	1,472
Net claims on government	384	325	1,015	1,240	1,273	1,273	1,167	1,167
of which: budget support	404	339	1,016	1,227	1,274	1,274	1,181	1,181
Claims on nongovernment	–7	–7	–7	–7	–7	–7	–7	–7
Claims on scheduled banks	218	272	219	224	249	249	249	279
Privatization account	–3	–3	–3	–3	–3	–3	–3	–3
Other items, net	–156	–164	–233	–204	–166	–100	–91	37
Reserve money, *of which*:	1,001	1,210	1,471	1,559	1,447	1,469	1,551	1,748
Banks' reserves	208	305	416	381	289	292	321	373
Currency	789	898	1,051	1,174	1,158	1,177	1,225	1,370
(12-month changes; in percent)								
Broad money	14.9	19.3	15.3	13.4	9.6	10.4	10.8	15.9
NFA, banking system (in percent of broad money) 1/	2.5	8.1	–7.8	–10.2	–11.4	–10.1	–4.9	1.8
NDA, banking system (in percent of broad money) 1/	12.4	11.3	23.1	22.0	20.2	19.6	15.7	14.1
Budgetary support (in percent of broad money) 1/	2.1	3.2	12.5	11.7	9.0	7.5	1.9	1.8
NFA, banking system	11.5	38.7	–32.1	–49.5	–65.1	–68.3	–34.5	20.9
NDA, banking system	15.8	14.2	30.5	32.6	27.3	25.8	18.4	15.4
Budgetary support	9.5	15.2	62.4	61.6	41.8	32.7	6.9	6.5
Private credit	23.2	17.2	16.4	20.2	16.8	18.4	25.2	19.6
Currency	11.2	13.5	16.9	26.6	15.9	21.2	17.7	12.6
Reserve money	10.2	20.9	21.6	27.9	5.8	9.8	5.4	12.7
NFA, SBP (in percent of reserve money) 1/	6.8	22.2	–25.4	–30.7	–43.1	–36.9	–16.6	2.6

(Continued)

TABLE 5.1 *(Continued)*

	2005/06	2006/07	2007/06	Est. Sep.	Proj. Dec.	Proj. Mar.	Jun.	Proj
					2008/09		**2009/10**	
NDA, SBP (in percent of reserve money) 1/	3.4	-1.4	46.9	52.5	48.6	45.8	22.0	10.2
Net claims on government (in percent of reserve money) 1/	14.8	-5.8	56.9	59.3	51.7	36.9	10.3	0.0
				(In units as indicated)				
Memorandum items:								
Velocity	2.2	2.1	2.2	3.0	—	—	2.6	2.6
Money multiplier	3.4	3.4	3.2	3.0	3.3	3.3	3.4	3.4
Currency to broad money ratio (percent)	21.7	20.7	20.9	23.7	24.2	24.5	22.2	21.6
Currency to deposit ratio (percent)	27.8	26.1	26.5	31.0	31.9	32.4	28.6	27.6
Reserves to deposit ratio (percent)	7.8	9.5	11.2	10.7	7.9	7.9	7.9	7.9
Budget bank financing (billions of Pakistani rupees) *of which:*	61	108	509	105	147	160	91	91
By commercial banks	-74	173	-167	-106	-111	-98	-74	91
By SBP	135	-65	677	211	258	258	165	0
NFA of SBP (change from beginning of the year in US dollar billions) 2/	1	4	-4.5	-2.2	-4.4	-5.0	-2.9	0.4
NFA of commercial banks (in billions of Pakistan billions rupees)	145	197	187	177	193	172	201	254
NDF of commercial banks (in billions of Pakistan billions rupees)	2,261	2,658	3,030	2,938	3,191	3,226	3,445	4,022
Excess reserves in percent of broad money	0.3	1.0	—	—	—	—	—	—

Source: International Monetary Fund (2008), *Pakistan: Request for Stand-By Arrangement*, Table 4.
1/ Denominator is the stock of broad (reserve) money at the end of the previous year.
2/ Includes valuation adjustments.

Particularly in earlier periods, when credit cards were less widely used and cash was more critical for purchases, households and firms needed reasonable stocks of readily available funds (e.g., balances in checking accounts) to finance purchases, particularly between the receipt of salary checks and payments from customers. Even today, households and firms need a certain amount of readily available funds to meet financing needs. The transactions motive thus explains why the demand for money is likely to bear a positive relationship to the level of economic activity, i.e., GDP (Y).

At the same time, money (cash and checking account balances) is part of each household's and firm's portfolio of financial assets. Since money typically earns little or no interest, the demand for money tends to decline as interest rates rise. Indeed, because inflation reduces the purchasing power of money, the demand for money (cash or near-cash balances) should be negatively related to the price level. Thus, one can describe the demand for nominal money balances as a function of three variables: income (Y), the nominal interest rate (i), and the price level (P):

$$M^D = f(\overset{+}{Y}, \bar{P}, \bar{i})$$

This expression can in turn be used to describe the demand for real money balances, (M^D/P):

$$M^D/P = f(\overset{+}{y}, \bar{r}),$$

where y is real GDP (Y/P), r is the real interest rate, and P is the GDP deflator.

The above reasoning helps explain why central banks try to set the money supply so as to meet demand. Too little money can inhibit transactions, limiting economic growth. Indeed, because monetary assets equal liabilities, too little money may mean, for example, less bank lending, thereby inhibiting output, investment, and commerce. However, too much money is also problematic. Because there is no long-run tradeoff between money growth and inflation, economists have traditionally believed that, over sufficient time, money bears a close relationship with the price level. Thus, supplying more money than the public (households and firms) demand can lead to inflation. As a consequence, central banks that follow a traditional approach to monetary policy, targeting the growth rate of broad money, aim to meet but not exceed the demand for broad money. Attaining this goal is hard for several reasons:

1. The monetary authorities control only "high powered" (reserve or base) money;
2. The total money supply depends on bank activities (lending policy and activity) and the public's use of money (the share of money held in banks, rather than in cash, and the public's demand for loans); and
3. Capital inflows (changes in net foreign assets) can also affect reserve (or base) money.

B. The Quantity Theory of Money and Velocity

The analysis of money demand and supply, and the presumed relationship among money, real income, and inflation, have led economists to develop what is called the quantity theory of money. Focusing only on the transactions demand for money, one can write that the demand for real balances is some multiple or fraction of real income, y:

$$M/P = ky,$$

where M is broad money, P is the price level (e.g., the GDP deflator), y is real GDP, and k is the multiple or fraction.

Multiplying both sides of the above equation by P and dividing both sides by k yields the following:

$$M \cdot V = P \cdot y = \text{nominal GDP } (Y),$$

where V is defined as the velocity of broad money, the ratio of nominal GDP ($P \cdot y$) to M, or how many times the money stock "turns over" while financing the sum of transactions representing nominal GDP. The quantity theory of money is useful, since it encapsulates the complex relationship between money supply and GDP: a certain amount of money is needed to finance a certain level of real transactions, but beyond that amount more money leads to higher prices. It also provides a way to forecast the demand for broad money. If money velocity can be estimated (e.g., by looking at velocity during the most recent period and assuming little change), money demand can be forecast as the ratio of nominal GDP to money velocity.

C. The Money Multiplier

The second point (the role of banks and the public in creating broad money) is sufficiently important that economists have developed a term, the money multiplier, to show the relationship between broad money and reserve (or base) money:

$$mm = \frac{M}{RM} = \frac{CY + D}{CY + R},$$

where mm is the multiplier, M is broad money (e.g., $M2$ or $M3$), RM is reserve (or base) money, CY is currency in circulation, D is deposits, and R is bank reserves held against deposits (both required reserves and "excess" reserves, i.e., reserves exceeding required levels). Because reserves are normally a small fraction of deposits, the money multiplier normally exceeds 1 and may be several times as big, e.g., 2, 3, or even larger. The size of the multiplier rises as the percentage of total money held in deposits increases and declines as the ratio of reserves to deposits rises.

If we define c as the ratio of currency to deposits and r as the ratio of reserves to deposits, the following expression is true:

$$M = \frac{(c+1)}{(c+r)} RM$$

where M is broad money ($M2$ or $M3$) and RM is reserve (base) money. We can thus express the money multiplier, mm, in terms of c and r:

$$mm = \frac{c+1}{c+r}.$$

Because of the money multiplier, one can say that two broad factors affect the money supply (Figure 5.6):

1. the amount of reserve ("high powered") money (the monetary base); and
2. the money multiplier.

Factors Affecting Money Supply

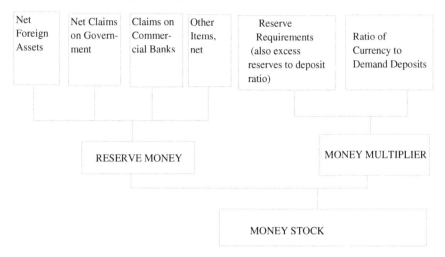

FIGURE 5.6. FACTORS AFFECTING MONEY SUPPLY

As noted earlier, in discussing the accounts of the monetary authorities, reserve money (the monetary base) depends from the asset side on (1) the net foreign assets of the monetary authorities and (2) the claims by the monetary authorities on government, deposit money banks, and other entities, i.e., the monetary authorities' net domestic assets. The money multiplier, in turn, depends on reserve requirements (plus bank holdings of excess reserves) and the ratio of currency to deposits. Figure 5.6 summarizes these relationships.

D. The Valuation Adjustment

The inclusion of several items (net foreign assets, foreign exchange deposits, and in some countries loans made in foreign currency) complicates the analysis of the monetary sector. Changes in the exchange rate of domestic currency will change the domestic currency value of these items, what appears in the monetary survey and the accounts of the monetary authorities and the deposit money banks. To prevent these changes from affecting the recorded changes in monetary aggregates such as broad money, other items net includes a revaluation account, which keeps track of valuation changes and records them in a way that offsets the impact of these changes on the monetary aggregates. If the valuation changes tend to increase total assets, the revaluation account records an offsetting decrease. If the changes tend to reduce total net assets (as in the case of a rise in recorded foreign deposits due to an exchange rate depreciation), the revaluation account records an offsetting increase.

The valuation adjustment is calculated as the difference between the change in net foreign assets (or foreign exchange deposits, or loans made in foreign currency) recorded in the monetary accounts and the "pure transactions" change in the item, measured at the average exchange rate during the observed period. For example, suppose net foreign assets in the banking system (recorded in the monetary survey) equal US$100 million at end-2015 and US$150 million at end-2016. Suppose also that the exchange rate is 2 units of local currency per US$1 at end-2015 and 3 units of local currency per US$1 at end-2016. In this case, net foreign assets will be recorded as 200 million local currency units at end-2015 and 450 million local currency units at end-2016. Assume that the exchange rate depreciated smoothly in 2016, so that the average exchange rate during the year was 2.5 units of local currency per US$1. In this case, the valuation adjustment would be calculated as follows:

(1) Total change in net foreign assets, in local currency = 450 million – 200 million = 250 million.
(2) The transactions change, measured at the average exchange rate = (50 million × 2.5) = 125 million.
(3) The valuation adjustment = total change — transactions change = 250 million – 125 million = 125 million.

Because the valuation adjustment affects net foreign assets, the revaluation account would be debited (reduced) by 125 million local currency units, to offset the effect of the valuation adjustment on net foreign assets. In other words, other items net would be 125 million less than otherwise because of the valuation adjustment for net foreign assets. Valuation adjustments for other items in the monetary survey would augment or diminish the overall change in the revaluation account.

The following steps provide a more general discussion of how to calculate the valuation adjustment.

Consider the stock of net foreign assets at the end of period t, denominated in local currency ($\text{NFA}_{L, t}$). The change in the stock of net foreign assets, denominated in local currency, between times t and $t-1$ can be decomposed into two parts: changes due to transaction flows (calculated using the average exchange rate over the period) and changes due to fluctuations in the exchange rate (valuation change):

$$(\Delta \text{NFA}_{L, t}) = \Delta \text{NFA Transactions} + \text{Valuation adjustment}$$

The following terms will be useful for this analysis:

$\text{NFA}_{L, t}$ = net foreign assets denominated in local currency at the end of period t

$\text{NFA}_{L, t-1}$ = net foreign assets denominated in local currency at the end of period $t-1$

Calculate the above using the end-of-period exchange rate.

$\text{NFA}_{\$, t}$ = net foreign assets denominated in foreign currency at the end of period t

$\text{NFA}_{\$, t-1}$ = net foreign assets denominated in foreign currency at the end of period $t-1$

EAV_t = average exchange rate in period t

The total change in stocks of net foreign assets, denominated in local currency, $= \text{NFA}_{L, t} - \text{NFA}_{L, t-1}$

Transaction flows (expressed in terms of local currency) $= \text{EAV}_t \times (\text{NFA}_{\$,t} - \text{NFA}_{\$, t-1})$.

The total change in stocks = transaction flows + valuation adjustment:

$\text{NFA}_{L, t} - \text{NFA}_{L, t-1} = \text{EAV}_t \times (\text{NFA}_{\$, t} - \text{NFA}_{\$, t-1}) + \text{Valuation adjustment}$.

Thus, the valuation adjustment is $(\text{NFA}_{L, t} - \text{NFA}_{L, t-1}) - [\text{EAV}_t \times (\text{NFA}_{\$, t} - \text{NFA}_{\$, t-1})]$.

IV. USING MONETARY ACCOUNTS: AN EXAMPLE FROM INDONESIA

Table 5.2 presents the monetary survey for Indonesia for the years 1999–2002, based on data available as of late 2004. The data show a sharp change in monetary developments between 2000 and 2002.

TABLE 5.2 INDONESIA: MONETARY SURVEY, 1999–2002

(end of period, in trillions of Rp unless otherwise indicated)

	1999	2000	2001	2002
Net foreign assets	121.3	163.2	210.8	228.4
NIR of BI	116.1	170.7	190.4	198.0
Other NFA	5.2	−7.5	20.4	30.3
		30%	3%	−4.1%
Net domestic assets	526.4	635.5	708.2	694.3
Net Claims on government	403.2	522.7	535.8	513.8
Budget	−50.8	−55.1	−54.0	−77.2
Other (including bank restructuring bonds)	454	577.8	589.8	591.1
Claims on business sector	253.7	335.3	376.3	412.9
Rupiah claims	175.3	186.1	232.0	304.0
Foreign exchange claims	78.4	149.2	144.3	108.9
Other items (net)	−130.5	−222.4	−203.9	−232.5
of which: adjustment due to consolidation	−93.6	−79.5	−100.4	−110.4
			12.3%	9.7%
Broad money (*M2*)	647.7	798.7	919.0	922.7
Rupiah broad money	533.2	606.8	689.3	743.4
Currency	58.4	72.4	76.3	80.7
Deposits 2/	474.9	534.4	612.9	662.8
Foreign exchange deposits	114.5	191.9	229.8	179.2
Changes in percent of broad money at end of previous period				
Net foreign assets		6.5	6.0	1.9
Net domestic assets		16.9	9.1	−1.5
Net claims on government		18.4	1.6	−2.4
Budget		−0.7	0.1	−2.5
Other (including bank restructuring bonds)		19.1	1.5	0.1
Claims on business sector		12.6	5.1	4.0
Rupiah claims		1.7	5.7	7.8
Foreign exchange claims		10.9	−0.6	−3.9
Other items (net)		−14.2	2.3	−3.1
Broad moncy (*M2*)		23.3	15.1	0.4
Rupiah broad money		11.4	10.3	5.9
Foreign exchange deposits		12.0	4.7	−5.5

(*Continued*)

TABLE 5.2   *(Continued)*

(end of period, in trillions of Rp unless otherwise indicated)

	1999	2000	2001	2002
Memorandum items:	(in US$ billions)			
Net foreign assets	17.1	17.0	20.3	25.5
NIR of BI	16.4	17.8	18.3	22.2
Net other FA	0.7	−0.8	2.0	3.4
Claims on business sector in foreign exchange	11.0	15.5	13.9	12.2
Foreign exchange deposits	16.1	20.0	22.1	20.0
Developments in interest rates, inflation, and exchange rate				
Interest rate developments				
Rupiah time deposit rates (average all banks for 1 month deposits)	24.0	11.2	14.5	12.8
Rupiah credit rates to business sector (working capital loans)	28.9	18.4	19.2	18.3
Rupiah credit rates to business sector (investment loans)				
Percent change in CPI	20.7	3.8	11.5	11.9
Real interest rates				
Using CPI inflation and Rupiah time deposit rates	2.7	7.1	2.7	0.8
Using CPI inflation and Rupiah credit rates for working capital loans	6.7	14.1	6.9	5.7
End of period exchange rate, Rupiah per U.S. dollar	7,100	9,595	10,400	8,940
Period average exchange rate, Rupiah per U.S. dollar	7,809	8,534	10,266	9,261
Percent change in exchange rate (period average, Rp per US$ 1.)	−20.9	9.3	20.3	−9.8

Sources: Bank Indonesia and IMF staff estimates.

In 2000, broad money grew by 23.3 percent, with 6.5 percentage points of that increase reflecting a rise in net foreign assets (mainly at Bank Indonesia, the central bank) and the remaining 16.9 percentage points (after rounding) from increases in net domestic assets. Much of that came from a large expansion in net credit to government, as a result of the central government's budget deficit and efforts to establish an asset management company to acquire bad loans and help banks recapitalize. However, credit to the private sector also increased, mainly in foreign currency loans. A sizable decline in other items net, in part from the effects of a large currency depreciation on foreign currency deposits, kept net domestic assets from rising further.

In 2001, broad money growth slowed to 15.1 percent. Net foreign assets contributed 6 percentage points of the increase, reflecting increases in net international reserves and other net foreign assets. However, the contribution from net domestic assets fell to 9.1 percentage points, as the growth in net claims on government slowed to about 3 percent from 30 percent in 2000, with the government financing most of its deficit through foreign borrowing and non-bank sources. In addition, the expansion of net claims on the business sector fell to 12 percent from 32 percent a year earlier with a decline in foreign currency loans outstanding.

In 2002, broad money growth fell to 0.4 percent, the rise in net foreign assets slowed considerably, and net domestic assets declined. A smaller budget deficit and continued recourse to non-bank financing led to a 4.1 percent decline in net credit to government. Moreover, credit to the private sector expanded by 9.7 percent, less than the 12.3 percent recorded in 2001. The monetary tightening limited the impact of subsidy removals on domestic inflation, which peaked at 11.9 percent in 2002 before declining to 6.8 percent in 2003 as the effect of subsidy removal waned.

V. SUMMARY

The monetary sector records financial sector developments, with focus on the banking system. Unlike the main accounts of the real, external, and fiscal sectors, the accounts in monetary sector record *stocks* — data at specific points in time. The main accounts in this sector are the balance sheet of the monetary authorities (central bank), the consolidated balance sheet of the deposit money (commercial) banks, and the monetary survey, which consolidates the balance sheets of the monetary authorities and the consolidated deposit money banks into a single table. The monetary survey reports, in local currency, net foreign assets, net domestic assets, and broad money (total currency and deposits) in the banking system. Together with information on debt, asset prices, the situation in non-bank financial institutions, and other macroeconomic developments, the monetary survey provides valuable information for the monetary authorities in setting monetary policy.

Useful monetary sector indicators include the growth rates of broad money, broad money in domestic currency, and reserve or base money (commercial banks' reserves plus currency in circulation); estimates of money demand; the velocity of money, defined as the ratio of nominal GDP to broad money or a component of broad money; and the money multiplier, the ratio of broad money to reserve or base money. Because monetary sector assets equal liabilities, changes in broad money can be explained by changes in net foreign assets and in various components of net domestic assets, such as the growth in net credit to government and credit to the non-government sector. The monetary authorities influence the growth in broad money by expanding or contracting reserve or base money (high powered money) through open market operations and changes in reserve requirements. However, commercial banks also play a role, by varying their loan volume and the extent of excess reserves. Changes in the percent of broad money held in deposits, rather than currency held outside the banks, also affect the rate of broad money expansion. The same growth rate of reserve or base money will yield a relatively high rate of broad money growth if bank lending is high, excess reserves are low, and deposits represent a large share of broad money. Broad money growth will be less if banks lend less, hold more excess reserves, and the share of deposits in broad money is smaller.

Because certain elements of the monetary survey — net foreign assets, foreign exchange deposits, and in some economies domestic lending in foreign currency — represent domestic currency equivalents of items denominated in foreign currency, the domestic currency value of these items can change with the exchange rate. To avoid reflecting the impact of these changes on broad money growth, the various accounts include a revaluation account, which keeps track of valuation adjustments, the impact of exchange rate changes on monetary items in foreign currency. Valuation adjustments are calculated as the difference between the total change in foreign currency items, measured in local currency, and the transactions change in these items, calculated as the product of the change in foreign currency items multiplied by the average exchange rate during the period.

Chapter 6

INTERRELATIONS AMONG MACROECONOMIC SECTORS AND THE FLOW OF FUNDS

Although the four macroeconomic sectors have thus far been treated separately, activities in each sector affect, and are affected by, activities in the other sectors. For example, as noted in Chapter 1, a rise in private consumption (part of the real sector) affects the balance of payments (since part of consumption involves imports), the fiscal sector (since most consumption goods are subject to tax), and the monetary sector (since bank deposits of some households may decline and, if automobiles or appliances are involved, consumer loans may increase). Likewise, a rise in income tax rates, which originates in the fiscal sector, will likely affect consumption and possibly investment (real sector), the balance of payments (imports and government borrowing from abroad may both decline), and the monetary accounts (net credit to government will likely decrease). An exchange rate depreciation, which should reduce imports and ultimately raise exports (external sector), will affect the real sector (a rise in net exports), the fiscal sector (higher import duties, measured in domestic currency, in the short run, and possibly higher profits taxes from exporters over time), and the monetary sector (changes in bank deposits and lending). A change in interest rates will affect lending and perhaps saving (monetary sector), investment and consumption (real sector), the government budget (interest payments and possibly tax revenues), and possibly net external capital flows (external sector).

I. INTERRELATIONS ACROSS MACROECONOMIC SECTORS

The four macroeconomic accounts have many linkages. Figure 6.1 shows the most important of these relationships.

As noted in Figure 6.1, the real and external sectors are closely linked, in that exports and imports of goods and (non-factor) services appear in each sector's accounts. Net exports (exports less imports of goods and (non-factor) services) are part of GDP by expenditure, while the trade balance (exports of goods f.o.b. less imports of goods f.o.b.) and the services balance (exports less imports of (non-factor) services) are an essential part of the current account of the balance of payments. The real sector is also linked to the fiscal sector, in that important elements of current government expenditure (payments for wages, salaries, and other goods and services) represent government consumption, while capital expenditure is

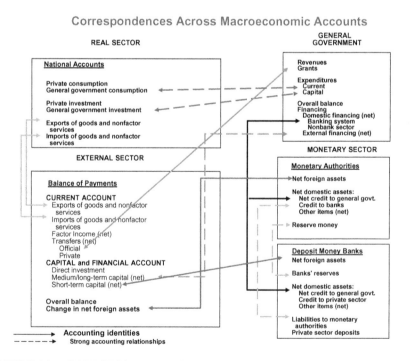

FIGURE 6.1.   CORRESPONDENCES ACROSS MACROECONOMIC ACCOUNTS

usually synonymous with government investment. The external sector, in turn, is related to the fiscal sector, in that grants to the budget represent official transfers in the balance of payments, while net external financing for the government budget is an important part of medium- and long-term net capital flows (or, in the Sixth BOP Manual approach, other investment). The external sector is linked to the monetary sector through changes in net foreign assets of the banking system. These items appear in short-term capital (net) and the change in net foreign assets (net international reserves) in the balance of payments and as changes in net foreign assets in the accounts of the monetary authorities and the consolidated commercial banks. Budget financing from the banking system corresponds to the sum of the change in net credit to government from the monetary authorities and the commercial banks in monetary sector. Finally, credit to banks from the monetary authorities should be closely related to banks' liabilities to the monetary authorities, while banks' reserves should be an important part of reserve money (the monetary base) in the accounts of the monetary authorities.

As Figure 6.1 indicates, many of these relationships are exact (accounting identities). Exports and imports of goods and (non-factor) services should be the same in both the national accounts and the balance of payments. Net official transfers in the balance of payments should match net grants in the budget. The changes in net foreign assets of the commercial banks and the monetary authorities should match the changes of these items recorded in the balance of payments. Likewise, net budget financing from the banking system in the fiscal accounts should match the change in net credit to government in the monetary accounts.

Other relationships are less exact. Nevertheless, government consumption in the national accounts should match those elements of consumption in the fiscal accounts. Similarly, that part of the monetary base comprised by banks' reserves should match banks' reserves in the consolidated accounts of the commercial banks.

II. THE FLOW OF FUNDS

Relations among economic sectors can also be seen using a "Flow of Funds" table or matrix. The Flow of Funds table is a matrix showing

Schematic Flow of Funds Accounts

Transactions/ Sectors		Domestic Economy			Banking System	Rest of the World	Horizontal Check
		Government	Private Sector				
	(1)= (2)+(3) + (4)	(2)	(3)	(4)	(5)	(1)+ (5)
Gross National Disposable Income (GNDI)	+ GNDI	+ GNDI g	+ GNDI p			
Final Consumption	- C	- Cg	- Cp			
Gross Investment	-I	-Ig	-Ip			
Exports of goods and nonfactor serv.					- X	
Imports of goods and nonfactor serv.					M	
Net factor income					- Yf	
Net Transfers					- TRf	
Non-Financial Balances	**(S-I)**	**(Sg-Ig)**	**(Sp-Ip)**	**0**	**- CAB**	**0**
Foreign Financing						
Nonmonetary Financing						
Direct Investment	FDI		FDI		-FDI	0
Net Foreign Borrowing	NFB	NFBg	NFBp		- NFB	0
Monetary Financing						
Change in Net Foreign Assets	-Δ NFA			-Δ NFA	+Δ NFA	0
Domestic Financing						
Monetary Financing						
Domestic Credit		+Δ NDCg	+Δ NDCp	-Δ NDC		0
Broad Money			-Δ M2	+Δ M2		0
Nonmonetary Financing						
Non Bank		NB	-NB			
Net Errors and Omissions	**-Δ OINd**	**Δ OINg**	**Δ OINp**	**-Δ OINb**	**Δ OINf**	**0**
Vertical Check	**0**	**0**	**0**	**0**	**0**	**0**

FIGURE 6.2. SCHEMATIC PRESENTATION OF THE FLOW OF FUNDS

income, expenditure, and financing between sectors of an economy and between that economy and the rest of the world. The name "Flow of Funds" reflects the fact that all the entries are flows, not stocks. Figure 6.2 provides a general illustration of the Flow of Funds table.

The Flow of Funds reveals two key points. One is which sectors of the economy have a resource – absorption surplus $(Y_d - C - I > 0)$ and which have a deficit $(Y_d - C - I < 0)$, where Y_d is the sector's disposable income, C is its consumption expenditure, and I is its expenditure for investment. This is the same as determining the savings – investment $(S - I)$ balance in each sector. The other point is how sectors in surplus finance those in deficit, and how those in deficit are financed by sectors in surplus.

A. Structure of the Flow of Funds Matrix

The Flow of Funds matrix has a particular structure. Columns measure a sector's imbalance between its income (Y_d) and expenditure $(C + I)$

and how the imbalance is financed. The sector's balance (surplus or deficit) appears in the "non-financial balances" line. Entries below that line show how the non-financial balance is financed. Since financing equals the imbalance but has the opposite sign, the columns each sum to zero.

Columns in the Flow of Funds matrix reflect the four sectors of the economy discussed in earlier chapters/sections, with the real sector replaced by the private or non-government sector. There are separate columns for the government sector, the private (non-government) sector, the financial (or banking) sector, and the external sector. To emphasize the role of the banking sector as a financing agent, non-financial transactions of the banking system are included in the private (non-government) sector. Activities of state enterprises are also included in the private sector, unless the government sector is redefined as the broad public sector to include the accounts of state enterprises. To facilitate analysis, the activities of the external sector are reported as those of the "rest of the world," with the opposite sign: exports, for example, are shown with a negative sign, while imports are positive. At the far left is a column summarizing the non-financial activities of the entire economy, the sum of the government and non-government sectors.

B. Conventions for the Flow of Funds Matrix

The Flow of Funds is prepared using the following conventions. When recording entries, an increase in an asset or a reduction in a liability takes a negative sign; an increase in a liability or decline in an asset takes a positive sign; and vice versa. Columns — the sum of all non-financial and financial transactions — should add to zero. The same rule applies to rows: the sum of all entries should be zero. Consider, for example, an increase in the money stock, reported in the "bottom half" (financing block) of the matrix. An increase in the money stock held by the private sector is a liability of the banking sector and an asset of the private sector. The transaction is recorded twice in the same row: as a negative entry in column 3 and as a positive entry in column 4. Thus, the horizontal sum is zero.

The Non-Financial Balances

Transactions/ Sectors		Domestic Economy			Rest of the World	Horizontal Check
		Government	Private Sector	Banking System		
	(1)= (2)+(3) + (4)	(2)	(3)	(4)	(5)	(1)+ (5)
Gross National Disposable Income (GNDI)	+ GNDI	+ GNDI g	+ GNDI p			
Final Consumption	- C	- Cg	- Cp			
Gross Investment	-I	-Ig	-Ip			
Exports of goods and nonfactor serv.					- X	
Imports of goods and nonfactor serv.					M	
Net factor income					- Yf	
Net Transfers					- TRf	
Non-Financial Balances	**(S-I)**	**(Sg-Ig)**	**(Sp-Ip)**	**0**	**- CAB**	**0**
Foreign Financing						
Nonmonetary Financing						
Direct Investment	FDI		FDI		-FDI	0
Net Foreign Borrowing	NFB	NFBg	NFBp		- NFB	0
Monetary Financing						
Change in Net Foreign Assets	-Δ NFA			-Δ NFA	+Δ NFA	0
Domestic Financing						
Monetary Financing						
Domestic Credit		+Δ NDCg	+Δ NDCp	-Δ NDC		0
Broad Money			-Δ M2	+Δ M2		0
Nonmonetary Financing						
Non Bank		NB	-NB			
Net Errors and Omissions	-Δ OINd	Δ OINg	Δ OINp	-Δ OINb	Δ OINf	0
Vertical Check	**0**	**0**	**0**	**0**	**0**	**0**

FIGURE 6.3.   NON-FINANCIAL BALANCES IN THE FLOW OF FUNDS

C. General Approach to Constructing the Flow of Funds Matrix

The first step in constructing a flow of funds matrix is to calculate each sector's non-financial transactions balance (Figure 6.3). These are calculated directly from the sectoral accounts, as follows:

1. the current account balance is derived from the balance of payments $(X–M, Y_F, TR_F)$;
2. the budget deficit (excluding net lending) is derived from the government accounts $(S–I)_g$; and
3. private sector net saving $(S–I)_p$ is derived from the national income accounts and the budget deficit, excluding net lending.

The second column in the flow of funds matrix presents transactions and financing for the government sector. The entries in this column appear in Figure 6.4.

Some points to note about the government sector are as follows:

The Government Sector

Transactions/ Sectors	Domestic Economy			Banking System	Rest of the World	Horizontal Check
		Government	Private Sector			
	(1)= (2)+(3) + (4)	(2)	(3)	(4)	(5)	(1)+ (5)
Gross National Disposable Income (GNDI)	+ GNDI	+ GNDI g	+ GNDI p			
Final Consumption	- C	- Cg	- Cp			
Gross Investment	-I	-Ig	-Ip			
Exports of goods and nonfactor serv.					- X	
Imports of goods and nonfactor serv.					M	
Net factor income					- Yf	
Net Transfers					- TRf	
Non-Financial Balances	**(S-I)**	**(Sg-Ig)**	**(Sp-Ip)**	**0**	**- CAB**	**0**
Foreign Financing						
Nonmonetary Financing						
Direct Investment	FDI		FDI		-FDI	0
Net Foreign Borrowing	NFB	NFBg	NFBp		- NFB	0
Monetary Financing						
Change in Net Foreign Assets	-Δ NFA			-Δ NFA	+Δ NFA	0
Domestic Financing						
Monetary Financing						
Domestic Credit		+Δ NDCg	+Δ NDCp	-Δ NDC		0
Broad Money			-Δ M2	+Δ M2		0
Nonmonetary Financing						
Non Bank		NB	-NB			
Net Errors and Omissions	-Δ OINd	Δ OINg	Δ OINp	-Δ OINb	Δ OINf	0
Vertical Check	**0**	**0**	**0**	**0**	**0**	**0**

FIGURE 6.4.   THE GOVERNMENT SECTOR IN THE FLOW OF FUNDS

1. In the national income accounts, net lending is considered a financing item. But net lending may be treated as expenditure in the government accounts if the 1986 GFS approach is used.

2. If the 2001 GFS approach is used, the non-financial transactions balance of the government is equal to the overall government balance, recalculated to remove net lending from expenditure.

3. When the government balance excludes net lending, net lending should be included in non-bank domestic financing in the flow of funds table, or shown as a separate financing item.

4. The non-financial sector balance for the economy as a whole, denoted as the sum of $(S–I)_g$ and $(S–I)_p$, is equal to the external current account balance of the balance of payments.

The third column of the matrix records the transactions involving the private (non-government) sector, as summarized in Figure 6.5. The numbers for disposable income, consumption, and investment are calculated as the difference between those for the economy and those identified for government.

The Private (Non-Government) Sector

Transactions/ Sectors		Domestic Economy		Banking System	Rest of the World	Horizontal Check
		Government	Private Sector			
	(1)= (2)+(3) + (4)	(2)	(3)	(4)	(5)	(1)+ (5)
Gross National Disposable Income (GNDI)	+ GNDI	+ GNDI g	+ GNDI p			
Final Consumption	- C	- Cg	- Cp			
Gross Investment	-I	-Ig	-Ip			
Exports of goods and nonfactor serv.					- X	
Imports of goods and nonfactor serv.					M	
Net factor income					- Yf	
Net Transfers					- TRf	
Non-Financial Balances	(S-I)	(Sg-Ig)	(Sp-Ip)	0	- CAB	0
Foreign Financing						
Nonmonetary Financing						
Direct Investment	FDI		FDI		-FDI	0
Net Foreign Borrowing	NFB	NFBg	NFBp		- NFB	0
Monetary Financing						
Change in Net Foreign Assets	-Δ NFA			-Δ NFA	+Δ NFA	0
Domestic Financing						
Monetary Financing						
Domestic Credit		+Δ NDCg	+Δ NDCp	-Δ NDC		0
Broad Money			-Δ M2	+Δ M2		0
Nonmonetary Financing						
Non Bank		NB	-NB			
Net Errors and Omissions	-Δ OINd	Δ OINg	Δ OINp	-Δ OINb	Δ OINf	0
Vertical Check	0	0	0	0	0	0

FIGURE 6.5.   THE PRIVATE (NON-GOVERNMENT) SECTOR

The fourth column of the matrix records the financing transactions provided by the banking (financial) sector. Figure 6.6 highlights these entries.

Following are some notes on compiling entries for the banking (financial) sector:

1. The change in net foreign assets, a form of external financing of the banking system, is obtained from the monetary survey.
2. Similarly, the changes in bank credit are obtained from the monetary survey.
3. The definition of broad money used here includes the total liabilities of the banking system to the private sector.

Figure 6.7 presents the entries in the fifth column, which records the external sector from the perspective of the rest of the world. Some points to note are the following:

The Banking (Financial) Sector

Transactions/ Sectors	Domestic Economy			Banking System	Rest of the World	Horizontal Check
	Government	Private Sector				
	(1)= (2)+(3) + (4)	(2)	(3)	(4)	(5)	(1)+ (5)
Gross National Disposable Income (GNDI)	+ GNDI	+ GNDI g	+ GNDI p			
Final Consumption	- C	- Cg	- Cp			
Gross Investment	-I	-Ig	-Ip			
Exports of goods and nonfactor serv.					- X	
Imports of goods and nonfactor serv.					M	
Net factor income					- Yf	
Net Transfers					- TRf	
Non-Financial Balances	**(S-I)**	**(Sg-Ig)**	**(Sp-Ip)**	**0**	**- CAB**	**0**
Foreign Financing						
Nonmonetary Financing						
Direct Investment	FDI		FDI		-FDI	0
Net Foreign Borrowing	NFB	NFBg	NFBp		- NFB	0
Monetary Financing						
Change in Net Foreign Assets	-Δ NFA			-Δ NFA	+Δ NFA	0
Domestic Financing						
Monetary Financing						
Domestic Credit		+Δ NDCg	+Δ NDCp	-Δ NDC		0
Broad Money			-Δ M2	+Δ M2		0
Nonmonetary Financing						
Non Bank		NB	-NB			
Net Errors and Omissions	-Δ OINd	Δ OINg	Δ OINp	-Δ OINb	Δ OINf	0
Vertical Check	**0**	**0**	**0**	**0**	**0**	**0**

FIGURE 6.6. THE BANKING (FINANCIAL) SECTOR IN THE FLOW OF FUNDS

The External Sector

Transactions/ Sectors	Domestic Economy			Banking System	Rest of the World	Horizontal Check
	Government	Private Sector				
	(1)= (2)+(3) + (4)	(2)	(3)	(4)	(5)	(1)+ (5)
Gross National Disposable Income (GNDI)	+ GNDI	+ GNDI g	+ GNDI p			
Final Consumption	- C	- Cg	- Cp			
Gross Investment	-I	-Ig	-Ip			
Exports of goods and nonfactor serv.					- X	
Imports of goods and nonfactor serv.					M	
Net factor income					- Yf	
Net Transfers					- TRf	
Non-Financial Balances	**(S-I)**	**(Sg-Ig)**	**(Sp-Ip)**	**0**	**- CAB**	**0**
Foreign Financing						
Nonmonetary Financing						
Direct Investment	FDI		FDI		-FDI	0
Net Foreign Borrowing	NFB	NFBg	NFBp		- NFB	0
Monetary Financing						
Change in Net Foreign Assets	-Δ NFA			-Δ NFA	+Δ NFA	0
Domestic Financing						
Monetary Financing						
Domestic Credit		+Δ NDCg	+Δ NDCp	-Λ NDC		0
Broad Money			-Δ M2	+Δ M2		0
Nonmonetary Financing						
Non Bank		NB	-NB			
Net Errors and Omissions	-Δ OINd	Δ OINg	Δ OINp	-Δ OINb	Δ OINf	0
Vertical Check	**0**	**0**	**0**	**0**	**0**	**0**

FIGURE 6.7. THE EXTERNAL SECTOR IN THE FLOW OF FUNDS

1. Total external borrowing is taken from the balance of payments (converted into local currency at the average exchange rate for the period).
2. Net external borrowing of the public sector is obtained from the fiscal accounts.
3. Net external borrowing by the banking system can be derived from the monetary survey (and reconciled with balance of payments data by taking account of valuation adjustments).
4. Private sector external flows are derived as a residual (e.g., net non-bank external borrowing less net external borrowing by government).

The next to last row in the matrix, labeled "Net Errors and Omissions," records items not otherwise accounting for in financing individual sectors. These items are labeled changes in "other items net," or ΔOIN with subscripts denoting the particular sector: d for the domestic economy, g for government, p for private sector, b for banking sector, and f for external sector. Following are some points to note about these entries:

1. The discrepancy in the banking sector column corresponds to the change in other items (net) of the monetary survey after removing valuation adjustments (which are not pure transactions).
2. The discrepancy in the external sector column represents the errors and omissions item in the balance of payments (here, Tables 6.2 and 6.7).
3. These two discrepancies have their counterparts in the discrepancy that remains in the accounts of the private sector.

III. ILLUSTRATIVE FLOW OF FUNDS: DATA FOR INDONESIA, 2001

The following tables, drawn from data on Indonesia, show how an illustrative flow of funds table can be derived, using data for Indonesia. The flow of funds is based on information from the real, external, fiscal, and monetary sectors. To compile the flow of funds table, data for the balance of payments must be presented in domestic currency (in this case, Indonesian rupiah), while monetary data must be presented in flows (meaning changes between stocks at two periods), excluding any valuation

TABLE 6.1 INDONESIA: EXPENDITURE ON GROSS DOMESTIC PRODUCT (IN CURRENT PRICES 2000–2002)

	2000	2001	2002
	(In billions of rupiah)		
Domestic demand	1,100,018	1,307,363	1,445,971
Consumption	824,136	993,297	1,119,806
Private	768,996	933,949	1,055,458
Public (central govt)	55,140	59,348	64,348
Investment	275,881	314,066	326,165
Fixed capital	275,881	314,066	326,165
Private sector	227,193	272,481	290,542
Government (central govt)	48,688	41,585	35,623
Change in stocks			
Net exports of g+nfs	164,901	160,292	164,594
Exports of goods and nonfactor services	600,670	632,742	597,479
Imports of goods and nonfactor services	435,768	472,450	432,885
Gross domestic product	1,264,919	1,467,655	1,610,565
Net factor service income	(109,966)	(110,766)	(92,189)
Net transfers	10,156	10,738	11,660
Gross national disposable income	1,165,109	1,367,627	1,530,036
Government disposable income	77,543	41,381	75,155
Private sector disposable income	1,087,566	1,326,246	1,454,882
Gross national savings (S)	340,973	374,330	410,230
Investment (I)	275,881	314,066	326,165
Savings – Investment (S – I)	65,091	60,264	84,065

Source: Developed from data provided by the Indonesian authorities.

adjustments for items denominated in foreign currency (net foreign assets, domestic loans in foreign currency, and foreign currency deposits in the case of Indonesia). In this case, data are taken from the tables labeled 6.1 (real sector), 6.2 (balance of payments in rupiah), 6.3 (fiscal sector), and 6.4 (monetary sector). The resulting flow of funds appears in Table 6.5, both in rupiah and in percent of GDP.

TABLE 6.2 INDONESIA: SUMMARY BALANCE OF PAYMENTS, 1998–2002
(IN BILLIONS OF RUPIAH)

	1998	1999	2000	2001	2002
Current account	43,840	49,434	65,091	60,264	84,065
Exports of goods and non factor services	539,399	434,129	600,670	632,742	597,479
Imports of goods and non factor services	−401,740	−305,151	−435,768	−472,450	−432,885
Factor service income, net	−103,289	−88,204	−109,966	−110,766	−92,189
Factor service receipts	16,263	13,103	18,750	18,714	11,076
Factor service payments	−119,552	−101,307	−128,716	−129480.376	−103,265
Transfers, net	9,470	8,660	10,156	10,738	11,660
Capital and financial account	−43,840	−49,434	−65,091	−60,264	−84,065
Government sector	98,459	41,793	27,455	10,584	10,891
Drawings	135,637	73,576	42,553	29,545	34,859
Amortization	−37,178	−31,782	−15,097	−18,961	−23,968
Private Sector	−119,144	−65,521	−93,217	−37,336	−46,125
Direct Investment	−3,515	−25,535	−38,832	−60,321	1,343
Other private capital	−133,090	−51,953	−46,419	−42,572	−22,440
Errors and omissions, net	17,461	11,967	−7,967	65,557	−25,028
Monetary Sector	−23,146	−25,707	670	−33,513	−48,831
Bank Indonesia	−23,146	−25,707	−12,286	−5,265	−35,625
Commerical banking system	—	—	12,956	−28,248	−13,206

Source: Developed from data provided by the Indonesian authorities.

TABLE 6.3   INDONESIA: CENTRAL GOVERNMENT BUDGET, 2000–2002 (IN BILLIONS OF RUPIAH)

		2000	2001	2002
Total Government Income	(1)	244,553	301,079	300,073
Transfers of Government	(2)	167,010	259,698	224,918
Interest Expenditures		72,188	101,201	86,384
Subsidies		74,514	77,443	40,006
Transfers to Regions		20,308	81,054	98,528
Government Disposable Income	(3) = (1) – (2)	77,543	41,381	75,155
Public Consumption	(4)	55,140	59,348	64,348
Public Fixed Capital Formation	(5)	48,688	41,585	35,623
Foreign Financed		24,342	20,214	10,928
Domestically Financed		24,346	21,371	24,695
Government Savings	(6) = (3) – (4)	22,403	–17,967	10,807
S – I for Government	(7) = (6) – (5)	–26,285	–59,552	–24,816
Financing of S – I for Government		26,285	59,552	24,816
Domestic		–1,170	48,968	13,925
Banking System		119,489	13,092	–21,935
Bank Indonesia		–19,447	30,743	5,182
Commercial Banks		138,936	–17,651	–27,117
Other Domestic		–120,659	35,876	35,860
External		27,455	10,584	10,891
Drawings		42,553	29,545	34,859
Amortizations		15,097	18,961	23,968

Source: Developed from data provided by the Indonesian authorities.

TABLE 6.4 INDONESIA: MONETARY SURVEY, 2000–2002 (CHANGES IN BILLIONS OF RUPIAH AND BY SOURCE OF CHANGE)

	Change in		
	2000	**2001**	**2002**
TOTAL CHANGE			
Change in NFA	41,874	47,641	17,542
Change in NDA	109,171	72,685	−13,908
Credit to Private Sector	81,589	41,071	36,584
Net credit to Government	119,489	13,092	−21,935
Change in OIN	−91,907	18,522	−28,557
Change in liabilities to private sector (*M*2)	151,045	120,327	3,634
CHANGE DUE TO EXCHANGE RATE ADJUSTMENT			
Change in NFA	42,544	14,129	−31,289
Change in NDA	1,790	2,252	−308
Credit to Private Sector	32,331	12,292	−19,716
Net credit to Government			
Change in OIN	−30,541	−10,040	19,408
Change in liabilities to private sector (*M*2)	44,335	16,381	−31,597
CHANGE DUE TO TRANSACTIONS & NON EXCHANGE RATE VALUATION ADJUSTMENTS			
Change in NFA	−670	33,513	48,831
Change in NDA	107,381	70,433	−13,600
Credit to Private Sector	49,258	28,779	56,300
Net credit to Government	119,489	13,092	−21,935
Change in OIN	−61,366	28,562	−47,965
Change in liabilities to private sector (*M*2)	106,711	103,946	35,231

Source: Developed from data provided by the Indonesian authorities.

TABLE 6.5   INDONESIA: FLOW OF FUNDS, 2001.

(in billions of Indonesian Rupiah)

	Economy	Government Sector	Non-Government Sector	Banking System	Rest of the World	Horizontal Check
Disposable Income 1/	1,367,627	41,381	1,326,246	—	—	
Consumption	993,297	59,348	933,949	—	—	
Gross investment	314,066	41,585	272,481	—	—	
Net exports of goods and nonfactor services	160,292	—	—	—	-160,292	
Net factor income	-110,766	—	—	—	110,766	
Net transfers	10,738	—	—	—	-10,738	
Statistical discrepancy						
Nonfinancial balances	60,264	-59,552	119,817	0	-60,264	
Government domestic nonbank financing	—	35,876	-35,876	—	—	
External financing of government	—	10,584	—	—	-10,584	
External financing of non-government sector	—	—	-37,336	—	37,336	
Change in net foreign assets	—	—	—	-33,513	33,513	
of which: Bank Indonesia	—	—	—	-5,265	5,265	
commercial banks	—	—	—	-28,248	28,248	

(Continued)

TABLE 6.5 (Continued)

	Economy	Government Sector	Non-Government Sector	Banking System	Rest of the World	Horizontal Check
Change in domestic bank credit	—	13,092	28,779	−41,872	—	—
Change in broad money stock	—	—	−103,946	103,946	—	—
Other items, net	—	—	28,562	−28,562	—	—
Vertical check	—	0	0	0	0	0
		(in percent of GDP)				
Nonfinancial balances	4.1	−4.1	8.2	0.0	−4.1	
Government domestic nonbank financing	—	2.4	−2.4	—	—	
External financing of government	—	0.7	—	—	−0.7	
External financing of non-govt sector	—	—	−2.5	—	2.5	
Change in net foreign assets	—	—	—	−2.3	2.3	
of which: Central bank	—	—	—	−0.4	0.4	
commercial banks	—	—	—	−1.9	1.9	
Change in domestic bank credit	—	0.9	2.0	−2.9	—	
Change in broad money stock	—	—	−7.1	7.1	—	
Other items, net	—	—	1.9	−1.9	—	
Vertical check	0	0	0	0	0	0

Nominal GDP 1,467,655

IV. SUMMARY

The four macroeconomic sectors are connected in a variety of ways. Developments in one sector, including changes in policy and autonomous developments such as external shocks and changes in savings and investment preferences, affect activities in other sectors. In addition, certain elements of one sector's accounts have direct counterparts in other sectors. For example, exports and imports of goods and (non-factor) services appear in both the national accounts (real sector) and the balance of payments, while net credit to the government from the monetary authorities and the commercial banks appears in both the fiscal and the monetary accounts.

The various linkages across sectors can be tracked by constructing a flow of funds table for the economy. The flow of funds indicates the savings minus investment (S–I) balances for the government and non-government sectors and for the economy as a whole. It also shows the economy's relations with the rest of the world, recording elements of the balance of payments from the perspective of those outside the economy, with opposite signs (e.g., exports appear as debits rather than credits). The flow of funds shows which sectors have surpluses (S exceeds I) and which have deficits (S is less than I). It also shows how surpluses are used and deficits are financed, noting flows of financing among the government and non-government sectors, the banking system, and the external sector (flows involving rest of the world). The flow of funds can identify data discrepancies across sectors, including differences between the economy's S–I balance and the external current account balance and shortfalls or excesses of financing for a specific sector. The flow of funds can also be used to show the impact of different ways of financing changes in government consumption and investment.

Chapter 7

FISCAL POLICY

Fiscal policy involves the use of the government budget to attain macroeconomic objectives. Although the overall budget balance — total revenues and grants minus total expenditures and net lending — has the greatest impact on macroeconomic activity, many specific elements of the budget, including the composition of revenues, expenditures, and financing, also have important macroeconomic implications.

1. The amount of revenue and expenditure relative to the size of the economy — the ratios of revenue and expenditure to GDP — help determine the scope of the government sector in the economy. Small island economies typically have relatively high ratios of revenue to GDP, normally 35 percent or larger, because a small economy is funding a broad array of government functions. Revenue and expenditure ratios can also be high in advanced economies — above 40 percent of GDP in a number of European OECD countries, although ratios are lower in the United States, Japan, and the Republic of Korea. In many developing countries, revenue can be 15 percent of GDP or less, with expenditure a bit higher. In middle income countries, revenues average 25–30 percent of GDP, again with expenditure somewhat higher. Table 7.1 presents data for general government revenue in several groups of countries for the years 2013 through 2016, while Table 7.2 does the same for expenditure.

TABLE 7.1   GENERAL GOVERNMENT REVENUE IN SELECTED GROUPS OF COUNTRIES, IN PERCENT OF GDP

	2013	2014	2015	2016 proj.
Emerging Market and Middle-income Countries	**29.3**	**29.7**	**27.7**	**26.7**
Asia	25.3	25.6	26.3	25.4
Europe	35.7	35.5	34.9	34.1
Latin America	30.1	29.2	28.2	27.3
Middle East, North Africa, and Pakistan	**35.9**	**33.1**	**26.1**	**23.9**
G-20 Emerging market countries	28.8	28.4	27.9	27.1
Advanced economies	**37.0**	**37.0**	**36.5**	**36.4**

Source: IMF (2016), *Fiscal Monitor*, October 2016, Statistical Tables A5 and A13. The drop in revenue for Middle East, North Africa, and Pakistan in 2014 and 2015 reflects the plunge in world petroleum prices.

TABLE 7.2   GENERAL GOVERNMENT EXPENDITURE IN SELECTED GROUPS OF COUNTRIES, IN PERCENT OF GDP

	2013	2014	2015	2016 proj.
Emerging Market and Middle-income Countries	**30.8**	**31.1**	**32.2**	**31.4**
Asia	27.2	27.5	29.4	28.8
Europe	37.2	36.8	37.7	37.4
Latin America	33.3	34.3	35.8	35.3
Middle East, North Africa, and Pakistan	31.6	33.9	34.5	32.3
G-20 Emerging market countries	30.7	30.9	32.3	31.5
Advanced economies	**40.7**	**40.2**	**39.3**	**39.4**

Source: IMF (2016), *Fiscal Monitor*, October 2016, Statistical Tables A6 and A14.

2. The composition of revenues can affect the economy's productivity, because taxing income imposes a "double taxation" of savings (savings come from after-tax income, while the earnings from savings — interest, dividends, and capital gains — are also taxed) unless income from capital is tax-exempt, as in Singapore. Relying more on consumption taxes, such as value-added and sales taxes, avoids this problem, although consumption taxes typically fall more heavily on low- and middle-income

households, which generally save less of their incomes than the rich. Complex revenue systems, with many exemptions and exclusions, can distort behavior, driving taxpayers into less-efficient but tax-sheltered investments and shifting purchases from high-tax to low-tax or tax-exempt goods and services.

3. The composition of expenditures can also affect the economy. Devoting a high share of expenditure to transfer payments, such as public pensions, or poorly targeted subsidies (such as subsidies for motor fuels), may preclude spending for maintaining and expanding public infrastructure. High interest payments, the result of heavy deficit spending in the past, may limit funds for education and health care.

4. The composition of budget financing also matters. Relying heavily on foreign financing often exposes the budget's debt service obligations to exchange rate risk, particularly in developing and emerging market countries that can only borrow externally in foreign currency. Extensive borrowing from the central bank, which leads to money creation, can prove inflationary, while extensive bank borrowing may crowd out financing for private investment if government borrowing represents a large share of total bank lending.

I. IMPACT OF FISCAL POLICY ON MACROECONOMIC ACTIVITY: AGGREGATE DEMAND

As noted in Chapter I, fiscal policy can affect the level of economic activity. How much the economy expands or contracts depends on the **fiscal multiplier**. The fiscal multiplier is the ratio of the change in nominal GDP to a change in revenues or expenditures that causes it. Fiscal multipliers arise because changes in revenues and expenditures affect aggregate demand. Tax cuts leave more after tax income available for consumption or investment, while higher expenditures raise spending directly (if government increases its purchases) or indirectly (if higher government benefit payments raise consumption). Fiscal multipliers typically increase over time, as the spending of one person or firm becomes the income of other firms or persons who, in turn, use that for further spending. Eventually, the size of the multiplier reaches a practical limit, as taxes and other withdrawals (e.g., spending for imports) gradually reduce the increment to spending from each additional receipt of income.

The size of the fiscal multiplier depends on a variety of factors. These include:

- *The type of fiscal measure*: multipliers for tax cuts and spending increases aimed at those more likely to spend the additional income are typically higher than for measures aimed at those who may save a notable part of additional income. Thus, raising unemployment benefits, creating temporary employment programs for the unemployed, and increasing transfers to the poor will likely have higher multipliers than tax cuts for the rich. In addition, spending increases often have higher multipliers than tax cuts, because the spending adds directly to aggregate demand, while only the part of a tax cut that is spent does so.
- *The nature of the economy (open or closed)*: in open economies, with a higher ratio of total trade to GDP, a higher share of any new spending is likely to go for imports (and thus not raise GDP directly) than is true in a more closed economy, with a lower ratio of trade to GDP.
- *The state of economic development*: fiscal multipliers are thought to be higher in more advanced economies, perhaps because in less advanced economies the formal sector is smaller.
- *The type of exchange regime*: Multipliers are typically lower in economies with flexible exchange rates, because the higher interest rates resulting from an increased deficit are more likely to appreciate the exchange rate, which reduces exports and raises imports, thereby generating less GDP. In economies with fixed exchange rates, the monetary authority can be expected to prevent any appreciation in the exchange rate, thereby avoiding this offset to the demand-inducing effects of fiscal expansion.
- *The type of budget financing*: non-bank and commercial bank financing are likely to have lower multipliers than central bank financing (money creation), because the new government bonds crowd out some private sector borrowing, thereby offsetting some of the growth-inducing effects of the fiscal measure.

- *Whether the fiscal measure is considered temporary or permanent*: temporary measures have smaller multipliers, because private firms and consumers recognize that they will end and consequently change their behavior less than with measures considered permanent.
- *The direction and size of the output gap*: multipliers are typically larger, the larger and more negative is the output gap, because the economy is further away from potential output and, thus, has more idle resources. As the output gap shrinks, fewer idle resources are available and the expansion will more likely increase inflation. The multiplier is smaller still in the case of a positive output gap, when the economy is operating above potential and the expansion will most likely raise prices rather than real GDP.
- *The degree of confidence in the economy and the authorities*: the multiplier will likely be higher in economies where people have more confidence in government and the economy is seen as stable. Many factors can affect confidence, including the rate of inflation and the ratio of government debt to GDP, with high levels of both typically undermining confidence. Confidence will also be low in countries where the higher budget deficits resulting from tax cuts or spending increases are expected to worsen the balance of payments and drain reserves. In these situations, expansionary fiscal policy could actually reduce GDP, as people anticipate a crisis and move to protect themselves, for example, by shifting assets into foreign currency or sending funds outside the economy.
- *Whether the policy crowds out or crowds in the private sector*: In the normal situation, the higher budget deficit will likely crowd out some private borrowing as interest rates rise, thereby reducing the multiplier. However, if the policy measure provides an incentive for the private sector to spend more — for example, an infrastructure project that causes private firms to increase their own investment, or a subsidy for fertilizer use that leads farmers to spend more in total on fertilizer — the "crowding in" of private spending could raise the multiplier.

Economists have done extensive research on the size of fiscal multipliers. Earlier research, conducted before the early 2000s, suggested that multipliers were generally positive but often less than one.[1] More recent research by IMF staff has suggested that fiscal multipliers vary with the stage of the business cycle and can be large, well above one, in the following circumstances:[2]

- When the economy is in recession and well below potential output;
- When the stimulus involves productive spending that uses unemployed resources (e.g., outlays for infrastructure);
- When monetary policy is supportive; and
- When the stimulus is coordinated with other countries.

Moreover, recent empirical research supports the view that fiscal multipliers are larger for more advanced economies, less open economies, and economies with fixed exchange rates. At the same time, multipliers are generally smaller for smaller, less developed, and more open economies, and for economies with floating exchange rate regimes.[3]

A. Fiscal Policy during Severe Recessions in Advanced Economies

During severe economic downturns, expansionary fiscal policy has proved able to limit losses in income and employment, with little impact on the inflation rate. During 2009, for example, interest and inflation rates remained very low in economies like the United States, despite fiscal stimulus approaching and, in some cases (e.g., the People's Republic of China (PRC)) equal to or exceeding, 2 percent of GDP. Here slow growth and a weak financial market in the wake of the financial crisis limited the

---

[1] Hemming, Richard, and others (2002), "The Effectiveness of Fiscal Policy in Stimulating Economic Activity: A Review of the Literature," IMF Working Paper 02/28 (Washington: International Monetary Fund). Available at: http://www.imf.org/external/pubs/ft/wp/2002/wp02208.pdf. Accessed July 16, 2017.

[2] See, e.g., Spilimbergo, Antonio, and others (2009), "Fiscal Multipliers," Staff Position Note 09/11 (Washington: International Monetary Fund, May). Available at: http://www.imf.org/external/pubs/ft/spn/2009/spn0911.pdf. Accessed July 16, 2017.

[3] Ilzetzki, Ethan, and others (2011), "How Big (Small?) Are Fiscal Multipliers?" IMF Working Paper 11/52 (Washington: International Monetary Fund, March). Available at: www.imf.org/external/pubs/ft/wp/2011/wp1152.pdf. Accessed July 16, 2017.

demand for funds from private firms. As a result, crowding out was hard to observe, and fiscal policy served to boost aggregate demand. Indeed, under these conditions, fiscal policy proved potent, even in advanced economies with flexible exchange rates and near-perfect capital mobility.[4] From 2014 onward, the challenge facing many advanced economies had become addressing the huge accumulation in government debt and rise in the government's debt-to-GDP ratio created by the recession and fiscal measures to combat it.

B. Fiscal Policy when Sustainability is Threatened

In times of large deficits, rising public debt, and lack of confidence, the fiscal multiplier can be small or even negative, by creating expectations of future tax increases. If the macroeconomic situation is sufficiently precarious, expansionary fiscal policy can lead to a sharp fall in activity by creating expectations of a fiscal or macroeconomic crisis. In these circumstances, fiscal stimulus can prove counterproductive. Developing countries offer many examples of this situation, a recent one being the adverse consequences of expanding the deficit by raising energy subsidies in Pakistan during 2008.

When fiscal policy is unsustainable, fiscal contraction may prove expansionary. The main examples of so-called "expansionary contraction" in advanced economies involved countries with high debt/GDP ratios and relatively high tax burdens, such as Denmark and Ireland in the 1980s. In these countries, cuts in spending that reduced budget deficits, accompanied by exchange rate depreciation, helped boost economic activity. Indeed, Ireland's reforms unleashed a wave of economic growth that dramatically raised per capita incomes from the late 1980s until 2008, when a banking crisis engulfed the economy. In developing and emerging market countries, fiscal contraction has often been the key to reducing current account deficits and restoring a viable balance of payments. Thus, macroeconomic stability has a critical bearing on the effectiveness of fiscal policy in stimulating economic activity.

---

[4] See, e.g., Christiano, Lawrence, and others (2009), "When Is the Government Spending Multiplier Large?" NBER Working Paper 15394 (Cambridge, MA: October).

C. Pro-Cyclical vs. Counter-Cyclical Fiscal Policy

The impact of fiscal policy on aggregate demand means that fiscal policy can play an important role in stabilizing macroeconomic activity by expanding policy (cutting taxes and raising expenditures) when the economy is in recession or below potential output and tightening policy (raising revenues and reducing expenditures) when economic activity exceeds potential output and inflation begins to accelerate. In most economies, revenues follow a natural counter-cyclical pattern, rising more than proportionately when the economy expands and falling significantly when it contracts, because of progressive income and profits taxes and the tendency for corporate profits to rise (and fall) even faster than changes in economic activity. In many advanced economies, programs such as unemployment insurance, disability pensions, and special benefits for the poor make expenditures follow a similar pattern, as outlays for these programs expand during slowdowns and contract as the economy recovers. Thus, fiscal policy tends to be counter-cyclical in these economies, unless overwhelmed by legislated tax cuts and spending increases when economic activity is buoyant.

In developing and emerging market economies, by comparison, fiscal policy has often been pro-cyclical, because of the inability of governments to restrain government expenditure during good times. In many of these economies, weak tax administration and low levels of per capita income constrain the ability to raise funds to finance public services. Thus, when the economy strengthens, governments have tended to expand spending, thereby augmenting aggregate demand and adding to inflationary pressures. The resulting rise in public debt makes it hard for governments to expand spending and cut taxes when the economy is weak. It is thus hard to make fiscal policy "lean against the wind," to stabilize the economy.

Research by Kaminsky and others (2004)[5] and Ilzetzki and Végh (2008)[6] confirms that developing and emerging market economies have

---

[5] Kaminsky, G., C. Reinhart, and C. Végh (2004), "When It Rains, It Pours: Procyclical Capital Flows and Macroeconomic Policies," NBER Working Paper 10780 (Cambridge, MA: National Bureau of Economic Research).

[6] Ilzetzki, E. and C. Végh (2008), "Procyclical Fiscal Policy in Developing Countries: Truth or Fiction?" NBER Working Paper 14191 (Cambridge, MA: National Bureau of Economic Research).

tended to practice more pro-cyclical fiscal policy, at least through the 1990s. More recent research suggests that fiscal policy has become more counter-cyclical in about a third of emerging market economies (Végh and Vuletin, 2012).[7]

II. IMPACT OF FISCAL POLICY ON THE MONETARY SECTOR AND MONETARY POLICY

Whatever its effect on aggregate demand, fiscal policy is important because of its impact on the monetary sector and monetary policy. Fiscal deficits require financing, and unless there is substantial demand for government securities from non-bank institutions and the general public, the domestic banking system will need to provide much, if not most, of this financing. Commercial bank purchases of government debt will crowd out lending to private firms and households, unless the central bank expands the money supply to accommodate the additional borrowing. Indeed, if the government deficit is sufficiently large and other sources of financing are not available, the government's financing needs will compel the central bank to expand the money supply to provide financing. This situation, called **fiscal dominance**, makes it difficult for the central bank to pursue other objectives, such as attaining low inflation. Ending fiscal dominance is a key precondition for enabling the monetary authorities to establish the monetary framework known as inflation targeting. More generally, limiting deficits so as to avoid fiscal dominance is an important objective for sound fiscal policy.

III. IMPACT OF FISCAL POLICY ON THE BALANCE OF PAYMENTS

Fiscal policy also affects the external sector through its relationship with the current account balance in the balance of payments. As noted in Chapter 2, one can show that the economy's savings minus investment

---

[7]Végh, C. and G. Vuletin (2012), "Overcoming the Fear of Free Falling: Monetary Policy Graduation in Emerging Markets," NBER Working Paper 18175 (Cambridge, MA: National Bureau of Economic Research).

balance — the difference between gross national savings and total investment — equals the current account balance in the balance of payments. Moreover, the economy's savings minus investment balance equals the sum of the savings minus investment balances for the government and the non-government sectors. The fiscal balance — total revenues less total expenditure (generally excluding expenditures for net lending) — turns out to be the savings minus investment balance for the government sector. Strengthening the fiscal balance, by reducing the budget deficit, can thus improve the external current account balance, provided that the decline in the deficit affects the demand for imports as well as domestic goods and services. For this reason, countries with unsustainably large current account deficits are often advised to reduce their fiscal deficits as part of a broader program of macroeconomic adjustment.

IV. FISCAL POLICY AND PUBLIC DEBT SUSTAINABILITY

The sustainability of fiscal policy represents still another important policy concern. The ability to maintain the current stance of fiscal policy depends, among other things, on the ability of government both to service its debt and to issue new debt, in the typical case where the budget is in deficit. Sustainability thus depends both on the government's liquidity, its ability to generate funds sufficient to pay interest and principal on existing debt obligations, and on its underlying solvency, its ability to replace debt falling due with new debt and to expand its debt in the event of a deficit.

Economists generally contend that a key measure of fiscal sustainability is the ratio of government (or public sector) debt to GDP and whether that ratio is forecast to decline, remain stable, or rise steadily. A continuing rise in the government's debt-to-GDP ratio means that the government is becoming steadily more indebted, even relative to the size of the nation's economy. Unless the initial debt-to-GDP ratio is modest, for example, less than 20 percent of GDP, many economists view the prospect of a steadily rising debt-to-GDP ratio as unsustainable. In addition, having public debt exceed a critical level — typically 40 percent of GDP for developing and emerging market countries and 60 percent of GDP for advanced economies — is itself considered a sign of risk. The 40 percent level reflects research and observations of the IMF on the risk of country default, while the 60 percent level for advanced economies is enshrined in the Maastricht Treaty binding countries in the euro zone and has been recognized as a key indicator in such other countries as the United Kingdom and the United States.

Keeping the ratio of debt to GDP below a critical level requires limiting the government's budget imbalance. Mathematics shows that the critical indicator is the government's primary balance — revenues less non-interest expenditures. The trend of the government's debt-to-GDP ratio reflects the following formula:

$$d_t = \frac{1+i^*}{1+n} d_{t-1} - pb_t + \frac{1+i^F}{1+n} \varepsilon_t \alpha_{t-1} d_{t-1}$$

where d_t is the debt-to-GDP ratio at the end of the current period, i^* is the average interest rate on all government debt, n is the growth rate of nominal GDP, d_{t-1} is the debt-to-GDP ratio at the end of the previous period, pb_t is the government's primary balance during the current period in percent of GDP, i^F is the nominal interest rate on foreign currency debt, ε_t is the percent change in the nominal exchange rate (units of domestic currency per unit of foreign currency) during the current period, and α_{t-1} is the percentage of debt denominated in foreign currency. If all debt is denominated in domestic currency, the formula can be simplified to one of the following expressions:

$$d_t = \frac{(1+i)}{(1+n)} d_{t-1} - pb_t \text{ or } d_t = \frac{(1+r)}{(1+g)} d_{t-1} - pb_t$$

where r is the average *real* interest rate on government debt, g is the average *real* growth rate of GDP, and d_t, d_{t-1}, i, n, and pb_t are as in the previous equation. Notice that, in all these expressions, the key factor that restrains the rise in the government's debt-to-GDP ratio is the primary budget balance. A sufficiently positive primary balance will reduce the debt-to-GDP ratio or keep it from rising, while too negative a balance (i.e., too large a primary deficit) will cause the ratio to increase. Maintaining the debt-to-GDP ratio requires setting the primary balance in accord with the following formula:

$$pb_t = \frac{(r-g)}{(1+g)} * d_{t-1}$$

If the real interest and growth rates are forecast to remain unchanged over the foreseeable future, reducing the current debt-to-GDP ratio d_0 to a targeted level d^* over a period of t years requires setting the primary balance to the following amount each year:

$$pb = \frac{1-\beta}{1-\beta^t} (\beta^t d_0 - d^*)$$

where pb is the required primary balance in percent of GDP and β is $\frac{(1+r)}{(1+g)}$.

V. FISCAL POLICY FOR PROMOTING GROWTH

Fiscal policy can promote growth by adopting a moderate level of taxation, comparable to that in similarly situated economies but sufficient to finance an adequate level of key public services and focused more on taxing consumption than income. Focusing expenditures on growth-supporting programs is also important. According to the 2008 *Report of the Commission on Growth and Development*, countries with sustained high rates of growth have typically had total investment equal to at least 25 percent of GDP; the *Report* recommended that about a third of the total comprise "public investment in physical infrastructure and 'human capital' (education and training)."[8] Productive spending on health care can also support growth, because sound health is an important prerequisite for children to succeed in school and for adults to function effectively in employment. The same applies to productive spending on education that promotes literacy and an appropriately skilled labor force. Adequate spending on maintaining public facilities also supports growth, by slowing the deterioration of public infrastructure and allowing more spending to go for new, rather than replacement, facilities.

VI. FISCAL POLICY FOR POVERTY REDUCTION

Fiscal policy is among the most effective tools government has for reducing poverty and addressing income and wealth inequality. On the revenue side

---

[8] Commission on Growth and Development (2008), "Highlights of the Growth Report," p. 2.

of the budget, progressive income taxation can moderate the inequality of incomes in the market place, while progressive estate and inheritance taxes can help reduce the transmission of inequality across generations by limiting the size of inheritances among the wealthy. In the United States, the earned income credit program, which provides refundable tax credits to low-income households with employed adults, has become a major part of the country's anti-poverty efforts. The expenditure side of the budget offers a wide array of programs for addressing poverty, including targeted cash transfers and food allowances for the poor and equal access to basic health care facilities. Making available high-quality public primary and secondary education to all children provides an important source for economic mobility, helping equalize the chances of the poor in improving their economic circumstances. In emerging market countries such as Brazil and Mexico, programs like Bolsa Familia, which condition the receipt of cash benefits on having children attend school and receive immunizations, have helped improve school attendance and health standards of low-income children. In a few advanced economies, such as the United States, programs offering subsidized housing have also helped reduce poverty. Finally, programs supporting effective job search and training programs, including programs supporting apprenticeships for students entering the labor force, can help reduce poverty while promoting higher employment and a more productive workforce.

VII. SPECIAL FISCAL ISSUES[9]

1. *Tax Expenditures.* Tax expenditures are provisions in an economy's tax code that give taxpayers benefits comparable to budget subsidies or transfers, except that they are provided in the form of reductions to tax liabilities. Thus, they appear on the revenue side of the budget.[10] Tax expenditures include exemptions or reduced rates for certain types of income, such as

---

[9] The text in this section is drawn from Greene, J. (2012), *Public Finance: An International Perspective*, Ch. 7.

[10] For the United States, the Congressional Budget Act of 1974 defines tax expenditures as "revenue losses attributable to provisions of the Federal tax laws which allow a special exclusion, exemption, or deduction from gross income or which provide a special credit, a preferential rate of tax, or a deferral of tax liability." Congressional Budget and Impoundment Control Act of 1974 (Pub. L. No. 93-344), Sec. 3(3).

dividends, as compared with the rates levied on wages or other types of income. Other tax expenditures provide subsidies, in the form of deductions from taxable income or credits against tax liability, for payments made for specified items. Tax expenditures are popular, because they let governments provide benefits off-budget, in a form readily available to qualifying tax-payers. However, they complicate the tax code and make filing and paying taxes harder. Being off-budget, tax expenditures are less visible than budgetary outlays and harder to control, because they serve as entitlements (see below). Thus, their cost is harder to estimate than comparable budget outlays. Nevertheless, many analysts estimate that tax expenditures cost governments substantial amounts of revenue. In the United States, for example, some researchers have estimated that tax expenditures reduced federal revenues by more than US$1 trillion, or more than 20 percent of household income tax liability, in fiscal year 2015.[11]

2. *Mandatory Expenditures* ("Entitlements"). Mandatory expenditures are outlays made automatically, as a matter of law, without need for appropriation or legislative approval during the formal budget process. **Entitlements** represent the most common mandatory expenditure programs. Entitlements are spending programs in which individuals or institutions qualify for benefits as a result of satisfying statutory requirements for eligibility. Once qualified, all such payments become automatic spending obligations for the government providing them. There is no need for government to authorize a specific amount of spending for the program. Indeed, total program spending can only be estimated in advance and known after the end of the fiscal year. Health insurance programs that provide approved benefits to certain individuals are a typical entitlement program. Other such programs include pensions for prior government employees and certain subsidy programs that governments have promised to pay. Discretionary expenditures, by comparison, must be approved each year, allowing the government to set the level of spending as conditions warrant.

Discretionary expenditures are easier to control than mandatory expenditures. Many mandatory spending programs include formulas that allow

---

[11] Center on Budget and Policy Priorities (2016), "Policy Basics: Federal Tax Expenditures." Available at: http://www.cbpp.org/sites/default/files/atoms/files/policy-basics-taxexpenditures.pdf. Accessed July 16, 2017.

steady increases from year to year, unless the legislature intervenes. Entitlements present a special problem in this regard. For example, unless subject to an explicit ceiling on total outlays, expenditures for government-funded health insurance or health care will automatically rise with the introduction of new medical procedures and pharmaceuticals. Likewise, outlays for government-funded pension programs will rise over time as life expectancy increases and consumer prices rise, if benefits are indexed to inflation. Discretionary programs typically do not face these problems, because the government sets overall spending limits through the budget process.

3. *Contingent expenditures.* Contingent expenditures are spending obligations that occur if specific events happen. The following are examples of continent expenditures:

- *Loan guarantees.* When a government guarantees a loan for a state enterprise or other institution, the government budget becomes liable for debt service payments if the agency with primary responsibility for the loan cannot meet its obligations.
- *Bank failures.* If the government has implicitly guaranteed some or all of the deposits in the country's banking system, the government will have to reimburse depositors for any losses. The same applies if the government has underwritten a deposit insurance fund and the fund has exhausted its resources. To prevent banks from closing, the government may also have to recapitalize insolvent financial institutions, either by providing these institutions with government debt in exchange for bad assets or by establishing an asset management company with funds to buy bad assets from these institutions.
- *Catastrophe-related expenditures.* Governments typically bear the burden of emergency relief and repairs in the event of natural disasters, such as earthquakes, floods, and hurricanes.

Contingent expenditures also include future outlays that will be triggered by foreseeable events. For example, certain age-related expenditures, such as rising outlays for health care and public pension programs, can be considered as contingent outlays, because they will materialize as the population ages.

4. *Quasi-fiscal expenditures.* As mentioned in Chapter 4, quasi-fiscal expenditures are outlays by off-budget public agencies that look and function like regular budgetary expenditures. Being off-budget, they are less transparent and far harder to control than regular budgetary outlays. Many quasi-fiscal activities occur at monetary authorities (central banks), because they have readily available funds and typically earn profits from their operations. Quasi-fiscal activities often carried out at monetary authorities include the following:

- *Providing exchange rate guarantees.* When the exchange rate depreciates, many importers who have ordered goods for domestic resale at fixed prices may lose money if contracts are honored at market exchange rates. Thus, the monetary authority may be pressured to sell foreign exchange at a more favorable (less depreciated) rate. Doing so amounts to giving an off-budget, non-transparent subsidy to the beneficiaries. If the authorities agree to provide unlimited amounts of foreign exchange at this rate, the subsidy is also uncontrollable. Exchange rate guarantees generally lose money for the monetary authority, reducing its profits and thus the revenue it can transfer to the government budget. The guarantees can also have broader economic effects, diverting foreign exchange from regular markets and creating the possibility for parallel exchange markets, if purchasers can resell to others the foreign exchange they receive at a higher (more depreciated) exchange rate.

- *Funding deposit guarantees.* If a country does not have a formal deposit insurance program, or if the program's resources are insufficient, a monetary authority may be asked to "bail out" depositors by covering their losses at failing banks. If it does, the monetary authority provides a non-transparent, hard-to-control subsidy to depositors that reduces its own profits and, thus, the revenues it can provide to the government budget. As with a program of unlimited deposit insurance, funding deposit guarantees, or serving as a back-up to an existing program, can create moral hazard for the banking system, because bankers no longer fear the consequences of bad loans that can decapitalize their banks. Under these circumstances a system-wide bank failure could decapitalize the monetary authority, requiring budgetary transfers to restore its financial viability.

*   *Sterilizing capital inflows.* Many central banks try to minimize the effects of capital inflows on their economies through sterilization. Sterilization involves selling government securities, or central bank securities, to commercial banks, to offset the impact of additional foreign exchange on the money supply. Sterilization, while effective at reducing the so-called monetary base (the amount of high-powered money in an economy), generally reduces the monetary authority's profits and, thus, the revenues it provides the budget. The reason is that the interest it earns on its foreign exchange reserves is typically less than the interest it had earned on the government securities it sells (or the interest it must pay when it issues its own securities).[12] For this reason, most monetary authorities can only engage in sterilization for a limited time and typically turn to exchange restrictions as a response to capital inflows, unless the exchange rate is allowed to appreciate. Economically, sterilization operations create distortions by allowing the exchange rate to be more depreciated than the market would otherwise allow. To that extent exports will be promoted and imports suppressed, reducing budget revenues from import duties.

VIII. SUMMARY

Fiscal policy involves the use of government budgets — revenues, expenditures, the budget balance, and budget financing — to affect macroeconomic activity. Theory and experience show that changes in these items can affect the real level of economic activity. Changes in the

---

[12] The People's Bank of China may be an exception to this rule, because interest rates on its securities are less than those on its foreign exchange reserves. See Ljungwall, C., Yi Xiong, and Zou Yutong (2009), "Central Bank Financial Strength and the Cost of Sterilization in China," Stockholm School of Economics, Available at: http://swopec.hhs.se/hacerc/papers/hacerc2009-008.pdf. Accessed July 16, 2017. Central banks in most other countries can only sell their own bills at interest rates well above those received from their foreign exchange reserves.

budget balance, for example, can affect output by raising and lowering aggregate demand. Changes in the composition of revenues and expenditures can affect both aggregate demand and aggregate supply. Indeed, the choice of revenue and spending measures can have a major impact on incentives for saving and investment, thereby affecting an economy's rate of growth. Finally, budget financing can have important implications for an economy's monetary sector and balance of payments.

Chapter 8
MONETARY POLICY

Monetary policy involves the use of certain policy instruments, typically interest rates, to achieve short- and intermediate targets as a way of attaining broader objectives, such as a desired rate of inflation. Figure 8.1 describes the basic framework for monetary policy, regardless of the particular policy regime the monetary authority uses.

Beginning in the upper left-hand corner of Figure 8.1, the monetary authority takes a policy decision and uses instruments to set an operating target — typically a very short-term interest rate, such as that in the overnight money market. The instruments involve activities such as *open market operations* (buying and selling government securities or its own securities to deposit money banks, sometimes through repurchase ("repo") or reverse repurchase ("reverse repo") operations), *changing its discount rate*, or *changing reserve requirements*. The monetary authority sets the operating target as a way of attaining an intermediate target — the growth rate of broad money, the exchange rate, or a forecast rate of inflation — in order to achieve an ultimate policy objective, such as a targeted rate of inflation. After attaining its operating target, the monetary authority reviews a broad set of indicator variables, to see how the economy has responded to its actions. Depending on the values of these variables, the authority decides whether to keep policy unchanged or make further changes to its operating target.

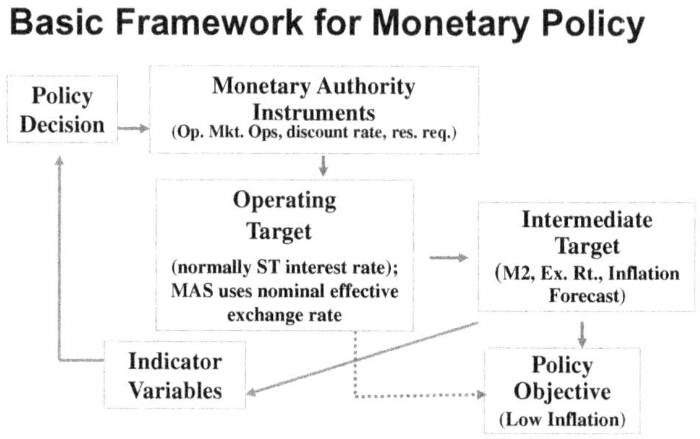

Basic Framework for Monetary Policy

FIGURE 8.1. BASIC FRAMEWORK FOR MONETARY POLICY

I. GENERAL DESCRIPTION OF THE FRAMEWORK FOR MONETARY POLICY

A. The Monetary Policy Objective

Monetary policy can focus on *price stability*, *exchange rate stability*, or *minimizing the variability in real output* (real GDP). Monetary policy cannot affect real output in the long run, because there is no long-run tradeoff between inflation and unemployment. However, if there is confidence in the authorities, monetary policy can affect real output in the short-run (e.g., respond to recession). As mentioned earlier in Chapter 5, external capital inflows affect the monetary system and the impact of monetary policy.

The monetary authorities may be tempted to use policy for multiple objectives, because it is relatively easy for them to adjust policy instruments. However, aiming monetary policy at more than one objective requires multiple instruments and may not be effective. So-called secondary instruments, such as reserve requirements, can be blunt, since they affect all banks and may require difficult actions, such as having banks call in loans to meet higher reserve obligations. Thus, these instruments may be less effective than subtler instruments, e.g., open market operations. At the same time, targeting the exchange rate can itself be an intermediate target for managing inflation: linking the national currency to that of a low-inflation trading partner may be a way of "importing" the partner's inflation rate, provided that the country can maintain competitiveness at the given exchange rate.

How should the authorities choose among objectives? Most economists favor making price stability the main goal for monetary policy. As mentioned earlier, there appears to be no long-run tradeoff between inflation and growth. In addition, inflation has many costs for an economy. These include the costs of having to economize on the use of money; overinvestment in the financial sector, as firms and households try to protect the real value of their financial assets; difficulties in deciding about future expenditures, since higher inflation usually also means greater variability in the inflation rate; and a higher nominal, if not real, cost of capital, which also deters investment. In addition, as mentioned in Chapter 1, above a certain modest level, higher inflation reduces economic growth.

Making price stability the overriding objective for monetary policy ordinarily promotes confidence, particularly among firms and investors. It also addresses what has been called the time inconsistency trap, whereby monetary authorities are tempted to announce one inflation target and then adjust policy instruments in a way so as to raise output above the level consistent with that inflation rate, hoping that firms, households, and workers will not notice the discrepancy and thus attain a higher level of real GDP. In practice, market participants will observe shortages, find prices rising, and adjust their own wages and prices, thereby defeating the efforts of the monetary authorities. When this happens, people lose confidence in the authorities, making it harder to attain low inflation. For this reason, economists urge the authorities to pursue price stability and act in a way to encourage trust, thereby avoiding the time inconsistency trap.

B. Choosing among Policy Instruments

The monetary authorities can choose between direct and indirect instruments when setting the operating target. Direct instruments include interest rate ceilings, ceilings on the growth of bank credit, and changes in rules directing credit toward particular industries or sectors of the economy (e.g., a requirement that banks dedicate a certain percentage of all loans to agriculture). Indirect instruments include open market operations,

interest rates on the rediscount or overdraft window, and reserve requirements. Some unusual instruments include targeting the level of reserve
money or the monetary base and changing the exchange rate, which
Singapore does because of the close relationship between the exchange
rate and inflation in its highly open economy, where total trade can be
several times GDP.

Most countries use indirect instruments, for several reasons. First, they
usually involve fewer distortions, since they avoid using credit controls or
interest rate ceilings. Second, they are more market friendly, since they
allow banks to set their own interest rates and respond to the market. With
open market operations, individual banks can decide whether or not to
accept the monetary authorities' offer to buy or sell government securities
or engage in repo operations. By comparison, credit ceilings on individual
banks bind each bank, whether or not it wants to lend as much or more
than its ceiling.

Open market operations are the main policy instrument that most
monetary authorities use. They are less blunt than changes in reserve
requirements, since they do not require banks suddenly to increase
reserves, which may require some banks to "call in" loans not yet due.
They also have a bigger impact than changing the discount rate, since typically only a few banks use the discount window at any time. In practice,
the main issue is whether to use government securities or central bank bills
for open market operations. Monetary authorities in advanced economies
typically use government securities, while those in some emerging market
economies, such as Tajikistan, also use central bank bills.

C. The Operating Target

As mentioned earlier, most monetary authorities use as their operating
target a very short-term policy interest rate that reflects the rate (cost) at
which banks obtain liquidity. Examples of policy interest rates include
Malaysia's *overnight policy rate* (the rate at which large banks lend to
each other overnight on the interbank money market); Australia's *cash
rate* (the interest rate in its overnight money market); and the *federal funds
rate* in the United States (the interest rate at which depository institutions
lend balances at the Federal Reserve to other depository institutions

overnight). Singapore, because of the close link between inflation and the exchange rate in its highly open economy, targets the nominal effective exchange rate of its (unannounced) currency basket, letting the rate fluctuate within an (unspecified) band but indicating an overall direction (appreciation, depreciation, or no change).

II. THE TRANSMISSION MECHANISM FOR MONETARY POLICY

Monetary policy works in various ways when reducing inflation or combatting recession is the broad policy objective. Figure 8.2 summarizes the main channels through which monetary policy operates.

A change in the operating target (e.g., policy interest rate) can affect inflation, for example, in at least four ways: through its impact on lending rates and the amount of credit; through its effect on asset prices; through its impact on inflation expectations; and through its influence on the exchange rate. The latter impact, in turn, can affect inflation in two ways: indirectly, through its influence on aggregate demand and, thus the output gap; and more directly, through its impact on import prices.

The Monetary Policy Transmission Mechanism

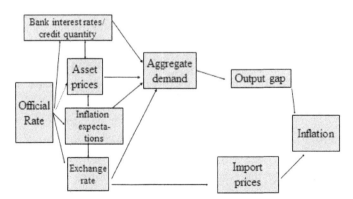

FIGURE 8.2. MAIN CHANNELS OF MONETARY POLICY TRANSMISSION

Source: Developed from Bank of England, Monetary Policy Committee, "The transmission mechanism of monetary policy." Available at www.bankofengland.co.uk/publications/Documents/other/monetary/montrans.pdf. Accessed July 16, 2017.

One way monetary policy can affect inflation is by changing bank interest rates, particularly loan rates. A rise in the policy interest rate, in most economies, causes banks to raise their lending rates, since it raises the cost of funds through the interbank market, even if deposit rates do not change. With a higher cost of funds, banks in turn generally raise lending rates, which should reduce the demand for loans as some investment projects become unprofitable. Higher lending rates may also leave banks with a less attractive set of potential borrowers, as those with less risky projects drop out of the lending queue. In either case, the volume of loans will likely decrease, thereby reducing aggregate demand and inflationary pressures.

A second way monetary policy can affect inflation is by altering asset prices. Because the prices of many assets — particularly stocks and bonds — are believed to depend on the ratio of expected earnings to the rate of return on similar assets, changing the policy interest rate can affect asset prices by changing market interest rates in the same direction. A rise in the policy interest rate, by raising other interest rates, will reduce the value of many financial assets, which in turn will have two effects. One is to reduce demand, because their decline in wealth causes asset owners to spend somewhat less. The other is to reduce the value of collateral available to support loans, which will reduce lending. Both effects will reduce aggregate demand, thereby helping diminish inflationary pressures.

A third way monetary policy can affect inflation is by changing the inflation expectations of firms, workers, and households. Raising the policy interest rate, for example, may signal that the monetary authorities view higher inflation as a risk and are moving to reduce it. If market participants have confidence in the authorities, the rise in the policy interest rate may cause them to reduce their expectations of future inflation, thereby dampening demand. Policy rate changes can have unexpected effects on expectations, however. For example, in uncertain times an unexpected decline in the policy interest may be interpreted not as a sign of smaller inflationary risks but as a signal that the authorities are worried about the strength of the economy. In this case, firms in particular may decide to reduce investment, as evidently occurred in the United States following an unexpected cut in the Federal Funds rate during the fall of 2007.

A fourth way monetary policy can affect inflation is by changing the exchange rate. Raising the policy interest rate, by raising most interest rates in financial markets, will likely increase the attractiveness of domestic financial assets, thereby encouraging a net rise in external capital inflows. In a flexible exchange rate environment, the increased demand for domestic assets should appreciate the exchange rate, thereby raising imports and reducing exports. The resulting decrease in net exports will reduce aggregate demand, thereby helping contain inflation. The exchange rate appreciation will also affect inflation directly, by reducing the prices of imported goods in the consumer price index (CPI).

Although the monetary authorities can change the policy interest rate very quickly, inflation typically adjusts only with a significant lag. Most of the channels require some time — weeks, sometimes months — to take effect. In turn, it takes time for changes in aggregate demand to affect inflation. For this reason, monetary authorities that use inflation targeting generally target an inflation rate 18–24 months in the future, even if they move quickly to respond to current inflation pressures.

In addition, the effects described above (and effects in the opposite direction, when the monetary authorities reduce the policy interest rate) are most likely to occur during "normal" economic times, when banks have at most modest amounts of nonperforming loans and firms are not burdened by large amounts of foreign currency debt. When banks have sizable nonperforming loans, or firms face the prospect of a serious recession, lowering the policy interest rate may have contrary effects. A rate cut, by helping to depreciate the exchange rate, could weaken company balance sheets, decreasing their willingness and ability to borrow as the domestic currency value of foreign currency liabilities rises. Banks with large foreign exchange exposure could likewise see their balance sheets deteriorate, making them less willing to lend. Both developments could cause aggregate demand to decline. If the resulting effects on firms increased the volume of nonperforming loans, banks would also be less willing to lend. Hence, the channels of monetary policy transmission are sensitive to general economic conditions, in particular foreign exchange liabilities among banks, firms, and households.

III. THE APPROACH TO MONETARY POLICY: ALTERNATIVE MONETARY FRAMEWORKS

As Figure 8.1 has noted, economies can choose among several options for intermediate targets of monetary policy. Each of these intermediate targets implies a different framework for monetary policy.

A. Exchange Rate Targeting (Using the Exchange Rate as a Nominal Anchor)

One such framework involves **exchange rate targeting**. In this framework the monetary authorities use their policy instruments to maintain the nominal exchange rate at a certain level, or within a certain range, of a particular currency or currency basket. For example, the Hong Kong Monetary Authority uses its policy instruments to link the HK dollar to the U.S. dollar within a narrow band around US$1 = HK$7.80. The authorities intervene to prevent the HK dollar from depreciating below US$1 = HK$7.85 or appreciating above US$1 = HK$7.75.

Until the past few decades, exchange rate targeting was arguably the most common monetary framework. Under the pre-World War II gold standard, for example, countries committed to ensure a certain relationship between their currencies and gold, or between their currency and another currency such as the British pound or the U.S. dollar that was pegged to gold. A similar rule applied under the Bretton Woods regime of 1945–1971, under which major world currencies were pegged at a fixed rate to the U.S. dollar and the U.S. dollar in turn was pegged to gold at US$35 per ounce. The European Exchange Rate Mechanism of 1979–1992, in which various currencies were linked at fixed exchange rates to the Deutsch (German) Mark, required the countries participating to commit their policy instruments to maintaining the exchange rate. Today, fewer countries maintain an exchange rate anchor for monetary policy. Nevertheless, as recently as April 2016 some 82 IMF member countries used an exchange rate anchor as their monetary framework. Thirty nine countries were linked to the U.S. dollar; 25 to the Euro, nine to some other currency, and nine to a basket of currencies. Of these 82 countries, 14 had no currency of their own, with eight using the U.S. dollar as legal tender.[1]

B. Monetary Aggregate Targeting

A second monetary policy framework is **monetary aggregate targeting**. In this framework the monetary authorities use their policy instruments to

---

[1] IMF (2016), *Annual Report on Exchange Arrangements and Exchange Restrictions* (Washington: October), Table 2, p. 6.

attain a targeted rate of growth in a monetary aggregate such as broad money (*M*2 or *M*3), either excluding or including foreign currency deposits. Monetary aggregate targeting rests on the assumption of a close link between money growth and inflation. Thus, it represents a rather traditional approach to monetary policy.

Monetary targeting used to be common among advanced economies, particularly during the 1970s and 1980s. The U.S. Federal Reserve Board under Chairman Volcker, for example, adopted monetary targeting in the late 1970s in its effort to reduce the inflation that resulted from petroleum price shocks and passive monetary policy. However, the observation that inflation often moved quite differently from changes in monetary aggregates led most advanced economies to abandon monetary aggregate targeting. As of April 2016, some 24 countries, all low or middle income, targeted a monetary aggregate.[2]

C. Inflation Targeting

A third and more common monetary policy framework is **inflation targeting**. A monetary authority that adopts inflation targeting uses its policy instruments to keep its *forecast rate of inflation* equal to an announced target, in most cases a range around a central inflation rate. Virtually all countries today use the annual rate of change in the official ("headline") CPI as their inflation target.[3] New Zealand was the first country to adopt inflation targeting as its monetary framework, in 1989. Inflation targeting was considered the most innovative monetary framework during the period through 2008, although enthusiasm for this approach diminished with the Global Financial Crisis and the subsequent desire of many countries to use monetary policy to minimize recession in the absence of noticeable inflation. As of April 2016, 38 countries, mainly advanced economies, followed inflation targeting.[4]

---

[2] *Ibid.*

[3] Until a few years ago, Thailand made the core inflation rate (the inflation rate after eliminating volatile elements such as food and energy prices) as its inflation target.

[4] IMF (2016), *op. cit.*, Table 2.

Although many developing and emerging market countries have expressed interest in adopting inflation targeting, experience suggests that successful adoption usually requires meeting certain preconditions. First, the monetary authority must have a *mandate to pursue price stability*. Second, the monetary authority requires *instrument independence*: the ability to use its policy instruments without restraint once an inflation target has been established. A third requirement is *accountability and transparency*. The monetary authority must be accountable to some unit of government (typically the Parliament or Congress) for trying to attain its target, although few countries have gone so far as New Zealand's original inflation targeting law in holding the central bank governor personally responsible for attaining (or trying to attain) the inflation target. In addition, the monetary authority must announce its inflation target and announce the decisions of its monetary policy committee, usually through published reports. A fourth precondition for successful inflation targeting is the *stability and development of the financial system*. This requires *adequate financial supervision and regulation*, to prevent fragility that could require bailouts or undermine the authorities' ability to raise interest rates; *deep and liquid credit markets*, to allow open market operations; and the *creation of any necessary financial infrastructure not yet present*, such as a financial clearinghouse.

Besides the foregoing conditions, successful inflation targeting requires a *good methodology for forecasting inflation* and a *reasonable understanding of the transmission channels between policy instruments and inflation*. In addition, the monetary authorities need to follow a *forward-looking operating procedure*, since any policy changes will only affect inflation with a lag, i.e., future inflation. Finally, inflation targeting is best introduced under certain macroeconomic conditions. An especially important one is the *absence of fiscal dominance*. Government budget deficits should be modest and not require central bank financing. Failing to satisfy this condition could make it impossible for the monetary authority to pursue inflation targeting, because of the need to provide budget financing. Successful implementation also requires a *reasonably well-developed and sound financial system*, as opposed to one requiring substantial capitalization for loss-making banks. Finally, inflation targeting is best adopted in an environment of *internal and external stability*, meaning low inflation, output close to potential, and a sustainable balance of payments. Absent this, the monetary authority might need to focus on avoiding a domestic or external crisis, to the detriment of targeting low inflation.

D. Eclectic Monetary Framework

The last approach to monetary policy is the **eclectic** or other monetary framework. In this framework, the monetary authority has no explicit monetary anchor. Instead, it monitors a variety of monetary indicators and uses its policy instruments to pursue stable growth and low inflation, typically without announcing a formal inflation target. The U.S. Federal Reserve Board, for example, has a dual mandate: attaining stable prices and maximum sustainable employment. This allows the Board to shift its focus between employment and inflation, depending on macroeconomic circumstances. As of April 2016, some 48 countries pursued some form of eclectic monetary framework, including the United States, Switzerland, and members of the Euro Zone.[5]

IV. DEVELOPMENTS IN MONETARY POLICY SINCE THE GLOBAL FINANCIAL CRISIS

A. Quantitative Easing

Quantitative easing involves efforts by monetary authorities to relax monetary conditions when the policy interest rate has reached a minimum level. It involves purchasing government securities and other debt to accelerate monetary growth and expand the capacity of banks to lend. Quantitative easing has been important in many advanced economies since 2009, where accommodative policy has cut policy interest rates to zero or near zero (in the case of the European Central Bank and the Bank of Japan, below zero).

In the United States, the Federal Reserve Board substantially raised its holdings of U.S. government securities and other debt from about US$800 billion before the Global Financial Crisis in mid-2008 to nearly

---

[5] *Ibid.*

US$2.1 trillion in mid-2010. Subsequent purchases raised holdings to more than US$4.5 trillion at the end of 2014, and holdings have remained about at that level since then, as further additions to the balance sheet effectively ended in October 2014. Buying debt other than U.S. government securities was a major innovation for the Federal Reserve Board. Since 2016, the Federal Reserve Board has begun raising its policy interest rate. Figure 8.3 charts the development of U.S. Federal Reserve System assets from 2003 through early 2017.

B. Monetary Policy in Selected Asian Economies

1. *Malaysia.* Malaysia, which uses an eclectic monetary framework, has pursued a careful monetary policy since the Global Financial Crisis. The monetary authorities kept the overnight policy rate unchanged at 3.5 percent during the first half of 2008 before the Crisis erupted worldwide, despite the sharp increase in global commodity prices. The rate was maintained during the rest of the year and cut to 2 percent in 2009 as part of the economy's response to the Crisis. During 2010, the rate was increased in three steps to 2.75 percent as the economy returned to a more normal growth rate and raised further, to 3 percent in May 2011, after inflation accelerated somewhat during the first quarter of the year. The rate remained at 3 percent until July 2014, when it was raised to 3.25 percent, with strong growth prospects and inflation reported as being above its long-term average, as inflation reached 3.4 percent during the first quarter of the year and 3.3 percent during the second quarter.[6] The authorities reduced the rate in July 2016, citing global uncertainty and a projection of less inflation in 2016 (2–3 percent) with inflation remaining stable in 2017.[7] The rate remained unchanged as of March 2017. Figure 8.4 shows the recent history of the policy rate.

The authorities have succeeded in keeping inflation at a moderate level while maintaining a reasonable rate of growth. Inflation averaged 1.7 percent during the fourth quarter of 2016 and 2.1 percent for the full year, the

---

[6] Bank Negara Malaysia (2014), *Quarterly Bulletin for the Second Quarter of 2014.*

[7] Bank Negara Malaysia (2016), "Monetary Policy Statement," Ref. No. 07/16/03 (July 13). Available at: http://www.bnm.gov.my/index.php?ch=en_press&pg=en_press&ac=4213& lang=en. Accessed July 16, 2017.

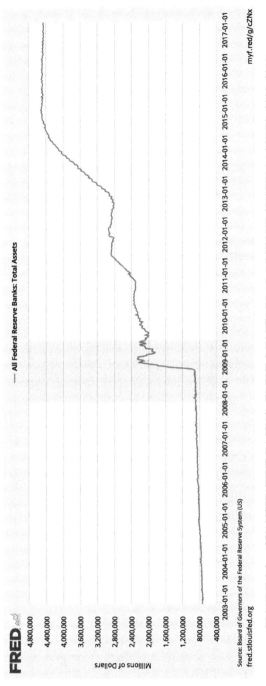

FIGURE 8.3. QUANTITATIVE EASING: TRENDS IN FEDERAL RESERVE SYSTEM ASSETS, 2003–2017

Daily Weighted Average Overnight Interbank Rate

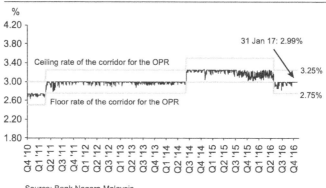

Source: Bank Negara Malaysia

FIGURE 8.4. MALAYSIA: TRENDS IN THE OVERNIGHT POLICY RATE, LATE 2010 THROUGH EARLY 2017
Source: Bank Negara Malaysia (2017), *Quarterly Bulletin for the Fourth Quarter of 2016.*

same as in 2015. Broad money (*M3*) growth, which had risen to an annual rate of near 8 percent during the last half of 2015, slowed thereafter, averaging 3 percent during 2016 (Figure 8.5). At the same time, real GDP grew by 4.5 percent during the fourth quarter of 2016 and at an average rate of 4.2 percent for all of 2016, down slightly from 5 percent during 2015 (Figure 8.6). The current account and balance of payments remained in surplus during 2016, with the overall surplus larger than in 2015. Net international reserves remained equivalent to 8.6 months of imports and about 4 times short-term debt, although the overall level of reserves, US$95 billion at the end of January 2017, was about 1/3 less than the recent peak of about US$130 billion during mid-2014 (Figure 8.7).[8] Moreover, the Malaysian ringgit depreciated to a near low of almost MYR 4.5 per US$ in March 2017, compared to about MYR 3.25 per US$ at the beginning of 2014.[9]

2. Philippines. The Philippines uses an inflation targeting framework, with the percent change in headline (CPI) inflation as its inflation target.

---

[8] All data taken from Bank Negara Malaysia (2017), *Quarterly Bulletin for the Fourth Quarter of 2016.*

[9] *Source*: Trading Economics. Available at: http://www.tradingeconomics.com/malaysia/currency. Accessed July 16, 2017.

Monetary Aggregates

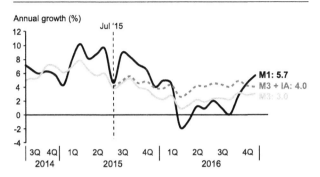

Note: From July 2015 onwards, the compilation of M3 is adjusted to exclude Islamic Investment Accounts (IA) due to a data reclassification exercise. This is reflected as a negative contribution through 'other influences'. The dotted line represents M3 growth had this reclassification not taken place

Source: Bank Negara Malaysia

FIGURE 8.5. MALAYSIA: BROAD MONEY GROWTH, MID-2014 THROUGH 2016

Source: Bank Negara Malaysia (2017), *Quarterly Bulletin for the Fourth Quarter of 2016.*

The Economy Expanded by 4.5% in the Fourth Quarter (at constant 2010 prices)

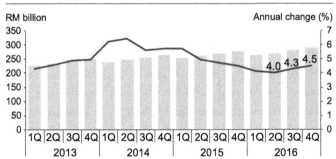

Source: Department of Statistics, Malaysia

FIGURE 8.6. MALAYSIA: GROWTH IN REAL GDP, 2013–2016

Source: Bank Negara Malaysia (2017), *Quarterly Bulletin for the Fourth Quarter of 2016.*

Net International Reserves (as at end period)

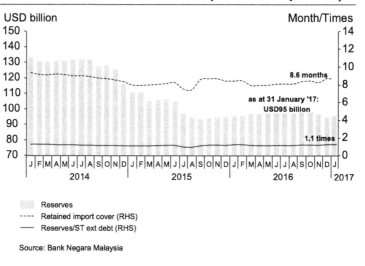

Reserves
---- Retained import cover (RHS)
—— Reserves/ST ext debt (RHS)

Source: Bank Negara Malaysia

FIGURE 8.7.   MALAYSIA: NET INTERNATIONAL RESERVES, 2013–2016

Source: Bank Negara Malaysia (2017), *Quarterly Bulletin for the Fourth Quarter of 2016.*

For much of the period through 2014, the inflation target was a range of 3 percent–5 percent. For the period 2015–2018, the target was reduced to 3 percent, plus or minus 1 percent.

The Bangko Sentral NG Pilipinas (BSP), the central bank, has adjusted its policy rates in response to changing economic circumstances. In 2009, as the Global Financial Crisis cut the annual growth rate to less than 2 percent, the BSP reduced its policy rate (the overnight borrowing or reverse repurchase rate) to 4 percent, with the overnight lending rate cut to 6 percent. Although growth rebounded early in 2010 to an annual rate of more than 6 percent during the first half of 2010, growth fell below 4 percent later in the year, and policy rate was kept steady through early 2011. After inflation accelerated to an annual rate of 4.8 percent during the early months of 2011, the BSP raised the overnight borrowing and overnight lending rates by 50 basis points in two steps during the first half of the year, to cool inflation. Although inflation subsided, the rates were kept unchanged for the rest of the year. When inflation remained subdued, the two rates were cut by 100 basis points during 2012 to support growth.

The policy rates remained at 3.5 percent and 5.5 percent through late July 2014 but were raised in two steps to 4 percent and 6 percent in September to address higher inflation. When inflation diminished, the two rates were cut by 50 basis points to 3.5 percent and 5.5 percent in June 2016 and kept there through March 2017. Figure 8.8 summarizes recent trends in the two policy interest rates.

The central bank has had considerable success in attaining its inflation targets. Although inflation rose during 2016, inflation equaled 2.5 percent during the fourth quarter, within the BSP's target range (Figure 8.9). At the same time, real growth in GDP and gross national income (GNI) averaged 6 percent or more (Figure 8.10).[10]

BSP Policy Rates
in percent

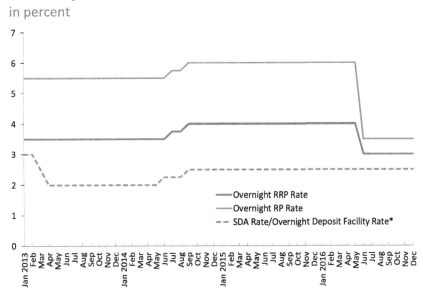

* On 3 June 2016, Special Deposit Accounts (SDAs) were replaced by the Overnight Deposit Facility (ODF) in line with the implementation of the Interest Rate Corridor (IRC) System.
Source: BSP

FIGURE 8.8. PHILIPPINES: POLICY INTEREST RATES, 2013–2016
Source: BSP (2017), *Inflation Report, 4th Quarter 2016.*

---

[10] BSP (2017), *Inflation Report, 4th Quarter 2016.*

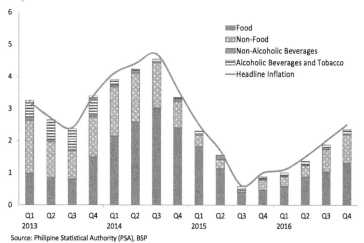

Source: Philipine Statistical Authority (PSA), BSP

FIGURE 8.9. PHILIPPINES: TRENDS IN QUARTERLY HEADLINE INFLATION, 2013–2016

Source: BSP (2017), *Inflation Report, 4th Quarter 2016.*

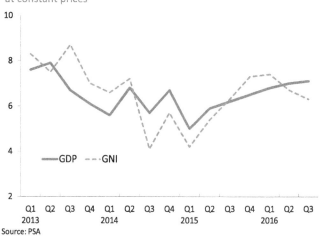

Source: PSA

FIGURE 8.10. PHILIPPINES: TRENDS IN REAL GROWTH, 2013–2016

Source: BSP (2017), *Inflation Report, 4th Quarter 2016.*

V. SUMMARY

Monetary policy involves using policy instruments, such as open market operations, to adjust an operating target (such as short-term interest rates) as a way of attaining an intermediate target, such as the growth rate of broad money, to achieve a broader macroeconomic objective such as reducing inflation. The type of monetary framework used determines the choice of intermediate target. Monetary authorities monitoring traditional monetary aggregates typically target a certain rate of growth in broad money or, on occasion, reserve money or the monetary base. Economies that have adopted inflation targeting aim to attain a forecast rate of inflation at some point (usually 18 to 24 months) in the future. Those with a fixed exchange rate regime use monetary instruments to attain a specific rate of exchange between the domestic currency and a specific foreign currency or a basket of currencies. Ultimately, most economies use monetary policy to attain and maintain low inflation, although during periods of slow growth or recession monetary authorities may use their instruments to support aggregate demand by lowering interest rates and providing banks with more funds to lend. Most monetary authorities use indirect policy instruments, such as open market operations (buying and selling government securities or central bank bills, either outright or using repurchase (repo) and reverse repurchase (reverse repo) operations), although a few use blunter instruments such as changes in reserve requirements.

Monetary policy affects aggregate demand and inflation through various transmission channels. These include the impact of changes in short-term interest rates on bank lending and market interest rates, on asset prices, on inflation expectations, and on the exchange rate. All of these channels affect inflation by stimulating or restraining aggregate demand. In addition, the exchange rate channel affects inflation by altering the domestic price of imports. From 2009 through 2017 monetary authorities in many advanced economies lowered interest rates nearly to (and in some cases below zero) to support demand. Some of these authorities supplemented these measures through quantitative easing, buying government bonds and unconventional financial assets such as mortgage backed securities to provide still more resources for bank lending. In Asia, various countries have altered their policy rates, depending on macroeconomic conditions, lowering rates following the crisis to support the economy and raising them when inflation appeared to accelerate.

Chapter 9
EXCHANGE RATE POLICY

Exchange rate policy involves two elements: establishing an exchange rate regime and setting the exchange rate. The exchange rate regime determines how the exchange rate for an economy's currency is determined. The exchange rate itself can be determined by the economy's authorities or, in the case of a freely-floating rate, the market for foreign exchange. Although a country's authorities can, for extended periods, determine the level of the exchange rate, over time it is hard for the exchange rate to deviate significantly from the level that would clear the market for foreign exchange without the development of a parallel exchange market — an unofficial or "black" market where the rate reflects a market clearing level. In addition, certain regimes are often linked to the economy's choice of a monetary policy framework. For example, countries adopting inflation targeting without capital controls generally adopt a floating rate regime, to allow an independent monetary policy while minimizing the risk of a speculative attack on the exchange rate.

I. VARIETIES OF EXCHANGE RATE REGIMES

Economies can choose among a wide array of exchange rate regimes. In practice, these cover a spectrum ranging from what are called "hard fixed" regimes to freely floating regimes, with many possibilities in between (see Figure 9.1). Table 9.1, reproduced from the IMF's 2016 Annual Report on Exchange Arrangements and Restrictions, provides a

Range of options

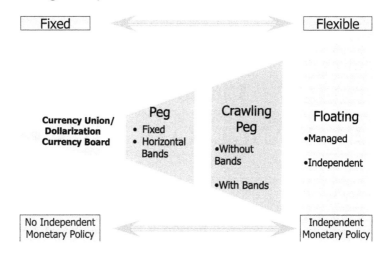

FIGURE 9.1. THE RANGE OF EXCHANGE RATE REGIMES
Source: Govil (2005).

TABLE 9.1 IMF CLASSIFICATION OF EXCHANGE RATE REGIMES

Type	Categories				
Hard pegs	Exchange arrangement with no separate legal tender	Currency board arrangement			
Soft pegs	Conventional peg	Pegged exchange rate within horizontal bands	Stabilized arrangement	Crawling peg	Crawl-like arrangement
Floating regimes (market-determined rates)	Floating	Free floating			
Residual	Other managed arrangement				

Source: IMF (2016), *Annual Report on Exchange Arrangements and Exchange Restrictions 2016* (Washington), Table 1, p. 1.

more detailed breakdown of the various types of exchange regimes. As of 2016, 14 IMF members had no separate legal tender, and 11 had currency boards. Some 40 members had floating regimes, and 31 had freely floating currencies. A total of 76 members had different types of soft peg regimes: 44 with conventional pegs, 18 with "stabilized arrangements", 3 with crawling pegs, 10 with crawl-like arrangements, and 1 pegged within horizontal bands. The remaining 20 had "other managed regimes." The period from 2008 to 2014 showed some movement away from floating regimes, mainly toward other managed arrangements.[1]

Each regime has certain advantages and disadvantages. Research has underscored the main consequences of choosing one regime instead of another.

A. "Hard Peg" Regimes

"Hard peg" exchange rate regimes are those in which the exchange rate is pegged in a way that makes it very difficult to adjust, even under pressure from financial markets. Hard fixed regimes typically come in one of three types. The first entails membership in a currency union, where several economies jointly create and use a single currency for all international transactions. Examples include the Euro zone in Europe, whose members all use the euro as a common currency, and the CFA Franc zone, comprising 14 countries in Sub-Saharan Africa that use the CFA franc as their currency. The second type involves economies that adopt another country's currency. One example is Panama, which has adopted the U.S. dollar as its official currency. The third variety involves countries with a currency board — a particular type of monetary regime in which the amount of official international reserves limits the amount of domestic currency that can be created. Hong Kong SAR and Brunei Darussalam are examples of economies with currency boards, with Hong Kong's currency pegged to the U.S. dollar and Brunei's tied to the Singapore dollar.

Having a hard peg provides certain advantages for an economy. Economies with such arrangements often have low inflation rates,

---

[1]IMF (2016), *Annual Report on Exchange Arrangements and Exchange Restrictions 2016*, pp. 6–8.

provided they observe fiscal policies consistent with the hard peg regime. Restrictions on currency issuance typically limit the growth rate of broad money, for example, while members of currency unions often face restrictions on the size of annual budget deficits and the ratio of public debt to GDP, such as those normally binding on members of the Euro zone. Economies that make another country's currency their own can often "import" the inflation rate of the country issuing the currency, so long as fiscal policy enables the country to maintain the peg.

Having a hard peg may also shield the economy from speculative attack on the currency, particularly in the case of currency union members and economies using another country's currency. The reason is that the currency in use is issued or controlled by another economy or group of economies. So long as the currency union or country issuing the currency appears financially sound, financial markets have no incentive to attack the currency.

However, a hard peg can severely constrain macroeconomic policy making, making it hard to stabilize the economy in the event of real or financial shocks. Unless monetary issuance is well below the legal limit, for example, central banks that are currency boards may have trouble acting as a lender of last resort, because of the inability to expand the money supply sufficiently to recapitalize failing banks. Similarly, countries in currency unions may have difficulty using fiscal policy to counteract recession, because of limitations on public debt and deficits, unless these are temporarily suspended. A hard peg also prevents economies from using exchange rate policy to respond to real shocks, such as a loss in external competitiveness. Some economists have argued, for example, that being part of the Euro zone has hindered Greece's ability to respond to its debt crisis by preventing any depreciation in the exchange rate.[2] As a consequence, adjustment has had to involve more painful cuts in income and expenditure. By comparison, the ability of the Icelandic krona to depreciate contributed to Iceland's recovery from its financial crisis, despite the

---

[2] See, for example, Tavlas, G. (2013), "For Greece, A Lesson in Addressing Structural Problems, Not Symptoms," Univ. of Chicago Becker Brown Bag Talk (November). Available at: https://bfi.uchicago.edu/news/feature-story/greece-lesson-addressing-structural-problems-not-symptoms. Accessed July 16, 2017.

hardships that depreciation imposed on the population.[3] In the case of economies adopting another country's currency, a real appreciation of that currency may undermine the economy's competitiveness, weakening the balance of payments and constraining growth. Indeed, the inability of the exchange rate to adjust eliminates a tool the authorities could use to promote exports and growth by establishing a "super-competitive" currency — a strategy some Asian countries have arguably used on occasion, to the chagrin of other economies.

Empirical research has shown that economies with fixed exchange rates tend to have less inflation. An early IMF study (Ghosh and others, 1996) reported that pegged regimes typically had lower inflation rates and less variability, although countries with frequent changes in the peg benefitted less than those maintaining a peg for an extended time. Subsequent research confirmed lower inflation in both pegged and intermediate regimes, but mainly in developing economies and not in emerging market and more advanced economies.[4] In emerging market and advanced economies, differences in inflation rates between economies with fixed and more flexible exchange rates appear insignificant. If anything, inflation is slightly higher in advanced economies with pegged exchange rates.[5]

The impact of a hard peg on economic growth also differs, depending on the type of economy. For developing and emerging market countries, the differences in growth rates between fixed and other exchange rate regimes appear insignificant. For advanced economies, however, growth tends to be lower with fixed rate regimes. The reason is that fixed rates tend to slow the pace of adjustment to various shocks. Thus, advanced economies appear to do better with floating rate regimes.[6]

---

[3] See, for example, Hammar, K. (2015), "IMF Survey: Iceland Makes Strong Recovery from 2008 Crisis" (March). Available at: http://www.imf.org/en/news/articles/2015/09/28/04/53/socar031315a. Accessed July 16, 2017.

[4] Rogoff, K., and others (2004), *Evolution and Performance of Exchange Rate Regimes*, IMF Occasional Paper 229 (Washington: IMF), p. 29.

[5] *Id*, p. 33.

[6] *Ibid.*

B. "Soft Peg" Regimes

Soft peg regimes encompass a range of exchange rate systems. One is the pegged but adjustable regime, in which the authorities commit to maintaining a peg but either lack the institutional mechanism (such as membership in a currency union) to prevent a change or choose to maintain the legal ability to adjust the rate if necessary. The currency regimes active under the pre-1972 Bretton Woods system were good examples of such a system, since member countries established a currency peg (usually to the U.S. dollar, with the U.S. dollar in turn pegged to gold at US$35 per ounce) but retained the right to adjust their exchange rate in the event of a "fundamental disequilibrium." [7]

Another such regime involves a peg within horizontal bands. In this system, the currency is typically linked to another at a central rate, but the rate is allowed to fluctuate within a certain range determined by two bands, one upper and one lower. The Hong Kong dollar (HK$) provides a good example of such as system. The HK$ has a central parity of HK$7.80 per U.S. dollar. However, the authorities allow the rate to fluctuate somewhat around that level, typically intervening to buy HK$ when the rate drops to HK$7.85 per U.S. dollar and intervening to sell HK$ when the rate appreciates to HK$7.75 per U.S. dollar.[8]

A third such regime is the stabilized arrangement. In this regime, the authorities limit the movement of the exchange rate within a 2 percent range for at least a 6-month period, without committing to a particular central rate.[9] The Singapore dollar during 2013 provides an example of such an arrangement, according to the IMF.[10] The IMF noted that, during 2013, the authorities kept the rate within 2 percent of a composite (but unannounced) basket of currencies. However, the authorities described their regime somewhat differently, as following a "modest and gradual

---

[7] See, for example, IMF Staff (2000), "Exchange Rate Regimes in an Increasingly Integrated World," (June).

[8] See Hong Kong Monetary Authority (2011), "Linked Exchange Rate System" (August). Available at: http://www.hkma.gov.hk/eng/key-functions/monetary-stability/linked-exchange-rate-system.shtml. Accessed July 16, 2017.

[9] IMF (2014), *Annual Report, op. cit.*, p. 69.

[10] *Id.*, p. 12.

appreciation path of the S$NEER policy band, with no change to its slope, width, and the level at which it was centred [sic]."[11]

A fourth soft peg regime is the crawling peg. In this regime, the authorities adjust the exchange rate according to a particular schedule, often announced publicly. Authorities sometimes adopt this regime when they want to provide assurances about the exchange rate but recognize that, because domestic inflation is higher than that of many trading partners, a downward adjustment of the rate is needed to maintain the competitiveness of the economy's exports. Hungary's exchange rate regime from 1995 through the early 2000s, in which the exchange rate of the forint against the U.S. dollar depreciated at a pre-announced rate of 1 percent a month, provides an example of such a regime.[12]

Soft pegs also include what are called crawl-like arrangements. In this regime, the authorities keep the exchange rate within 2 percent of a statistically identified trend for at least 6 months. Armenia's dram, which appreciated within a 2 percent band against the U.S. dollar for a time after March 12, 2013, and the Belarus ruble, which followed a depreciating trend of about 2 percent from late 2012 through 2013, represent examples of crawl-like arrangements, according to the IMF.[13]

C. Floating Regimes

Floating regimes are exchange rate systems in which the market largely or fully determines the exchange rate. In a floating regime intervention in the foreign exchange market may occur to "moderate the rate of change or prevent undue fluctuations in the rate." However the authorities do not

---

[11] Monetary Authority of Singapore (2013), "MAS Monetary Policy Statement" (October). Available at: http://www.mas.gov.sg/news-and-publications/speeches-and-monetary-policy-statements/monetary-policy-statements/2013/monetary-policy-statement-14-oct-13.aspx. From the MAS rule, one could argue that the Singapore dollar actually followed a crawl-like arrangement, despite its relative stability during 2013.

[12] For a description, see Koptis, G. (1995), "Hungary's Preannounced Crawling Peg," *Acta Oeconomica*, 47, 3/4, pp. 267–86. Available at: www.jstor.org/stable/40729631. Accessed July 16, 2017.

[13] IMF (2014), *op. cit.*, pp. 8, 9.

intervene to target a particular exchange rate.[14] The IMF defines as freely floating regimes in which

> Intervention occurs only exceptionally and aims to address disorderly market conditions and if the authorities have provided information or data confirming that intervention has been limited to at most three instances in the previous six months, each lasting no more than three business days.[15]

In 2016, the IMF classified 40 economies as having floating rate regimes, including Kenya, Uruguay, Albania, Brazil, India, and Mauritius. Some 31 economies were classified as having freely floating regimes, including Canada, Japan, the U.K., the U.S., and the Euro zone countries.[16]

As noted earlier, floating rate regimes appear to offer certain economic advantages over more fixed rate regimes. First, they provide a buffer against external shocks, allowing the exchange rate to adjust when, under fixed rate regimes, domestic wages and prices would need to adjust (or adjust far more) to preserve competitiveness. As noted above, the rigidity of Greece's exchange rate regime has made it harder to adjust to the heavy burden of public debt and lack of competitiveness than has been true for countries like Iceland, with relatively flexible exchange rates. Second, advanced economies with more flexible exchange rates appear to grow somewhat faster than those with more fixed exchange rates.[17]

II. INTERACTIONS BETWEEN EXCHANGE RATE AND MONETARY REGIMES

Economists have increasingly noted the importance of the exchange rate regime for the choice of monetary policy framework. Part of this results from the experience of the Asian Crisis of 1997–1998. During this period, several Asian economies that maintained a soft peg regime while pursuing an independent monetary policy in a setting of few restrictions on capital movements found their currencies attacked, and most ultimately had to

---

[14] *Id.*, p. 70.

[15] *Id.*, p. 71.

[16] *Supra*, Note 1, p. 7.

[17] See Note 6 above.

FIGURE 9.2. THE "IMPOSSIBLE TRINITY": A PEGGED EXCHANGE RATE, INDEPENDENT MONETARY POLICY, AND FEW CAPITAL CONTROLS

abandon the peg after exhausting their foreign exchange reserves. This led many economists to develop the idea of the "Impossible Trinity": that countries wishing to pursue an independent monetary policy cannot simultaneously maintain a fixed but adjustable exchange rate and limited capital account restrictions (see Figure 9.2). Pursuing an independent monetary policy requires either a floating exchange rate regime or maintaining capital account restrictions. With countries increasingly choosing to have limited capital account restrictions, an independent monetary policy requires a floating rate regime. Indeed, as noted earlier, most countries using inflation targeting as their monetary policy framework have adopted a floating rate regime, with varying degrees of management. As of early 2016, for example, of 38 IMF member countries using an inflation targeting framework, 11 had freely floating exchange regimes and 27 had regimes classified as "floating," i.e., "largely market determined," with intervention to "moderate the rate of change and prevent undue fluctuations in the exchange rate," but not targeting a specific level of the rate.[18] However, the Impossible Trinity suggests that countries can choose to pursue an independent monetary policy and a fixed but

---

[18] IMF (2016), p. 7. The quotations are from IMF (2016), *op. cit.*, p. 48.

adjustable (soft peg) regime if they maintain effective capital account restrictions. Malaysia chose to do so beginning on September 1, 1998, although the restrictions were gradually removed beginning in 1999. Some analysts have argued that Malaysia's choice enabled it to recover from the Asian Crisis faster and in better shape than countries that opted to avoid restrictions and maintain a floating exchange rate.[19]

III. OBJECTIVES FOR EXCHANGE RATE POLICY

From a macroeconomic perspective, exchange rate policy can and should address various objectives. One is ensuring external competitiveness. The exchange rate should enable the economy to earn sufficient foreign exchange from exports of goods and services, plus net income and transfers, to cover the cost of imports, debt service and other income payments, and outward transfers without having to accumulate high levels of external debt — in practice, external debt exceeding 40–50 percent of GDP. Economies, and particularly developing economies, do not necessarily require current account surpluses. However, any deficits should be financed in a sustainable way: through a combination of foreign direct investment and other capital flows that keep the debt-to-GDP ratio at a moderate level while ensuring external liquidity: the ability to cover short-term debt service obligations, along with other payment obligations, smoothly. This requires that the real exchange rate — the exchange rate between the national currency and other currencies after taking into account changes in relative prices — remains competitive.

The exchange rate system must also maintain exchange market equilibrium. The market for foreign exchange must clear at market rates, meaning that the official rate must equal the market rate. Without such equality the demand foreign exchange will not equal the supply and parallel markets can develop. Research indicates that parallel markets inhibit growth,[20] so avoiding them is important.

---

[19] See, for example, Kaplan, E., and D. Rodrik (2001), "Did the Malaysian Capital Controls Work?" NBER Working Paper 8142 (Cambridge, MA: February).

[20] See, for example, Fischer, S. (1993), "Role of Macroeconomic Factors in Growth," *Journal of Monetary Economics*, Vol. 32, No. 3, pp. 485–512.

IV. ASSESSING THE APPROPRIATENESS OF THE EXCHANGE RATE

In addition to whether the nominal exchange rate clears the foreign exchange market, the appropriateness of the exchange rate depends largely on the level of the real exchange rate, in particular the real effective exchange rate, a weighted average of bilateral real exchange rates with weights representing the shares of each trading partner in the economy's exports, imports, or total trade, depending on which seems most appropriate. A steady appreciation in the real exchange rate, for example, may indicate a decline in competitiveness, particularly if the current account balance has worsened over the period. A large and continuing current account deficit, particularly when financed by short-term capital flows, may also signal a competitiveness problem and the need for adjustment. The real exchange rate is especially important for countries maintaining a fixed exchange rate. Keeping the real rate at a competitive level is essential for maintaining the viability of the nominal rate. An overvalued rate, by weakening competitiveness, may undermine the peg itself, encouraging speculative attacks on the currency in a soft peg regime when financial markets believe that the peg will be hard to maintain.

Besides monitoring the real exchange rate, other tools are available for assessing the appropriateness of a currency's level. As mentioned in Chapters 1 and 3, the IMF, for example, uses a method called the "External Balance Assessment" (EBA) approach, which relies on regression-based analyses to determine whether an exchange rate is over- or under-valued.[21] The IMF has used the EBA approach as part of its annual External Sector Reports, which assess the external positions of 29 of the world's largest economies, plus the Euro zone. The most recent of these reports appeared in 2016.[22]

It is important to remember that the real exchange rate itself is a critical price in an economy, providing signals not only about competitiveness,

---

[21] For details, see Phillips, S., and others (2013), "External Balance Assessment (EBA) Methodology," IMF Working Paper 13/272 (Washington: December). Available at: http://www.imf.org/external/pubs/ft/wp/2013/wp13272.pdf. Accessed July 16, 2017.

[22] IMF (2016), *2016 External Sector Report* (July). Available at: https://www.imf.org/external/np/pp/eng/2016/072716.pdf. Accessed July 16, 2017.

but also for the external position generally. An overvalued exchange rate discourages exports and boosts imports, because import prices are kept lower than would be consistent with a more equilibrium current account position. An undervalued exchange rate will boost exports and discourage imports. However, the increased price of imports will raise the consumer price index both directly and indirectly, as prices of imported goods and the cost of products for which imports serve as inputs to production will themselves be higher.

V. USING EXCHANGE RATE POLICY

Exchange rate policy can be a useful tool for addressing external competitiveness. Economies with "fixed but adjustable" exchange rates, i.e., soft pegs, facing competitiveness issues can use exchange rate adjustment to address the problem. Provided that domestic prices do not rise so much as to offset the impact of a change, devaluing the nominal exchange rate can lead to a depreciation in the real rate, making exports less expensive for prospective foreign purchasers. Devaluation can also provide confidence to financial markets that have been imposing pressure on the exchange rate, when the market believe that the initial rate is not sustainable. The IMF often recommends such an adjustment to countries with protracted external problems as part of a comprehensive adjustment program to address the situation.

The IMF-supported adjustment program for Brazil in the late 1990s offers an example of this use of exchange rate policy. Before the adjustment, inflation higher than in its trading partners had caused the Brazilian real (the currency of the time) to become over-valued, contributing to chronic current account deficits and a drain on the country's international reserves. A one-time, 8 percent devaluation in the currency, accompanied by tightened fiscal and monetary policy and a subsequent move to a floating exchange rate system, helped restore the competitiveness of Brazilian exports and strengthen the current account balance. Following an initial, sharp depreciation in the exchange rate, the rate stabilized against the U.S. dollar, supported by a much tighter fiscal policy that included higher revenues and expenditure cuts. For the next several years, the program led to a considerable improvement in Brazil's macroeconomic performance, as inflation slowed and the balance of payments turned positive.[23]

If imports represent a sizable share of the consumer price index, or if domestic prices are closely linked to the exchange rate (as can happen in economies with significant "dollarization" or use of foreign currency in place of domestic currency), exchange rate policy can also help moderate inflation. Provided that the current account balance appears sustainable, for example, when the current account is in surplus and appears likely to remain so for the foreseeable future, efforts to appreciate the nominal exchange rate, or at least avoid a depreciation, can limit the rise in prices of imported goods, thereby slowing inflation. In Indonesia, for example, where research suggested that exchange rate changes explained perhaps half of all variation in inflation during the 1990s and early 2000s,[24] and where the current account balance was in surplus from 1998 through 2002, efforts to maintain or appreciate the exchange rate might have helped trim inflation during 2003, particularly if combined with tighter fiscal and monetary policy. In Singapore, where trade is equivalent to several times GDP, the close connection between the exchange rate and domestic prices helps explain why the Monetary Authority of Singapore typically appreciates the nominal effective exchange rate if it wishes to slow the rate of inflation.

VI. SUMMARY

Exchange rate policy involves choosing an exchange rate regime and setting the level of the exchange rate relative to one or more foreign currencies. Although a country's authorities can strive to fix the exchange rate,

---

[23] See, for example, Li Xiaolin (2013), "Course Project: Brazil's Crisis, 1998–1999," unpub. course paper for ECON 656, Singapore Management University, December; and Fraga, A. (2000), "Monetary Policy during the Transition to a Floating Exchange Rate: Brazil's Recent Experience," *Finance & Development*, Vol. 37, No. 1, pp. 16–18 (March). Available at: http://www.imf.org/external/pubs/ft/fandd/2000/03/fraga.htm.

[24] See Ramakrishnan, U., and A. Vamvakidis (2002), "Forecasting Inflation in Indonesia," IMF Working Paper 02/111 (June), especially Table 2, p. 11.

it is hard for the rate to deviate for long periods from the level that would clear the foreign exchange market without developing a parallel exchange market — an unofficial or "black" market where the rate reflects a market clearing level. Countries can choose from a variety of possible exchange rate regimes. At one extreme are "hard pegs," involving the use of a currency board, membership in a currency union, or adopting another country's currency. At the other extreme are freely floating and managed floating regimes. Intermediate regimes involve the use of so-called "soft pegs", including conventional pegs (fixed but adjustable rates), pegging within horizontal bands, and crawling pegs or other crawling rate regimes. Different exchange rate regimes have different advantages and disadvantages. Pegged and intermediate regimes appear to bring lower inflation rates to developing countries, provided they can implement fiscal and monetary policies consistent with the pegged regime, to avoid an appreciation in the real exchange rate. Floating rate regimes help moderate the effects of external shocks, allowing the exchange rate to adjust when, under fixed rate regimes, domestic wages and prices would need to adjust (or adjust far more) to preserve competitiveness. In addition, advanced economies with floating rates appear to grow faster than those with pegged rates. Countries with inflation targeting as their monetary framework typically also adopt floating rate regimes. Doing so enables them to pursue an independent monetary policy while also maintaining low capital account barriers. This is consistent with the so-called "Impossible Trinity," under which countries can only have two of the following at any one time: an independent monetary policy, a fixed exchange rate, and few if any restrictions on capital flows.

Exchange rate policy can help an economy attain and maintain competitiveness, by setting the nominal rate a level where the real rate leads to a current account balance that can be financed with foreign direct investment and relatively inexpensive borrowing, such as concessional financing or long-term debt at relatively low interest rates. The successful use of exchange rate policy requires supporting monetary and fiscal policy, so that adjustments in the nominal rate are not undermined by offsetting increases in domestic wages and prices.

Chapter 10

USING MACROECONOMIC AND STRUCTURAL POLICIES TO ATTAIN MACROECONOMIC OBJECTIVES

As mentioned in Chapter 1 of this book, most governments aim to achieve several broad macroeconomic objectives. These include operating near potential output and attaining an acceptable level of economic growth; achieving relative price stability (low inflation); and maintaining a sustainable external position, meaning a sound balance of payments and a modest level of external debt. We can group these objectives under two broad headings: macroeconomic stability and growth. Stability implies operating close to potential output, with low inflation and a sustainable external position. To be compatible with stability, growth must allow the economy to expand at a rate consistent with potential output, without threatening excessive inflation or an unsustainable balance of payments as productive capacity expands.

Because stability in particular has both internal (domestic) and external aspects, economists sometimes describe macroeconomic stability as achieving internal and external balance. As mentioned in Chapter 1, internal balance implies attaining relative price stability (low inflation) and operating near potential output, ideally with low unemployment. External balance involves attaining an external current account balance that can be sustained with projected capital flows, preferably without accumulating excessive ratios of external debt to GDP and debt service payments to exports of goods and services. To be sustainable, growth should be consistent with macroeconomic stability, i.e., both internal and external balance. Stability and growth also require a sound financial system, with well capitalized financial institutions and low levels of nonperforming loans (NPLs) and other signs of financial distress, to avoid the risk of financial crises that can trigger balance of payments difficulties and severe recession.

I. ASSESSING INTERNAL AND EXTERNAL BALANCE: THE SWAN DIAGRAM

Determining whether an economy has attained internal and external balance can be done in various ways. One involves using the so-called Swan Diagram, initially developed by the Australian economist Trevor Swan to show the joint determination of employment and the balance of payments.[1] The Swan Diagram is a two-dimensional graph, with a vertical axis showing the economy's real exchange rate and a horizontal axis indicating real domestic demand (Figure 10.1). On this graph two schedules can be drawn, one representing external balance (labeled "CA") and one representing internal balance (labeled "YY"). The external balance schedule slopes downward because external sustainability with a more appreciated real exchange rate requires lower imports and, thus, less domestic demand. The internal balance schedule slopes upward because higher domestic demand raises the demand for domestic output, unless a more appreciated real exchange rate increases the demand for foreign rather than domestic goods.[2] An economy that has attained internal balance lies on the YY line, while one satisfying external balance lies on the CA line. In each case, the economy's position is determined by its real exchange

---

[1] Swan, T. (1963), "Longer-Run Problems of the Balance of Payments" in *The Australian Economy: A Volume of Readings*, H. Arndt and M. Corden (eds.), (Melbourne: Cheshire), pp. 384–395.

[2] See Wong, C.-H. (2002) "Adjustment and Internal-External Balance," in M. Khan, S. Nsouli, and C.-H. Wong, eds. *Macroeconomic Management: Programs and Policies*, (Washington: International Monetary Fund), Ch. 2, pp. 10–37.

Internal and External Balance

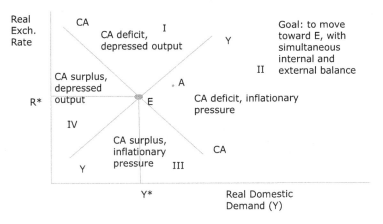

FIGURE 10.1. THE SWAN DIAGRAM

rate and level of real domestic demand. An economy satisfying both conditions will lie at the intersection of the YY and CA schedules (point E in Figure 10.1).

The Swan Diagram is useful because it provides a way to classify economies based on their imbalances. Economies not situated on one or both schedules can be described as lying in one of four quadrants, depending on whether they lie above or below the CA (external balance) schedule and to the right or left of the YY (internal balance) line. Economies situated above the CA schedule (with a real exchange rate too appreciated for external balance, given their level of real domestic demand), to the left of the YY line (with real domestic demand below the level of internal balance) lie in Quadrant I. They have a current account deficit (since they lie above the CA schedule) but depressed output (because they lie to the left of the YY schedule). Economies located above the CA schedule but to the right of the YY line (with real domestic demand too high for internal balance), such as the economy at point *A*, lie in Quadrant II. They have a current account deficit and inflationary pressure. Economies found below the CA schedule but to the right of the YY line lie in Quadrant III. These economies have a current account surplus (since they lie below the CA line) and inflationary pressure. Finally, economies lying below the CA schedule and to the left of the YY line have a current account surplus and depressed output.

TABLE 10.1 TYPICAL ECONOMIES IN EACH QUADRANT OF THE SWAN DIAGRAM

Location	General Condition	Typical Cases
Quadrant I	Current account deficit, depressed output	Many low-income economies
Quadrant II	Current account deficit, excess demand (inflation)	Economies with excessive spending that creates external problems; includes many countries seeking support from the IMF
Quadrant III	Current account surplus, excess demand (inflation)	Oil and mineral exporters where spending strains productive capacity
Quadrant IV	Current account surplus, depressed output	Many slowly growing post-crisis economies in Asia

Each of the four quadrants represents a different type of macroeconomic difficultly (Table 10.1). Economies in Quadrant I, with a current account deficit and depressed output, often have low per capita income or slow growth and lack the competitiveness for a sustainable external position. Many low-income developing economies fall into this situation, and many of them seek assistance from the IMF and the World Bank to accelerate growth in a way that maintains or strengthens their balance of payments. Economies in Quadrant II, with a current account deficit and inflationary pressure, often have overly expansionary fiscal and monetary policies that generate "overheating" (operating above potential output) that spills over into the external sector. Such economies usually need to cool domestic demand by tightening fiscal and monetary policies, often accompanied by exchange rate adjustment. Many countries requesting support from the International Monetary Fund (IMF) fall into this category. In Asia, Pakistan, which experienced severe balance of payments difficulties stemming from expansionary fiscal policies in 2008 and again in 2013, provides such an example. Vietnam, which experienced overheating and a current account deficit in 2008 and again in 2011 but did not approach the IMF for assistance, provides another example. Economies in Quadrant III, with a current account surplus and domestic demand that exceeds internal balance, include many oil producing countries in which heavy spending, often by governments financing public investment, strains available resources, generating inflation. Quadrant IV, representing economies with current account surpluses but depressed demand, includes countries like Japan, where high saving and weak domestic demand have produced a strong current account but little or no economic growth. It also includes countries such as Indonesia, which, during the first few years after the Asian Crisis, experienced persistent current account surpluses and low growth as efforts by firms to repay foreign currency debt kept domestic investment well below pre-crisis levels.

II. USING THE SWAN DIAGRAM TO DEVELOP POLICY RESPONSES TO MACROECONOMIC PROBLEMS

The Swan Diagram can be used to suggest policy responses to various combinations of domestic and external macroeconomic difficulties. For example, countries with current account deficits in Quadrant I may benefit from depreciating their exchange rate, which will boost exports by making them more competitive, thereby strengthening the current account balance, although inflation will likely accelerate. Countries in Quadrant II, which have current account deficits and excess demand, may also benefit from exchange rate depreciation. Here, however, tighter fiscal and monetary policies will probably also be important, to contain inflation and reduce excess demand, although growth will likely decrease in the short run. IMF-supported adjustment programs often include such a combination of domestic and external policies, frequently accompanied by structural reforms to improve efficiency and boost growth over time. Countries in Quadrant III will typically benefit from tighter monetary and fiscal policies, along with structural reforms to raise productive capacity (potential output). Countries in Quadrant IV, by comparison, may benefit from more relaxed monetary and fiscal policies to return the economy to potential output, along with structural reforms to raise potential output and growth over time.

Policy choices involve tradeoffs and may have side effects. For example, exchange rate depreciation will typically improve the current account balance and contribute to long-run growth, although inflation may rise if domestic policies are not tightened. However, depreciation will weaken the balance sheets of banks and firms with large debts in foreign currency, possibly curbing investment (because firms must use profits to recapitalize) and contributing to non-performing loans (NPLs). Thus, economies with substantial foreign currency debt may need to consider bank recapitalization and possibly some support for heavily indebted firms if exchange rate depreciation is part of the policy response. Tighter monetary policy can support the balance of payments by raising interest rates, thereby encouraging capital inflows and discouraging outflows, although investment may decline, slowing growth. Tighter fiscal policy can support the balance of payments by reducing the government's savings-investment imbalance and curbing aggregate demand, thereby reducing imports. By decreasing the government's demand for credit, tightening may also free up credit for the private sector, reducing interest rates and encouraging private investment. A tighter budget, however, may also reduce aggregate demand, possibly outweighing the positive effect of lower interest rates on investment and thus slowing growth. Relaxing fiscal policy, by comparison, should increase demand and growth, at the risk of higher inflation (if the economy is at or near potential output), higher imports, and a weaker current account balance. Well-chosen structural reforms can boost growth by raising efficiency and productivity, possibly even reducing inflation if measures reduce costs. However, structural reforms often require significant time to be implemented and take effect. For example, benefits from the bankruptcy reform introduced in Thailand after the Asian Crisis took several years to be realized, because of the time needed to enact the law, write interpretative regulations, and instruct judges and lawyers on how to use the new system.

Different policy mixes can be used to achieve various results. For example, tighter fiscal and monetary policy can be helpful in reducing inflation, thereby boosting an economy's competitiveness. Exchange rate depreciation can yield the same result, provided that any consequent inflation is limited. Combining depreciation with tighter monetary and fiscal policy will typically boost competitiveness with less need for domestic price adjustment. Thus, combining fiscal and monetary changes with exchange rate adjustment is often a more effective, or less costly, way to attain both internal and external balance. However, economies for which a fixed exchange rate is very important — for example, small economies closely linked to a single, large trading partner, such as Bhutan to India or

TABLE 10.2 CHARACTERISTICS OF DIFFERENT POLICIES FOR STABILIZATION AND GROWTH

Type of Policy	Implementation Speed	Speed of Impact	Comparative Advantage
Monetary Policy	Quick	Often long lags	Reducing inflation
Fiscal Policy	Slow, esp. with separate executive and legislature	Depends; quick for some measures	Fiscal sustainability; boosting growth
Exchange Rate Policy	Quick	Faster for imports	External balance
Structural Policies	Slow to Very slow	Slow	Growth

some Pacific island countries to Australia — may prefer to preserve the exchange rate peg and rely mainly on tightening monetary and fiscal policies. In this case, however, greater monetary and particularly fiscal policy adjustment will likely be required, at a cost of slower growth and more need for structural reform to boost productivity.

The policy mix should also take into consideration the strengths and weaknesses of each measure. Table 10.2 provides a useful summary of these features.

Monetary policy has the advantage of being very fast to implement, as a monetary authority board can change interest rates in a day or even delegate to the chair the ability to do so in between board meetings. For this reason, monetary policy is typically the preferred measure to combat inflation or revive an economy in recession. However, monetary policy typically affects inflation or aggregate demand only with a lag of several quarters — in some cases, as much as 2 years. Thus, monetary authorities generally need to anticipate future circumstances and act in advance, although changes in policy can affect market behavior by changing expectations for inflation and growth.

Fiscal policy typically takes longer to implement than monetary policy, because governments need to formulate a specific set of revenue and spending measures, even if they agree on the broad direction of policy change. Policy change can be particularly slow in countries with separate executive and legislative branches, such as Indonesia, the Philippines, and the United States, because the legislature must approve measures proposed by the President. Occasionally, however, such countries can adjust policy quickly if there is broad consensus on the direction and need for reform. The tax cuts approved in the United States during 2001 and 2009, which were enacted within a few months in response to the threat or experience of severe recession, are an example. The impact of fiscal policy may also come with a lag, depending on the type of measures. However, expanded unemployment benefits and cuts in income taxes that lead to higher disposable income may help boost demand in as little as a few months, as households increase spending, boosting consumption. Fiscal adjustment is particularly useful for addressing problems of public debt sustainability and for providing a more supportive environment for monetary policy. Fiscal policy can also help in spurring economic growth, particularly where expenditure is reallocated to boost growth-enhancing programs for productive infrastructure, health, and education.

Exchange rate adjustment, like monetary policy, has the benefit of being easy to implement, since the monetary authority can typically change the rate in a day. Its speed of impact can vary, however. Often imports adjust faster to exchange rate changes, because exports may be linked to long-term contracts and time may be needed to attract new customers, even with lower prices. Where petroleum products or food represent a high share of imports, even imports may take time to adjust, because depreciation will initially raise the cost of so-called "essential" goods and consumers may initially be reluctant to purchase (or firms may find it difficult to develop) domestically produced substitutes for imported items. Nevertheless, exchange rate adjustment is typically most effective at addressing external imbalances, provided that inflationary responses to depreciation can be contained and balance sheet effects are limited. Exchange rate adjustment is also essential to eliminate parallel markets in foreign exchange.

Structural reforms, as noted earlier, often require a long time to implement. Their impact may also involve long lags, although on occasion regulatory reforms can produce results within a year by facilitating investment. At the same time, structural reforms can be especially useful for promoting growth, particularly in economies where inappropriate and burdensome regulation weaken the investment climate.

III. POLICY MODALITIES AND COORDINATION

Fiscal policy involves changes in revenue and expenditures, with revenue increases and expenditure cuts representing fiscal tightening, while revenue cuts and spending increases constitute relaxation. If tightening is desired, research has shown that, in advanced economies, cutting the government wage bill, subsidies, and transfers has proved more durable than raising taxes or reducing public investment, because cuts in investment projects or maintenance for infrastructure are less visible and easier to disguise via "creative accounting" but are ultimately reversed with need.[3] In emerging market countries, cuts in unproductive spending generally and, where revenues are small share of GDP, higher taxes have both proved to be durable sources of fiscal consolidation.[4]

Monetary policy generally involves using open market operations — typically buying and selling government securities and/or securities of the monetary authority (e.g., central bank bills), or repurchase ("repo") and reverse repurchase ("reverse repo") agreements involving such securities, to banks, since most economies use indirect instruments to implement monetary policy. In a few economies such as Vietnam, the authorities also use changes in reserve requirements, either on their own or in combination with open market operations. Open market operations affect a short-term target, usually the policy interest rate, with increases (resulting from selling securities or repos to banks) tightening policy because liquidity is reduced.[5] The effect of these adjustments on broader objectives — an intermediate target, such as market interest rates, the growth in broad money, or an inflation forecast — depends on the transmission channel for

---

[3] Alesina, A. and R. Perrotti (1996), "Fiscal Adjustments in OECD Countries: Composition and Macroeconomic Effects," NBER Working Paper 5730 (August). Available at: http://www.nber.org/papers/w5730.pdf. Accessed July 16, 2017.

[4] Gupta, S., F. Baldacci, B. Clements, and E. Tiongsen (2003), "What Sustains Fiscal Consolidations in Emerging Market Countries?" IMF Working Paper 03/224 (November). Available at: http://www.imf.org/external/pubs/ft/wp/2003/wp03224.pdf. Accessed July 16, 2017.

[5] In Singapore, as noted earlier, the monetary authorities use the slope and width of the band surrounding the nominal effective exchange rate of the Singapore dollar, which is linked to an unannounced basket of currencies.

monetary policy. When the channel is effective, as in economies with limited excess reserves and reasonable competition among banks, such as Malaysia, market interest rates usually adjust quickly in response. In other economies with less competition among banks and more excess reserves, market interest rates may show little response, particularly if a large share of loans and deposits are in foreign currency. Such has been the experience in the Kyrgyz Republic, where about 44 percent of deposits and 56 percent of loans were in foreign currency in 2016.

Structural reform usually requires changes in laws, regulations, or both. Adjusting prices set by government for key commodities, such as the price of petroleum products or subsidized food items, represents one example. Another is a change in bankruptcy or commercial law or a simplification of the rules for opening a business or laying off workers. Structural reform can also involve administrative changes, such as a reorganization of the judicial system or a rationalization of state-owned enterprises. Except for changing prices, most of these measures require considerable time to implement and have impact, particularly when applicable law provides time for affected parties and the public to comment on proposed regulatory changes. They also tend to be controversial, which also explains why their implementation can be slow.

Effective adjustment usually requires policy coordination. Coordinating fiscal and monetary policy, in particular, is especially important. Expansionary fiscal policy can negate monetary tightening or lead to sharp reductions in private investment, as a result of crowding out. Similarly, tight monetary policy can limit the effectiveness of fiscal expansion aimed at promoting growth. Thus, the two policies work better when oriented in the same direction. However, the two policies attain their objective in different ways. Fiscal expansion, for example, typically raises output by boosting consumption and public investment, often at the expense of private investment, as a larger budget deficit raises interest rates, crowding out some private borrowing. Monetary expansion, by comparison, typically raises output by lowering interest rates and encouraging more private borrowing, thereby boosting private investment and consumption. For this reason, tightening fiscal policy to allow a more relaxed monetary policy can sometimes be useful, particularly if private investment has been weak. This is one reason why, in the United States, the Clinton Administration encouraged the Congress to approve a tax increase in 1993, in the hope that tighter fiscal policy would encourage the Federal Reserve Board to lower interest rates, which it ultimately did, starting in July 1995.

Coordinating monetary and regulatory policy can also be important for cooling an overheated financial sector, for example, if speculative behavior leads to sharp increases in equity (stock) or housing prices. Monetary tightening can be a blunt way of responding to so-called "bubbles" in the financial sector, cooling demand generally and raising unemployment. The resulting higher interest rates can also attract capital inflows and appreciate the exchange rate, reducing exports. Thus, tightening financial sector regulation often provides a more effective response. Regulatory measures to cool overheated asset markets can include reducing or limiting the loan-to-value ratio for housing and equity loans, raising bank capital requirements (to reduce the availability of funds for lending), limiting loan exposure (in volume or percent of lending) to sectors such as real estate that are prone to speculative activity, and adjusting collateral and margin requirements, particularly for loans to purchase equity (stock). Some economists have advocated establishing counter-cyclical rules for the above measures, so that maximum loan-to-value ratios automatically fall, and bank capital and margin requirements automatically rise, when an economy approaches potential output and then reverse automatically as an economy starts to contract.

During severe recessions, when monetary policy may have little impact because interest rates are already low and weak balance sheets may deter banks from lending and limit the demand for loans, fiscal policy may prove more effective at reviving economic activity. But the ability to use fiscal policy during recession may require tightening policy when the economy is strong, running primary surpluses and reducing the public debt-to-GDP ratio, to create the fiscal space for expansionary policy when the economy contracts. Fiscal policy can also be made more effective by expanding the use of so-called "automatic stabilizers," measures that automatically increase demand when an economy weakens and contract when an economy strengthens. Income and consumption taxes typically do this on the revenue side of the budget. On the expenditure side, creating more programs in which spending expands automatically when the unemployment rate or another cyclical indicator automatically crosses a threshold, for example, extending the duration of unemployment benefits or broadening eligibility for food subsidies, would have this effect.[6]

Addressing supply-side shocks, such as rise in petroleum or food prices, poses special difficulties, because the rise in prices raises inflation while curbing growth. Macroeconomic policy faces a dilemma, because tightening policy will curb inflation at the cost of lower growth, while avoiding action may entrench inflationary expectations. In this situation, economists have traditionally advocated allowing the first round of increases to pass through the economy but tightening policy if inflation expectations rise. Targeted relief from price increases can be given to low-income households, but not general subsidies, which are inefficient and more expensive. Measures can also be taken to boost alternative sources of supply and encourage conservation, to help slow inflation by limiting demand. During the summer of 2008, following a sharp rise in petroleum and food prices in the first half of the year, many emerging market countries raised interest rates after initially staying passive. A few countries reduced general subsidies. However, others cut excises to limit price increases, and some food exporters banned exports, to conserve supplies for their own residents. When the Global Financial Crisis spread and commodity prices fell, many countries used the occasion to reverse earlier price increases for petroleum products.

IV. USING MACROECONOMIC INDICATORS FOR ANALYSIS AND POLICY PRESCRIPTION: THREE CASE STUDIES

A. Pakistan, 2013

Table 10.3, drawn from an IMF staff report,[7] presents a number of macroeconomic indicators for Pakistan, estimated and forecast as of mid-to-late 2013.

---

[6]See Blanchard, O., G. Dell'Ariccia, and P. Mauro (2010), "Rethinking Macroeconomic Policy," IMF Staff Position Note (February), and *Journal of Money, Credit and Banking*, 42 (September), pp. 199–215, Available at: http://onlinelibrary.wiley.com/doi/10.1111/ j.1538-4616.2010.00334.x/full. Accessed July 16, 2017.

[7]IMF (2013), *Pakistan: 2013 Article IV Consultation and Request for an Extended Arrangement under the Extended Fund Facility* (Washington: September), IMF Country Report 13/287.

The table shows that, in mid-2013, at the end of its 2012/2013 fiscal year, Pakistan faced declining growth, notable inflation (although slightly less than in previous years), and a savings-investment (current account) balance of −1 percent of GDP, mainly because of a large government budget deficit, equivalent to 8.5 percent of GDP. Although gross capital formation, at 14.2 percent of GDP, was not high, gross national saving was even lower, at 13.3 percent of GDP. This reflected government dissaving of 5.2 percent of GDP, as revenue and grants totaled only 13.2 percent of GDP, with tax revenue only 9.7 percent of GDP. Although external debt, at 26.9 percent of GDP, was not so large, total public debt equaled 66.6 percent of GDP, well above prudent levels for an emerging market economy. This reflected a large primary fiscal deficit, equal to 3.9 percent of GDP. Besides a current account deficit, the external sector recorded a net capital outflow, and gross official reserves fell by more than 40 percent to US$6 billion, equivalent only to 1.4 months of imports.

A forecast of the economy by IMF staff showed that maintaining existing policies would lead to further, large fiscal deficits, a steady rise in the public debt to GDP ratio, and a continued decline in reserves to a projected US$2.3 billion at the end of fiscal year 2013/2014, barely equal to 0.4 months of imports. Pakistan thus faced the possibility of a balance of payments and currency crisis. Under these circumstances, Pakistan approached the IMF for financial assistance and agreed to a major adjustment program involving fiscal tightening, higher electricity charges, a reorientation of monetary policy toward building reserves, and major structural reforms, including improved tax administration, trade liberalization, and measures to improve the investment climate. Pakistan ultimately made significant progress under the arrangement, tripling its external reserves, slowing inflation to 3 percent, and reducing both its overall and primary fiscal deficits. However, public debt remained high at 64.8 percent of GDP, and growth was sluggish at about 3 percent of GDP.[8]

---

[8]See IMF (2016), *Pakistan: Twelfth and Final Review under the Extended Arrangement, Request for Waivers of Nonperformance of Performance Criteria, and Proposal for Post Program Monitoring* (Washington: October), IMF Country Report 16/325, Table 3, p. 32.

TABLE 10.3 PAKISTAN: MEDIUM-TERM BASELINE MACROECONOMIC FRAMEWORK, 2009/10–2017/18

		Estimates			Baseline Projections				
	2009/2010	2010/2011	2011/2012	2012/2013	2013/2014	2014/2015	2015/2016	2016/2017	2017/2018
Output and prices									
(Annual changes in percent)									
Real GDP at factor cost	2.6	3.7	4.4	3.6	3.3	3.1	3.0	3.0	3.0
Consumer prices (period average)	10.1	13.7	11.0	7.4	8.2	10.8	11.3	11.8	11.8
(In percent of GDP)									
Saving and investment balance	-2.2	0.1	-2.1	-1.0	-1.6	-1.1	-1.5	-1.6	-1.5
Government	-5.9	-6.7	-8.4	-8.5	-7.8	-8.0	-8.7	-9.8	-10.4
Non-government (including public sector enterprises)	3.7	6.8	6.3	7.5	6.2	6.9	7.2	8.3	8.9
Gross national saving	13.6	14.2	12.9	13.3	12.5	12.3	11.7	11.5	11.6
Government	-2.4	-4.2	-5.1	-5.2	-4.5	-4.8	-5.5	-6.6	-7.1
Non-government (including public sector enterprises)	16.0	18.4	17.9	18.4	16.9	17.1	17.1	18.1	18.7
Gross capital formation	15.8	14.1	14.9	14.2	14.1	13.3	13.2	13.0	13.0
Government	3.5	2.5	3.3	3.3	3.3	3.2	3.2	3.2	3.2
Non-government (including public sector enterprises)	12.3	11.6	11.6	10.9	10.8	10.1	9.9	9.8	9.8
(In billions of U.S. dollars, unless otherwise indicated)									
Balance of payments									
Current account balance	-3.9	0.2	-4.7	-2.3	-3.8	-2.5	-3.5	-3.6	-3.5
Net capital flows 1/	5.2	2.3	1.4	-0.1	3.2	3.2	4.0	3.5	3.3

Of which: foreign direct investment 2/	2.2	1.6	0.8	1.4	2.1	2.2	2.8	2.6	2.7
Gross official reserves	13.0	14.8	10.8	6.0	2.3	1.7	2.2	2.0	1.8
In months of imports 3/	3.6	3.6	2.7	1.4	0.5	0.4	0.4	0.4	0.4
External debt (in percent of GDP)	34.7	31.1	29.1	26.9	26.0	25.9	26.5	26.8	25.7
(In percent of GDP)									
Public finances									
Revenue and grants	14.3	12.6	13.1	13.2	13.0	12.8	12.7	12.1	12.1
Of which: tax revenue	10.1	9.5	10.3	9.7	9.8	9.8	9.8	9.8	9.8
Expenditure (inc. stat discr.), *of which:*	20.2	19.5	21.5	21.7	20.8	20.8	21.4	22.0	22.5
Current	16.7	16.5	17.8	17.0	17.4	17.6	18.2	18.7	19.2
Development (incl. net lending)	3.8	2.6	3.4	4.7	3.3	3.2	3.3	3.3	3.3
Primary balance 4/	–1.6	–3.1	–4.0	–3.9	–3.0	–3.1	–3.1	–3.8	–3.8
Overall fiscal balance 4/	–5.9	–6.9	–8.4	–8.5	–7.8	–8.0	–8.7	–9.9	–10.4
Total public debt (including obligations to the IMF)	61.5	59.5	63.8	66.6	69.2	71.9	75.5	79.9	82.2

Sources: Pakistani authorities for historical data: and Fund staff estimates and projections.
1/ Difference between the overall balance and the current account balance.
2/ Including privatization.
3/ In months of next year's imports of goods and services.
4/ Including grants.

Source: IMF (2013), *Pakistan: 2013 Article IV Consultation and Request for an Extended Arrangement under the Extended Fund Facility* (Washington: September), IMF Country Report 13/287, Table 2.

B. Iceland, 2008

Table 10.4, drawn from a 2008 IMF staff report,[9] provides important macroeconomic indicators for Iceland at the end of 2007 and IMF staff projections for 2008 and 2009. By 2007, real GDP growth had slowed to just
under 5 percent, with domestic demand declining by 1.5 percent after
several years of increases. The unemployment rate remained low at 1 percent, with consumer price inflation notable at 5 percent, although less than
in 2006. The fiscal position suggested stability, with an overall surplus
equal to 5.5 percent of GDP and a structural balance at 1.5 percent of
GDP. However, the monetary accounts suggested serious risks, with total
credit expanding by 56.6 percent, of which only half represented growth
in credit to residents, following several years of credit growth exceeding
20 percent. Data for the external sector pointed to more difficulties, with
the current account deficit estimated at 14.6 percent of GDP and external
debt equivalent to more than five times (551.5) percent of GDP. Table 10.5,
which provides fiscal data for Iceland, showed that gross public debt
equaled less than 29 percent of GDP. Thus, most of the external debt came
from the private sector. Indeed, Iceland's banks had accumulated massive
obligations to non-residents, as a result of attracting huge deposits from
abroad and using these to fund a variety of loans, both domestic and
foreign. If any significant fraction of these loans became non-performing,
Iceland's banks were likely to fail, leaving the country with not only a
domestic banking crisis but also massive external obligations. This, in
fact, occurred during 2008, at which point Iceland approached the IMF for
financial assistance. An IMF-supported adjustment program helped
stabilize Iceland's economy, ultimately enabling the country to return to
world financial markets after a severe depreciation of its currency and
substantial strengthening of financial regulation.[10]

---

[9]IMF (2008), *Iceland: Request for Stand-By Arrangement — Staff Report; Staff
Supplement; Press release on the Executive Board Discussion; and Statement by the
Executive Director for Iceland* (Washington: November), IMF Country Report 08/362,
Table 1, p. 26.

[10]Katsimi, M., and G. Zoega (2015), "The Greek and Icelandic IMF Programmes
Compared," VOXEU (Accessed on November 19, 2015), Available at: http://voxeu.org/
article/imf-programmes-greece-vs-iceland.

TABLE 10.4   ICELAND: SELECTED ECONOMIC INDICATORS, 2003–2009

	2003	2004	2005	2006	2007 est.	2008 staff proj.	2009 staff proj.
				(Percentage change unless otherwise noted)			
National Accounts (constant prices)							
Gross domestic product	2.4	7.7	7.4	4.4	4.9	1.6	–9.6
Total domestic demand	5.6	10.0	16.0	9.9	–1.5	–9.1	–19.7
Private consumption	6.1	7.0	12.9	4.4	4.3	–8.7	–23.7
Public consumption	1.8	2.2	3.5	4.0	4.2	3.2	2.9
Gross fixed investment	11.1	28.1	35.7	20.4	–13.7	–19.7	–33.6
Export of goods and services	1.6	8.4	7.2	–5.0	18.1	12.1	1.9
Imports of goods and services	10.7	14.5	29.4	10.2	–1.4	–15.2	–23.1
Output gap 1/	–4.7	–1.2	2.3	3.2	4.8	4.6	–5.4
Selected Indicators							
Nominal GDP (bln ISK)	841.3	928.9	1,026.4	1,167.9	1,293.2	1,490.1	1,495.1
Central bank gross reserves (bln ISK)	58.1	65.6	67.3	167.8	162.8	686.5	562.7

(Continued)

TABLE 10.4 *(Continued)*

	2003	2004	2005	2006	2007 est.	2008 staff proj.	2009 staff proj.
Unemployment rate 2/	3.4	3.1	2.1	1.3	1.0	1.4	5.7
Real disposable income per capita	–1.7	3.8	6.6	–2.0	5.4	—	—
Consumer price index	2.1	3.2	4.0	6.8	5.0	12.7	14.3
Nominal wage index	5.6	4.6	6.5	9.1	9.3	6.7	2.3
Nominal effective exchange rate 3/	6.2	1.8	10.4	–10.7	2.8	—	—
Real effective exchange rate (CPI) 3/	6.3	2.8	12.7	–6.8	5.7	—	—
Terms of trade	–4.1	–1.3	1.0	3.5	0.1	—	—
Money and Credit							
Deposit money bank credit (end-period)	26.7	41.9	76.0	44.4	56.6	—	—
of which to residents (end-period)	20.0	37.2	54.7	33.6	28.3	—	—
Broad money (end-period)	17.5	15.0	23.2	19.6	56.4	—	—
CBI policy rate (period average) 4/	5.3	8.2	10.5	14.1	13.8	—	—
Public Finance (in percent of GDP)							
General government 5/							
Revenue	44.6	45.9	48.8	49.7	50.0	45.3	41.7

Expenditure	47.5	45.9	44.0	43.4	44.5	45.5	55.2
Balance	-2.8	0.0	4.9	6.3	5.5	-0.2	-13.5
Structural balance	0.5	1.0	2.9	3.5	1.5	-3.4	-8.7
Balance of Payments (in percent of GDP)							
Current account balance	-4.8	-9.8	-16.1	-25.4	-14.6	-10.7	1.0
Trade balance (goods)	-1.9	-3.9	-9.1	-13.4	-6.8	1.0	6.4
Financial and capital account	1.2	12.7	13.5	36.4	13.2	-119.7	-11.4
o/w: reserve assets 6/	-2.8	-1.5	-0.5	-7.3	-0.5	-17.6	4.1
Net errors and omissions	3.6	-2.9	2.6	-11.0	1.4	2.4	0.0
Gross external debt	139.6	179.1	285.7	445.9	551.5	670.2	159.5
Central bank gross reserves (in months of imports of goods and services) 7/	2.2	2.1	1.8	3.4	3.3	11.0	9.9

Sources: Statistics Iceland: Central Bank of Iceland: Ministry of Finance, and staff estimates.

1/ Staff estimates. Actual minus potential ouput. in percent of potential ouput.
2/ In percent of labor force.
3/ A Positive (negative) sign indicates an appreciation (depreciation).
4/ Data prior to 2007 refers to annual rate of return. 2007 and on, refers to nominal interest rate.
5/ National account basis.
6/ A Positive (negative) sign indicates a decrease (increase) in gross official foreign reserves.
7/ Excluding imports from the construction of hydropower facility and smelters in 2003–2004.

Source: IMF (2008), *Iceland: Request for Stand-By Arrangement — Staff Report*, Table 1.

TABLE 10.5   ICELAND: SUMMARY OPERATIONS OF THE GENERAL GOVERNMENT, 2007–2013 (IN PERCENT OF GDP)

		Prel.			Staff Projection			
	2006	2007	2008	2009	2010	2011	2012	2013
Total revenue 1/	49.7	50.0	45.3	41.7	43.0	44.0	44.3	44.5
Current revenue	48.0	48.2	43.8	40.0	41.1	42.1	42.4	42.7
of which:								
Direct taxes	21.6	21.8	19.2	17.5	19.1	19.2	19.3	19.3
of which:								
Corporate income tax	2.4	2.7	1.7	1.3	2.0	2.0	2.0	2.0
Personal income tax	13.9	13.9	12.6	12.4	13.1	13.1	13.2	13.2
Social security contributions	3.3	3.1	2.8	2.8	2.9	2.9	2.9	2.9
Capital tax and rental income	1.9	2.2	2.1	1.1	1.1	1.2	1.2	1.3
Indirect taxes	19.8	19.2	17.0	15.2	14.7	15.6	16.0	16.3
Interest income	1.7	2.3	2.5	2.2	2.3	2.1	2.0	1.9
Other current income	4.8	4.9	5.1	5.1	5.1	5.1	5.1	5.1
Capital revenue	1.8	1.8	1.5	1.7	1.9	1.9	1.9	1.9
Total expenditure (incl. measures needed 1/)	43.4	44.5	45.5	55.2	53.6	51.3	46.0	42.6
Current expenditure	38.9	39.7	39.7	48.7	50.1	49.5	46.4	44.9
of which:								
Operational cost	27.7	27.7	27.2	29.9	30.6	29.8	29.0	28.4
of which:								

Wages and salaries	15.3	15.3	16.2	17.3	—	—	—	—
Purchase of goods and services	7.3	7.2	9.5	10.8	—	—	—	—
Interest expenditure	2.2	2.6	2.1	7.3	7.6	8.3	6.5	6.1
Subsidies	1.7	1.8	1.6	1.6	1.7	1.6	1.5	1.5
Income transfers	6.3	6.4	7.3	8.4	8.6	8.2	7.9	7.5
Other expense	1.0	1.2	1.4	1.6	1.6	1.6	1.5	1.4
Capital expenditure	4.6	4.8	5.8	6.5	6.7	6.4	6.1	5.9
Discretionary measures needed 1/	0.0	0.0	0.0	0.0	-3.2	-4.7	-6.6	-8.2
Primary balance	6.7	5.8	-0.6	-8.5	-5.2	-1.1	2.8	6.2
Overall balance	6.3	5.5	-0.2	-13.5	-10.5	-7.3	-1.7	2.0
Financing	-6.3	-5.5	0.2	13.5	10.5	7.3	1.7	-2.0
Net domestic financing 2/	—	—	0.2	13.5	10.5	7.3	1.7	-2.0
Net external financing	—	—	0.0	0.0	0.0	0.0	0.0	0.0
Debt position								
General government gross debt 3/	30.1	28.9	108.9	108.6	104.4	105.7	100.7	92.6
General government net debt 3/	7.8	7.3	90.6	97.0	92.8	94.8	90.5	83.0
Cyclically adjusted 4/								
Primary revenue	46.5	45.7	41.6	41.4	41.6	42.5	42.5	42.7
Primary expenditure	42.6	43.9	45.4	45.4	43.1	41.3	38.8	36.5

(Continued)

TABLE 10.5   *(Continued)*

	Prel.			Staff Projection				
	2006	**2007**	**2008**	**2009**	**2010**	**2011**	**2012**	**2013**
Primary balance	3.9	1.8	−3.8	−3.9	−1.4	1.1	3.7	6.1
Total revenue 5/	48.3	48.1	44.2	43.6	43.7	44.5	44.4	44.5
Total expenditure	44.8	46.6	47.6	52.2	50.2	49.3	45.2	42.6
Overall balance	3.5	1.5	−3.4	−8.7	−6.5	−4.8	−0.7	1.9
Memorandum items:								
Output gap 6/	3.2	4.8	4.6	−5.4	−6.3	−3.8	−1.8	0.0
Change in structural primary balance	−0.2	−2.1	−5.6	−0.1	2.5	2.6	2.5	2.4
Bank restructuring debt	0.0	0.0	25.8	25.8	25.7	24.2	22.7	21.3
Assumed liability to honor foreign depositor obligations 3/	0.0	0.0	47.0	32.8	18.7	17.7	16.5	15.5
Central Bank recapitalization costs	0.0	0.0	0.0	10.0	10.0	9.4	8.8	8.3

Sources: Ministry of Finance: and Fund staff estimates and calculations.

1/ Measures needed have been reflected as expenditure measures, but could also include revenue measures.
2/ In 2009, it is assumed that the government draws down on its deposits at the central bank to finance half of the deficit.
3/ Includes the liability assumed by the government from the deposit insurance to honor foreign depositor obligations.
4/ In percent of potential GDP.
5/ Structural revenue estimates were adjusted to account for the impact of the asset boom/bust price cycle.
6/ Actual output less potential in percent of potential.

Source: IMF (2008), *Iceland: Request for Stand-By Arrangement — Staff Report*, Table 5.

C. Russian Federation, 2015

Table 10.6, drawn from an IMF staff report on the Russian Federation,[11] presents key macroeconomic indicators for the Russian Federation at the end of 2015, with IMF staff projections for 2016 and 2017. The data show problems in three areas: the real sector, oil prices, and the exchange rate. Growth slowed to 0.7 percent in 2014 and turned sharply negative in 2015, with real GDP falling by 3.7 percent, while average inflation doubled to 15.5 percent from a year earlier. The overall deficit of the general government expanded to 3.5 percent of GDP from 1.1 percent in 2014, as revenue slipped to 32.8 percent of GDP while expenditure rose nearly 1 percentage point to 36.3 percent of GDP. The deterioration in revenue reflected the plunge in the average oil price from US$96 per barrel to US$51, as the non-oil fiscal balance showed little change at 11.7 percent of GDP. The drop in petroleum prices led to a 32 percent decline in exports, from US$498 billion to US$340 billion, as the volume of oil and gas exports increased. A sharp decline in imports of goods helped keep the current account balance from worsening. However, gross reserves, which had fallen sharply in 2014 as the authorities struggled to limit the depreciation in the ruble, declined further, to US$368 billion, with the ruble depreciating to 60.9 per U.S. dollar, a decline of about 37 percent. With the sharp nominal depreciation, the real effective exchange rate depreciated by about 17 percent, despite inflation. Because of the sharp compression of imports, reserves were equivalent to 15.7 months of imports at the end of 2015, up from 10.8 months a year earlier. However, the decline in imports helps explain the drop in real GDP, as fewer imports were available for consumption or as inputs to production. Under these circumstances, the IMF's Executive Directors urged the Russian Federation to pursue fiscal adjustment and use the real depreciation rate to diversify economic activity, supported by institutional reforms to improve the business climate.[12]

---

[11]IMF (2016), *Russian Federation: Staff Report for the 2016 Article IV Consultation — Press Release; and Staff Report* (Washington: June), IMF Country Report 16/229.

[12]*Id.*, Press Release.

TABLE 10.6   RUSSIAN FEDERATION: SELECTED MACROECONOMIC INDICATORS, 2013–2017

	2013	2014	2015	2016	2017
				Projections	
			(Annual percent change)		
Production and prices					
Real GDP	1.3	0.7	–3.7	–1.2	1.0
Consumer prices					
Period average	6.8	7.8	15.5	7.5	5.7
End of period	6.5	11.4	12.9	6.6	5.2
GDP deflator	4.8	9.0	7.7	7.4	5.5
Public sector[1]		(Percent of GDP)			
General government					
Net lending/borrowing (overall balance)	–1.2	–1.1	–3.5	–3.7	–1.6
Revenue	34.4	34.3	32.8	31.2	32.2
Expenditures	35.6	35.4	36.3	34.9	33.8
Primary balance	–0.6	–0.4	–2.7	–2.7	–0.4
Nonoil balance	–11.1	–11.5	–11.7	–10.0	–8.3
Federal government					
Net lending/borrowing (overall balance)	–0.5	–0.4	–2.4	–3.2	–1.5
Nonoil balance	–9.8	–10.1	–9.8	–9.0	–7.5

(Annual percent change)

Money					
Base money	8.0	6.3	-4.3	4.6	5.4
Ruble broad money	14.6	2.2	11.5	6.8	7.7
External sector					
Export volumes	1.9	0.1	2.6	1.1	2.3
Oil	2.7	0.1	10.9	-1.3	-1.6
Gas	9.9	-11.3	13.8	6.0	2.7
Non-energy	5.8	7.9	-5.5	2.2	6.4
Import volumes	3.2	-6.9	-28.4	-3.6	2.7

(Billions of U.S. dollars; unless otherwise indicated)

External sector					
Total merchandise exports, fob	523.3	497.8	339.6	299.0	332.2
Total merchandise imports, fob	-341.3	-308.0	-194.0	-180.1	-185.9
External current account	34.1	59.5	65.8	51.3	69.3
External current account (in percent of GDP)	1.5	2.9	5.0	4.0	4.9
Gross international reserves					
Billions of U.S. dollars	509.6	385.5	368.4	373.1	387.8
Months of imports[2]	13.0	10.8	15.7	17.2	17.3

(Continued)

TABLE 10.6   *(Continued)*

	2013	2014	2015	2016 projections	2017
Percent of short-term debt	251	302	478	257	274
Memorandum items:					
Nominal GDP (billions of U.S.D)	2,231	2,031	1,326	1,270	1,410
Exchange rate (rubles per U.S.D., period average)	31.8	38.4	60.9	—	—
World oil price (U.S.D per barrel)	104.1	96.2	50.8	42.2	48.8
Real effective exchange rate (average percent change)	1.8	−8.5	−17.4	—	—

Sources: Russian authorities; and IMF staff estimates.

1/ Cash basis.

2/ In months of imports of goods and non-factor services.

Source: IMF (2016), *Russian Federation: Staff Report for the 2016 Article IV Consultation — Press Release.*

V. PROMOTING STABILIZATION AND GROWTH THROUGH FINANCIAL SECTOR REFORM

Many recent crises have shown that macroeconomic stability is not enough for general economic health if the financial system is weak. Thus, a sound financial sector is critical for stability and growth. Attaining a sound financial sector in turn requires strengthening laws, regulations, and standards to increase the health of the financial system. Financial repression, in the form of interest rate ceilings and directed lending that keep the financial system from performing effectively, must also be remedied.

Strengthening the financial sector requires creating and enforcing appropriate prudential standards for the safety and soundness of financial institutions. In addition, financial sector institutions need appropriate regulation. For commercial banks, appropriate measures could include the following:

• Strengthening the prudential framework for capital adequacy, loan classification and provisioning, loan concentration, licensing, and the entry and exit of banks from the domestic market;
• Establishing and maintaining an effective deposit insurance system that protects small to medium depositors while maintaining exposure for large depositors, to avoid incentives for risky behavior by banks;
• Establishing and maintaining credible supervisory agencies that conduct both off-site and on-site inspections; and
• Ensuring adequate competition among banks, through measures to limit concentration, reduce the favored position of state-owned banks (in some cases by privatization), and allow foreign banks to enter the market.

As noted earlier, financial regulators may also consider establishing "cyclical regulatory tools" whose values vary over the business cycle. For example, the maximum loan-to-value ratio, particularly for housing, could be raised when the economy is strong and house prices begin to rise quickly, and then lowered when the economy weakens. Similarly, capital requirements can be made counter-cyclical, rising in good times to deter speculative lending and declining as the economy slows to make it easier for banks to lend. Requirements for loan collateral and margin, particularly for purchases of stock (equity), could also be made counter-cyclical. In addition, the authorities could limit the share of bank lending to sectors such as real estate that are prone to speculative bubbles.

Adequate regulation also requires close attention to NPLs in the banking system. Financial regulators should monitor their extent and their impact on bank capital. When NPLs expand significantly, regulators should explore appropriate ways to recapitalize banks that are considered fundamentally sound. Methods can include removing bad loans from bank balance sheets and providing fresh capital, along with measures such as restructuring and the removal of bank management to keep recapitalization from encouraging further inappropriate lending ("moral hazard"). When banks are recapitalized, the government should take into account the impact on the government budget, for example, if funds are needed for an asset management company to hold troubled loans. If state banks are involved, the authorities may consider the appropriateness of privatization as part of the response.

Where financial repression is contributing to an unsound financial sector, regulators should explore ways to address it. This could include eliminating, if they exist, directed lending, interest rate controls, restrictions on entry into the financial services industry, a lack of bank autonomy, extensive state ownership of banks or unfair competition between these institutions and private banks, foreign exchange controls and other restrictions on international capital flows, and taxes on financial transactions such as checks that weaken the ability of the financial system to provide intermediation.

In some countries, central bank reform is itself an issue. To enhance their credibility and improve their functioning, central banks should be granted adequate control over monetary policy instruments and encouraged to use indirect rather than direct instruments for monetary policy. The role of the monetary authorities in financial sector supervision and their relationship with other financial regulators, such as a deposit insurance system or capital market regulators, may also need clarification. In addition, whether and when the monetary authorities can serve as a lender of last resort should be defined.

Where appropriate, the authorities may consider careful liberalization of the banking system. Liberalization can bring benefits, in the form of financial innovation and a more efficient allocation of financial assets. However, the experience of the U.S. Savings and Loan Crisis of the late 1970s and early 1980s, the Nordic Banking Crisis of the early 1990s, and the Asian Crisis of 1997–1998 has shown that deregulation without sufficient safeguards can lead to financial crisis. Thus, liberalization needs to be appropriately sequenced (typically, domestic before international liberalization) and implemented in the right macroeconomic environment, normally when the economy is growing but not overheating. Strengthening financial sector regulation, to counteract the incentives for liberalized institutions to assume too much risk, is often a precondition for successful deregulation. Liberalizing capital controls should normally come toward the end of the reform process, after stabilizing the economy, establishing a sound system of prudential supervision and regulation, and deregulating domestic financial markets.

If a financial crisis occurs, macroeconomic stabilization may require providing temporary support for financial institutions, to avoid a massive economic contraction. The authorities may have to liberalize access to the central bank's lender of last resort facility, as the U.S. Federal Reserve Board did during 2007 and 2008. They may also need to recapitalize and, in some cases, assume control of systemically important financial institutions. Fiscal and monetary policy will need to be carefully coordinated, with greater use of fiscal policy if interest rates approach zero and the deterioration of bank and corporate balance sheets limits the ability of monetary expansion to spur private lending. During the 2007–2009 Financial Crisis, many advanced economies lowered policy interest rates and used "quantitative easing" to support lending. This included providing liquidity support to institutions other than commercial banks, accepting non-traditional collateral, and buying government debt in economies where this was unusual. Many emerging market economies temporarily provided full deposit insurance, to avoid the risk of bank runs. These and other measures could be appropriate responses to a future crisis.

VI. SUMMARY

Using macroeconomic and structural policies to address problems and attain particular objectives requires a proper assessment of the macroeconomic situation. A good understanding of macroeconomic accounts is essential for this task. So, too, is an appreciation of macroeconomic stability and the circumstances that can lead to internal and external imbalances. The Swan Diagram can help in this assessment. When problems arise, officials should keep in mind the strengths and weaknesses of different kinds of measures, in particular changes in monetary, fiscal, exchange rate, and structural policies. While monetary policy is most often used to address imbalances in normal times, during financial crises fiscal policy may prove more effective, particularly when the policy interest rate has been reduced almost to zero. In addition, exchange rate adjustment may be essential for addressing a systemic current account deficit that reflects underlying problems of competitiveness. Structural reforms, including a reallocation of fiscal expenditure toward productive investment, health, and education programs, can be especially important for boosting economic growth. At the same time, these reforms typically require time to be introduced and take effect. Policy making is particularly challenging during supply-side shocks, when a rise in commodity prices forces the authorities to choose between letting prices rise, to avoid cutting output, and tightening policy to limit inflation, at the cost of further economic slowdown.

While monetary, fiscal, exchange rate, and structural policies remain the principal means for responding to macroeconomic problems, officials should remember that stability and growth also require a sound financial system. Strengthening the financial system through appropriate supervision and regulation and eliminating financial repression are thus part of the toolkit for attaining stability and growth.

BIBLIOGRAPHY

Alesina, A. and R. Perrotti (1996), "Fiscal Adjustments in OECD Countries: Composition and Macroeconomic Effects," NBER Working Paper 5730 (August), http://www.nber.org/papers/w5730.pdf.

Bangko Sentral NG Pilipinas (2017), *Inflation Report, 4th Quarter 2016*, http://www.bsp.gov.ph/downloads/Publications/2016/IR4qtr_2016.pdf.

Bank Negara Malaysia (2014), *Quarterly Bulletin, Second Quarter 2014*, http://www.bnm.gov.my/files/publication/qb/2014/Q2/2Q2014_fullbook_en.pdf.

Bank Negara Malaysia (2016), "Monetary Policy Statement", Ref. No. 07/16/03 (July 13), http://www.bnm.gov.my/index.php?ch=en_press&pg=en_press&ac=4213&lang=en.

Bank Negara Malaysia (2017), *Quarterly Bulletin, Fourth Quarter 2016*, http://www.bnm.gov.my/files/publication/qb/2016/Q4/4Q2016_fullbook_en.pdf.

Bank of England, Monetary Policy Committee, "The transmission mechanism of monetary policy," Available at www.bankofengland.co.uk/publications/Documents/other/monetary/montrans.pdf .

Blanchard, Olivier, Giovanni Dell'Ariccia, and Paolo Mauro (2010), "Rethinking Macroeconomic Policy," IMF Staff Position Note (February), and *Journal of Money, Credit and Banking*, vol. 42 (September), pp. 199–215, http://onlinelibrary.wiley.com/doi/10.1111/j.1538-4616.2010.00334.x/full.

Blejer, M. and A. Cheasty (1991), *How to Measure the Fiscal Deficit* (Washington: IMF).

Calafell, Javier, and Rodolfo Padilla del Bosque (2002), "The Ratio of International Reserves to Short-Term External Debt as Indicator of External Vulnerability: Some Lessons from the Experience of Mexico and Other

Emerging Economies," https://www.g24.org/wp-content/uploads/2016/01/ THE-RATIO-OF-INTERNATIONAL-RESERVES-TO-SHORT-TERM.pdf.

Center on Budget and Policy Priorities (2016), "Policy Basics: Federal Tax Expenditures," http://www.cbpp.org/sites/default/files/atoms/files/policybasics-taxexpenditures.pdf .

Christiano, Lawrence, and others (2009), "When Is the Government Spending Multiplier Large?" NBER Working Paper 15394 (Cambridge, MA: October).

Commission on Growth and Development (2008), *Growth Report: Strategies for Sustained Growth and Inclusive Development* (Washington: World Bank), http://siteresources.worldbank.org/EXTPREMNET/Resources/489960-1338997241035/Growth_Commission_Final_Report.pdf.

Commission on Growth and Development (2008), "Highlights of the Growth Report."

Congressional Budget and Impoundment Control Act of 1974 (Pub. L. No. 93–344).

Fischer, S. (1993), "Role of Macroeconomic Factors in Growth," *J. of Monetary Economics*, vol. 32 (3), pp. 485–512.

Fraga, A. (2000), "Monetary Policy during the Transition to a Floating Exchange Rate: Brazil's Recent Experience," *Finance & Development*, Vol. 37 (1), March, http://www.imf.org/external/pubs/ft/fandd/2000/03/fraga.htm.

Govil, R. (2005), Presentation on Exchange Rate Regimes.

Greene, J. (2001), Overview of Macroeconomic Adjustment and Structural Reform," unpub., https://rbidocs.rbi.org.in/rdocs/content/PDFs/88174.pdf.

Greene, J. (2012), *Public Finance: An International Perspective* (Singapore: World Scientific).

Gupta, S.,E. Baldacci, B. Clements, and E. Tiongson (2003), "What Sustains Fiscal Consolidations in Emerging Market Countries?" IMF Working Paper 03/224 (November), http://www.imf.org/external/pubs/ft/wp/2003/wp03224.pdf.

Hammar, K. (2015), "IMF Survey: Iceland Makes Strong Recovery from 2008 Crisis" (March), http://www.imf.org/en/news/articles/2015/09/28/04/53/socar031315a.

Heller, Peter (2005), "Understanding Fiscal Space," IMF Policy Discussion Paper 05/4 (Washington: International Monetary Fund, March), http://www.imf. org/external/pubs/ft/pdp/2005/pdp04.pdf.

Hemming, Richard, and others (2002), "The Effectiveness of Fiscal Policy in Stimulating Economic Activity: A Review of the Literature," IMF Working Paper 02/28 (Washington: International Monetary Fund), http://www.imf. org/external/pubs/ft/wp/2002/wp02208.pdf.

Hong Kong Monetary Authority (2011), "Linked Exchange Rate System" (August), http://www.hkma.gov.hk/eng/key-functions/monetary-stability/ linked-exchange-rate-system.shtml.

Ilzetzki, Ethan, and Carolos A. Végh (2008), "Procyclical Fiscal Policy in Developing Countries: Truth or Fiction?" NBER Working Paper 14191 (Cambridge, MA: National Bureau of Economic Research).

Ilzetzki, Ethan, and others (2011), "How Big (Small?) Are Fiscal Multipliers?" IMF Working Paper 11/52 (Washington: International Monetary Fund, March), www.imf.org/external/pubs/ft/wp/2011/wp1152.pdf.

IMF Staff (2000), "Exchange Rate Regimes in an Increasingly Integrated World," Issue Brief 00/06 (June), https://www.imf.org/external/np/exr/ib/2000/ 062600.htm.

International Monetary Fund (1986), *Manual on Government Finance Statistics* (Washington), https://www.imf.org/external/pubs/ft/gfs/manual/1986/eng/ .

International Monetary Fund (1993), *Balance of Payments Manual, Fifth Edition* (Washington), https://www.imf.org/external/pubs/ft/bopman/bopman.pdf.

International Monetary Fund (1995), "Unproductive Public Expenditures: A Pragmatic Approach to Policy Analysis," IMF Pamphlet No. 48, http:// www.imf.org/external/pubs/ft/pam/pam48/pam4801.htm.

International Monetary Fund (2001), *Government Finance Statistics Manual 2001* (Washington), https://www.imf.org/external/pubs/ft/gfs/manual/.

International Monetary Fund (2007), *Balance of Payments and International Investment Position Manual, Sixth Edition (BPM6)*, https://www.imf.org/ external/pubs/ft/bop/2007/pdf/bpm6.pdf.

International Monetary Fund (2008), *Iceland: Request for Stand-By Arrangement — Staff Report; Staff Supplement; Press release on the Executive Board Discussion; and Statement by the Executive Director for Iceland* (Washington: November), IMF Country Report 08/362, https://www.imf.org/external/pubs/ft/scr/2008/ cr08362.pdf.

International Monetary Fund (2008), *Pakistan — Request for Stand-By Arrangement,* (Washington: December), IMF Country Report 08/364, https://www.imf.org/external/pubs/ft/scr/2008/cr08364.pdf .

International Monetary Fund (2013), "Staff Guidance Note on the Application of the Joint Bank-Fund Debt Sustainability Framework for Low-Income Countries," www.imf.org/external/np/pp/eng/2013/110513.pdf.

International Monetary Fund (2013), *Pakistan: 2013 Article IV Consultation and Request for an Extended Arrangement under the Extended Fund Facility* (Washington: September), IMF Country Report 13/287, https://www.imf. org/external/pubs/ft/scr/2013/cr13287.pdf.

International Monetary Fund (2014), *Annual Report on Exchange Arrangements and Exchange Restrictions 2014* (Washington: October), https://www.imf.org/external/pubs/nft/2014/areaers/ar2014.pdf.

International Monetary Fund (2014), *Government Finance Statistics Manual 2014* (Washington), https://www.imf.org/external/pubs/FT/GFS/Manual/2014/gfsfinal.pdf .

International Monetary Fund (2015), *Republic of Korea: Staff Report for the 2015 Article IV Consultation*, (Washington: May), IMF Country Report 15/130, https://www.imf.org/en/Publications/CR/Issues/2016/12/31/Republic-of-Korea-Staff-Report-for-the-2015-Article-IV-Consultation-42952.

International Monetary Fund (2016), *Annual Report on Exchange Arrangements and Exchange Restrictions 2016* (Washington: November), https://www.imf.org/en/Publications/Annual-Report-on-Exchange-Arrangements-and-Exchange-Restrictions/Issues/2017/01/25/Annual-Report-on-Exchange-Arrangements-and-Exchange-Restrictions-2016-43741.

International Monetary Fund (2016), *2016 External Sector Report* (July), https://www.imf.org/external/np/pp/eng/2016/072716.pdf.

International Monetary Fund (2016), *Fiscal Monitor, October 2016,* https://www.imf.org/external/pubs/ft/fm/2016/02/pdf/fm1602.pdf.

International Monetary Fund (2016), *Indonesia: 2015 Article IV Consultation — Press release; Staff Report; and Statement by the Executive Director for Indonesia* (Washington: March), IMF Country Report 16/81, https://www.imf.org/external/pubs/ft/fm/2016/02/pdf/fm1602.pdf.

International Monetary Fund (2016), *Pakistan: Twelfth and Final Review under the Extended Arrangement, Request for Waivers of Nonperformance of Performance Criteria, and Proposal for Post Program Monitoring* (Washington: October), IMF Country Report 16/325, https://www.imf.org/external/pubs/ft/scr/2016/cr16325.pdf.

International Monetary Fund (2016), *Philippines: 2016 Article IV Consultation — Press Release; Staff Report; and Statement by the Executive Director for the Philippines* (Washington: September), IMF Country Report 16/309, https://www.imf.org/external/pubs/ft/scr/2016/cr16309.pdf.

International Monetary Fund (2016), *Russian Federation: Staff Report for the 2016 Article IV Consultation — Press Release; and Staff Report* (Washington: July), IMF Country Report 16/229, www.imf.org/external/pubs/ft/scr/2016/cr16229.pdf.

International Monetary Fund (2016), *Singapore: 2016 Article IV Consultation — Press Release; Staff Report; and Statement by the Executive Director for Singapore* (Washington: July), IMF Country Report 16/263, https://www.imf.org/external/pubs/ft/scr/2016/cr16263.pdf

Jawan, S. (2012), "Inflation Targeting: Holding the Line," *Finance and Development* (March 28), http://www.imf.org/external/pubs/ft/fandd/basics/target.htm.

Kaminsky, G., C. Reinhart, and C. Végh (2004), "When It Rains, It Pours: Procyclical Capital Flows and Macroeconomic Policies," NBER Working Paper 10780 (Cambridge, MA: National Bureau of Economic Research).

Kaplan, E., and D. Rodrik (2001), "Did the Malaysian Capital Controls Work?" NBER Working Paper 8142 (Cambridge, MA: February).

Katsimi, M., and G. Zoega (2015), "The Greek and Icelandic IMF Programmes Compared," VOXEU (November 19, 2015), http://voxeu.org/article/imf-programmes-greece-vs-iceland.

Khan, M. and A. Senhadji (2001), "Threshold Effects in the relationship Between Inflation and Growth," *IMF Staff Papers*, vol. 48, No. 1, pp. 1-21 (December), https://www.imf.org/External/Pubs/FT/staffp/2001/01a/pdf/khan.pdf.

Knowledge @ Wharton (2005), "Reform of China's Banks, Burdened by Bad Loans, Is Priority for Government," (June 1), http://knowledge.wharton.upenn.edu/article/reform-of-chinas-banks-burdened-by-bad-loans-is-priority-for-government/.

Koptis, G. (1995), "Hungary's Preannounced Crawling Peg," *Acta Oeconomica* vol. 47, No. 3/4, pp. 267–86, www.jstor.org/stable/40729631.

Lee, Jaewoo, and others (2008), *Exchange Rate Assessments: CGER Methodologies*, Occasional Paper 261 (Washington, DC: International Monetary Fund, April).

Li Xiaolin (2013), "Course Project: Brazil's Crisis, 1998-99," unpub. course paper for ECON 656, Singapore Management University, December.

Ljungwall, C., Yi Xiong, and Zou Yutong (2009), "Central Bank Financial Strength and the Cost of Sterilization in China," Stockholm School of Economics, http://swopec.hhs.se/hacerc/papers/hacerc2009-008.pdf .

Mauro, P. (1995), "Corruption and Growth," *Quarterly Journal of Economics*, vol. 110, No. 3, pp. 681–712 (August).

Monetary Authority of Singapore (2013), "MAS Monetary Policy Statement" (October), http://www.mas.gov.sg/news-and-publications/speeches-and-monetary-policy-statements/monetary-policy-statements/2013/monetary-policy-statement-14-oct-13.aspx.

Ouanes, A. and S. Thakur (1997), *Macroeconomic Analysis and Accounting in Transition Economies* (Washington: International Monetary Fund).

Phillips, S. and others (2013), "External Balance Assessment (EBA) Methodology," IMF Working Paper 13/272 (Washington: December), http://www.imf.org/external/pubs/ft/wp/2013/wp13272.pdf.

Ramakrishnan, U., and A. Vamvakidis (2002), "Forecasting Inflation in Indonesia," IMF Working Paper 02/111 (Washington: June), https://www.imf.org/external/pubs/ft/wp/2002/wp02111.pdf.

Reinhart, Carmen, and others (2003), "Debt Intolerance," NBER Working Paper 9908 (Cambridge, MA: National Bureau of Economic Research, August).

Rogoff, K., and others (2004), *Evolution and Performance of Exchange Rate Regimes*, IMF Occasional Paper 229 (Washington: IMF).

Sayce, K. (2009), "Output Gap Indicates There Won't Be Any Inflation," Money Morning (June), https://www.moneymorning.com.au/20090629/output-gap-indicates-there-wont-be-any-inflation.html.

Spilimbergo, Antonio, and others (2009), "Fiscal Multipliers," Staff Position Note 09/11 (Washington, DC: International Monetary Fund, May),http://www.imf.org/external/pubs/ft/spn/2009/spn0911.pdf.

Swan, T. (1963), "Longer-Run Problems of the Balance of Payments" in *The Australian Economy: A Volume of Readings*, edited by H. Arndt and M. Corden (Melbourne: Cheshire), pp. 384–95.

Tavlas, G. (2013), "For Greece, A Lesson in Addressing Structural Problems, Not Symptoms," Univ. of Chicago Becker Brown Bag Talk (November), https://bfi.uchicago.edu/news/feature-story/greece-lesson-addressing-structural-problems-not-symptoms.

Trading Economics, http://www.tradingeconomics.com/malaysia/currency.

Végh, Carlos, and Guillermo Vuletin (2012), "Overcoming the Fear of Free Falling: Monetary Policy Graduation in Emerging Markets," NBER Working Paper 18175 (Cambridge, MA: National Bureau of Economic Research).

Wong, C.-H., "Adjustment and Internal-External Balance," in Khan, M., S. Nsouli, and C.-H. Wong, eds. (2002), *Macroeconomic Management: Programs and Policies* (Washington: International Monetary Fund), Ch. 2, pp. 10–37.

INDEX

ABOUT THE AUTHOR

Dr. Joshua Greene is a macroeconomist with a specialization in public finance, who has worked in both national and international organizations since 1976. Retired from the International Monetary Fund, where he served for 28 years, most recently as Deputy Director of the IMF-Singapore Regional Training Institute in Singapore, he has taught a variety of courses and led many training programs in macroeconomics and public finance, both for university students and for officials from countries around the world. Dr. Greene has served periodically as a visiting professor at Singapore Management University in the Master's Program for Applied Economics and as a consultant for the ASEAN Macroeconomic Research Office, Asian Development Bank, Bank Negara Malaysia, and the International Monetary Fund. He has also taught macroeconomics at George Mason University in the United States. Dr. Greene has done research on a variety of subjects, including African debt, factors affecting private investment in developing countries, and the U.S. balance of payments. His work has been published in *IMF Staff Papers, World Development,* the *Journal of African Finance and Economic Development,* and other journals. He has a Ph.D. in economics and a law degree from the University of Michigan and an undergraduate degree from Princeton University.

Printed in the United States
By Bookmasters